The Palgrave Macmillan Asian Business Series

Series Editor

Rosalie Tung
Beedie School of Business
Simon Fraser University
Burnaby, British Columbia, Canada

Aim of the Series
The Palgrave Macmillan Asian Business Series publishes theoretical and empirical studies that contribute forward-looking social perspectives on the study of management issues not just in Asia, but by implication elsewhere. The series specifically aims at the development of new frontiers in the scope, themes and methods of business and management studies in Asia, a region which is seen as key to studies of modern management, organization, strategies, human resources and technologies. The series invites practitioners, policy-makers and academic researchers to join us at the cutting edge of constructive perspectives on Asian management, seeking to contribute towards the development of civil societies in Asia and further a field.

More information about this series at
http://www.springer.com/series/14420

Young-Chan Kim
Editor

China and Africa

A New Paradigm of Global Business

palgrave
macmillan

Editor
Young-Chan Kim
International Business and Economics
University of Greenwich
London, United Kingdom

The Palgrave Macmillan Asian Business Series
ISBN 978-3-319-83643-0 ISBN 978-3-319-47030-6 (eBook)
DOI 10.1007/978-3-319-47030-6

Printed on acid-free paper

This Palgrave Macmillan imprint is published by Springer Nature
The registered company is Springer International Publishing AG
The registered company Address is: Gewerbestrasse 11, 6330 Cham, Switzerland

Acknowledgement

Since joining the China Research Centre at the University of Greenwich and working in the West–East academic collaboration project for British students, I gradually became accustomed to the Chinese research practices which paved the way for further research projects with distinguished Chinese researchers. Furthermore, via further collaborations with partner universities from several Chinese provinces such as Shenzhen, Guangzhou, Beijing and Hong Kong I successfully managed to bridge the dichotomy between our institution and the East by increasing the provision of internship schemes with companies that had significant affiliations with China and the East. Growing up in a Confucius society, and embarking on a compilation of research projects in British universities from the outset of my Master's and Ph.D.'s Degree permitted me to illustrate an 'impartial' view of China and her global status, unalike the general consensus re China that is prevalent in the West. Nevertheless, as far as research regarding China is concerned, there still exist two disparate perspectives regarding her global status. The Western perspective of a 'Red China' and the Chinese perspective of her is the alternate superpower to the USA. As a South Korean, I endeavoured to exhibit a view that served as the *via media*, concerning China's progress in line with the Asian development theory, while further attempting to evaluate the concerns that were presented in the Western argument. Hence, the desire to reach a common ground was the fundamental reason for pursuing the *Asian Business* series.

Ever since the China series was launched to commemorate the 70th anniversary of Chinese independence, many individuals from the business and academic sector alike encouraged me to pursue projects such as this and for that I am eternally grateful. Furthermore, since the publication of the *Chinese Global Production Networks in the ASEAN*, and the *US Firms' Business Competence in the Taiwanese IT Industry* as part of the *Asian Business* series, various communication channels have formed in academics and business between the USA, EU and China. Researching for subsequent projects which are in their preliminary stages, such as 'China and Digital Economy', 'China and Western Europe', 'China and the US' and 'China, Japan and Korea,' has made me realise the unfathomable nature of research into a nation like China.

From the outset of the project, the response was remarkable with a plethora of apt individuals pledging their support for the book. First and foremost, my sincere thanks go to all of the contributors, who throughout the last 20 months have ceaselessly worked to enable this proposal to materialise. Despite their demanding schedules, they have continuously worked alongside I to ensure that the disparate disciplines of the participants synthesised with ease to produce a refined piece of literature. Further thanks go to all my colleagues, especially Professor Bruce Cronin, Dr Adotey Bing-Pappoe who are also at the University of Greenwich, and the two anonymous reviewers from Royal Holloway and the SOAS, University of London, and Professor Gunter Schubert from University Tubingen, Professor Kjeld Erik Brodsgarrd from Copenhagen Business School, Professor Hsin-Huang Michael Hsiao from Academia Sinica whose invaluable input laid the foundations for the project. The reviewer from Palgrave Macmillan, who introduced us to a revolutionised theory that harmonised with our core objectives, enabled our project to gain greater prestige. Special thanks further go to Ms Liz Barlow and Ms Madeleine Holder from Palgrave for her continuous support and invaluable editorial advice throughout the course of the entire project. Without the input of every individual mentioned afore, the project would still be in its infancy; thus, I am sincerely thankful to each and every one of you.

Last but not least, many thanks go to my next generation—Seung-Gyum and Yong-Gyum and Gichan Yoon—their continuous support and constructive suggestions from the perspectives of the future generation that are due to collaborate on a greater scale with China, greatly enriched the contents of the book. I furthermore wish to extend my deep gratitude to Mr Ye Liu Chun, Mrs He Hui Mei and Ye Ying from Hakka family in Xining and Meizhou, Guangdong China, who inspired and helped my study of Chinese research since 2010.

Contents

Notes on Contributors

Simplice A. Asongu is the Director and Lead Economist of the African Governance and Development Institute, a self-funded research institute and think tank in Cameroon. His research interests include political sciences, knowledge economy, inclusive development, development models and financial development.

Ai-qin Cheng is a Ph.D. candidate of History at Sun Yat-sen University, professor of History at Hebei University, also a standing director of China Society for Southeast Asian Studies and Henan Institute of Religious Studies, director of Henan Association of Hakka Research and Association for Central Plains Economic Region Research. The leading area of study includes relationships of China and Asian-African, Maritime rights and sovereignty disputes over the South China Sea and Chinese national history.

Hany ElShamy is Associate Professor of Economics, Tanta University, Faculty of Commerce and Economics Department. El Shamy's main research interests are economic growth and productivity. His articles have appeared in international journals and he has presented papers in international conferences, which were published as full papers in their online proceedings.

Jianhong-Cai is a Ph.D. candidate from the Asia Pacific Department of Graduate School of Chinese Academy of Social Sciences (GSCASS), majored in international politics. Now she is pursuing her dissertation on the 'One Belt and One Road Policy'.

Young-Chan Kim, a senior lecturer at the University of Greenwich, has intensely researched on China and the Asian Pacific region, with six publications including 'Chinese Global Production Networks in the ASEAN' and 'US Firms' Business Competence in the Taiwanese IT Industry' and also wrote articles for other academic books and journals.

Okolo Abutu Lawrence received his Ph.D. in World Economy from Xiamen University, China. His core research interest includes international political economy with a clear focus on Asia–Africa economic relations. He has published different books and articles on China–Africa relations. His recent research articles have appeared in the journals such as *The Grin*, *Africa Review*, *International Journal of African Renaissance Studies*, *Fudan Journal of the Humanities*, *Asian Journal Research in Business Economics and Management*, *African East-Asia Affairs*, *Contemporary Social Sciences*, *Review of Education Institute of Education Journal* and *Quarterly Journal of Chinese Studies*.

Henning Melber is Director Emeritus of The Dag Hammarskjöld Foundation and Senior Research Associate at the Nordic Africa Institute, both in Uppsala, Sweden. He is Extraordinary Professor at the Department of Political Sciences at the University of Pretoria and at the Centre for Africa Studies at the University of the Free State in Bloemfontein, and Senior Research Fellow at the Institute for Commonwealth Studies/School for Advanced Study of the University of London.

Dong Niu is a postdoctoral fellow in School of Public Policy and Management, Tsinghua University, China. He studies Africans in Guangzhou, international migration theories, global migration governance and social work with immigrants. Dong has been conducting empirical works on a new analytic framework for understanding transnational mobility, especially making efforts to solve the problem on conceptualisation and typology of migrants. His publications appear in *Sociological Studies*, *Open Times*, *Guangzhou Daily* and *China Daily*.

Ute Röschenthaler is Professor of Social and Cultural Anthropology at the Johannes Gutenberg University of Mainz, and member of the research programme 'Africa's Asian Options' at Goethe University Frankfurt. She works on cultural mobility, entrepreneurship, intellectual property and the emerging markets in Africa and its trade networks with the Global South. Her recent books include *Cultural Entrepreneurship in Africa* (ed. with Dorothea Schulz, 2016).

Antoine Socpa is Associate Professor of Anthropology at Université de Yaounde I, executive secretary of the Pan African Association of Anthropologists and

Coordinator of the Cameroon Association of Anthropologists. His research interests focus on development and health issues in cultural perspective, political anthropology, citizenship, food security, migration and trade networks between Asia and Africa. His publications include a book on Democratization and Autochthony in Cameroon (2003) and articles in international journals and edited volumes.

Irene Yuan Sun is an engagement manager at McKinsey & Company's Washington, D.C. office. She is the author of a book about Chinese investment in Africa that will be published by Harvard Business Review Press in 2017. She is a graduate of Harvard Business School, Harvard Kennedy School and Harvard College.

Marina Thorborg is a professor at Sodertorn University, Stockholm, Sweden, since 1997, and has intensively researched gender role studies in South Asian and China with several publications including 'Women in China, Pirates, Iron-girls, and Financial Wizzards', and 'Chinese Workers and Labour Conditions from State Industry to Globalized Factories. How to Stop the Race to the Bottom'.

Yuan Wang is a consultant at the United Nations Development Programme's China office. She has extensive research experience in Chinese multinationals' engagement in Africa and Asia. She is the co-author of the Business Perception Index Kenya 2014, published by Globalethics.net; Sustainable Impacts of Chinese ODI: a review of literature, published by IISD and the UDNP publication: 2015 Report on the Sustainable Development of Chinese Enterprises Overseas. She is a graduate of Harvard Kennedy School and Shanghai International Studies University.

Liang Xu is a doctoral candidate in African History at Harvard University. Liang received his BA in 2005 from Peking University where he also completed his first Ph.D. in International Relations in 2010. Liang's previous dissertation investigated Japan–South African relations in the post-apartheid era. Currently, Liang is working on a thesis that examines homeland development under apartheid, Chinese family clothing firms and the making and unmaking of industrial Zulu women.

List of Figures

List of Tables

1

Introduction: The Global Shift in Economic Power to Asia and the Challenges of Africa's Industrialisation in the Twenty-First Century

Lauren Okolo

1.1 Introduction

The entry point for the chapter is the premise that the globalisation of the world economy is one of the most distinctive trends that shape the present environment for economic development. When assessing the different regional performances within the background of globalisation, there has been a tendency to contrast the sustained and rapid growth in Asian economies over the last four decades with the stagnation in the sub-Saharan African nations. Also significant in the transformation of the world economy has been the redistribution of the world industry away from the older industrialised countries—chiefly, Western Europe,

L. Okolo (✉)
Xiamen University, Xiamen, China
e-mail: lauren4all2003@yahoo.com

Y. C. Kim (ed.), *China and Africa*, The Palgrave Macmillan Asian Business Series, DOI 10.1007/978-3-319-47030-6_1

the United States of America and, to a lesser extent, Japan-towards Pacific Asia, Latin America, and other industrialising economies. Perhaps, these emerging economics or markets have been facing serious challenges since 1997, with their economic "fundamentals" especially in East Asia being sound; they possess high savings and investments rates as well as efficient workforces. Even though the United States and other industrialised economies still possess a preponderant share of global wealth and industry, they have declined in relative (not absolute) terms while the industrialising economies, especially China, have gained in economic importance over the course of the post-war era. Significantly, the impact of the Pacific Asian economic catastrophe on the larger global economy provides powerful evidence of the magnitude of change that has taken place (Gilpin 2000). Thus, as per the words of Ralph L. Woods, "there are no permanent changes because change itself is permanent. It behooves the industrialist to research and the investor to be vigilant."

On the other hand, immediately after World War II ended in 1945, intellectuals and political leaders alike in the less developed countries also known as LDCs accused the big economies of being "imperialists" and "exploiters" (Gilpin 2000). Furthermore, Robert Gilpin (2000) opined that the dependency theory accused the underdevelopment and poverty of the less developed countries on the dominant capitalist economies and on the multinational cooperations. For example, in an effort to break away from the web of dependency, many less developed countries especially in Latin America closed their markets to the outside world and pursued nationalist import substitution policies in order to become self-sufficient. Perhaps their efforts to overturn the developed countries control of the global economy climaxed in the mid-1970s with the unsuccessful effort of an LDC coalition to introduce a New International Economic Order (NIEO). Unfortunately, by the 1980s, this effort had failed; a significant number of less developed countries had become greatly burdened by huge debts, their governments were running unmanageable budget deficits, and their economies suffered from high inflation rates that discouraged productive economic activities and foreign investment (Gilpin 2000). However, the objective of this chapter is to analyse and examine the global economic shift to Asia and the policies of export-oriented growth employed by some of these countries. On the other hand, the research seeks to find out the major challenges facing Africa's industrialisation process in the twenty-first century.

1.2 The Dilemma of South–South Cooperation and the Emergence of Newly Industrialising Countries in Asia

Robert Gilpin (2001) asserts that individual LDCs were not able to exert any influence on the international system and its institutions, many of the countries, mostly from the southern developing regions of the world, attempted to promote a collective identity but to no avail. During the Afro-Asian Bandung Conference in 1955, Indonesia was famously regarded as being the first major nation to take the first step to forging that identity and is the genesis of what came to be viewed as the Southern perspective. Led by Achmed Sukarno of Indonesia, Jawaharlal Nehru of India, Marshal Tito of Yugoslavia, and Gamal Abdel Nasser of Egypt, heads of states from the developing nations initiated a dialogue among themselves that subsequently led to the formation of the Non-Aligned Movement in 1961 (Balaam and Veseth 1996). As a political banner of many newly independent LDCs, the Non-Aligned Movement expanded to include a number of nations from Latin America. However, this movement served three important purposes. First, it was to be the LDCs' political arm for addressing initiatives against the remaining remnants of colonialism, especially in Africa. Another purpose was to be their vehicle for positioning themselves outside the sphere of the Cold War scenario and lastly, it was to promote the interests of the LDCs.

Thwarted by their efforts to develop, increasing numbers of LDCs resorted to their membership in international organisations to foster third-world solidarity and momentum for a change in the international political economy. More importantly, in 1964, the United Nations Conference on Trade and Development also known as UNCTAD was established largely through the efforts of the 77 LDCs that became known as the Group of 77 (G-77). UNCTAD meets roughly every four years in the capital city of an LDC. With its membership seeing vast increases in numbers over the years, G-77 has been the LDCs' representative organisation at the UNCTAD sessions. The G-77 sought to make UNCTAD a means for dialogue and negotiation between the LDCs and the developed economies on trade, finance, and other development issues. At the first meeting, the G-77 proposed a new international trade organisation to replace General Agreement on Trade and Tariff (GATT). For the most part, the advanced economies resisted UNCTAD initiatives when it came to trade and other economic activities. Nevertheless, via UNCTAD, LDCs were slowly able to secure some significant concessions and preferential treatment—a Generalised System of Preference (GSPs)—on tariffs for their exports to developed countries (Balaam and Veseth 1996). Moreover, the shift in global trends is on such a scale that it is almost impossible to perceive the full impact of the changes as they happen. The present transition to a new global order has been developing for some time, but in the last two decades there have been some significant milestones (Gordhan 2007).

Another perspective is that over the past three decades there have been distinct changes in the economic development models in a number of countries, especially in Asia and Latin America. By the 1980s, South Korea, Hong Kong, Taiwan, and Singapore were now recognised as the new economic "tigers" in East Asia. The marvellous increase in these countries led many scholars and international analysts to increasingly group them as being "newcomers" on the part of industrialisation and development. Given the current increase in Malaysia and Thailand, these two nations have also been regarded as potential Newly Industrialized Countries (NICs). Paradoxically, the level of expectation since the 1950s for the third world to catch up with the industrial countries rested with the anticipated success of major Latin American countries like Brazil, Argentina, and Mexico, but as an alternative, it has been the success of the East Asian NICs that astonished, puzzled, and intrigued many. Sunil Kukreje (1996) states that: "*The Asian NICs-Hong Kong, Taiwan, Singapore, and South Korea-have achieved growth rates virtually without historical precedent... The speed with which the NICs have industrialized is astonishing. Nineteenth-century development in Europe and North America...pale in comparison with the record of the NICs.*"

The Industrialisation process in Asia is mystifying; South Korea and Taiwan, for instance, have pursued a strategy known as *export-oriented growth*; export-oriented strategy is based on a combination of liberal and mercantilist prescriptions for economic development and growth. For one, it calls for the state to strongly and firmly emphasise a country's comparative advantage in selected sectors of the economy and promote exports from these sectors (Hong 1987). Instead of relying on a non-interventionist state and free-trade policies, the East Asian NICs vehemently pursued specific national and international policies that changed the basic structure and function of their economies.

The four Asian tigers employed export-oriented strategies. For example, by the late 1960s, South Korea and Taiwan began to ease into the next phase of restructuring. Hong Kong and Singapore seized the advantage of their ports to export their goods abroad. Specifically, these countries increased their international market share by promoting the export of domestically manufactured durable goods. State intervention again played a strategic role in launching this initial export promotion effort. Prior to the initiation of vigorous export promotions, the comparative advantage of Korea in labour-intensive manufactures remained merely a potential one. In this sense, Korea's export-oriented growth in the 1960s and thereafter may be regarded as the process of opening up the Korean economy to semi-free trade. According to Corden (1971), the opening up of an economy to trade generates a "static" efficiency gain, which is very similar to a "once-and-for-all" technical progress in raising the absorption possibility frontier of a country at the given factor supplies.

Wontack Hong (1987) maintained that the major labour-intensive manufactured export sectors of Korea may be divided into three major groups. The first group represents those which were the leading export sectors in the late 1960s and early 1970s but whose export growth rates became much lower in the late 1970s. This group consists of wearing apparel, miscellaneous manufactures (mostly wigs), fish products, textile fabrics (including miscellaneous textile products), natural fibre yarns, and veneers and plywood. The second group represents those which revealed high rates of growth in exports only at the end of the 1970s. This group consists of footwear, watches and optical instruments, radios and televisions (including phonographs and tape recorders), metal products, and non-metallic mineral products (excluding cement). The third group represents those which maintained more or less the same rates of growth throughout the 1960s and 1970s. This group consists of electronic products, wood products, and leather products. Apparently, the rise and fall of various labour-intensive manufactured exports over time do not occur strictly in relation to the order of capital intensity. That is, the magnitude of the adverse impact inflicted by the tripling of the real wage rate during 1968–80 does not seem to have been proportional to the capital intensity of the sectors (Hong 1987).

In South Korea, for example, the four principle policy measures that were adopted to pursue an export-oriented strategy consisted of vigorous administrative supports for export promotion, a preferential tax system and subsidy allocation for export activities, and reduction of the import substitution biases in the Korean economy. There already exists a vast amount of literature dealing with the details of the export promotion policies that were initiated by the Korean government (see Hong 1979; Frank et al. 1975; Krueger 1977; Gilpin 2000), the study concentrates on the subsidy allocation in the form of low-interest-rate bank loans in relation to the sectoral orientation of investments and the characteristics of the leading export sectors.

In addition, the combined impact of investment policies in education and job training in the NICs have resulted in a better quality of labour; creating increased economic efficiency, industrial flexibility, and greater economic equality. Government initiatives in reducing the illiteracy rate and providing adequate access to job training is evident in the comparatively high enrolment rates and the increase in government expenditure directed towards creating an educated and skilled workforce. For example, by 1972, government spending on education was almost 16 per cent of the government's public expenditures in South Korea and Singapore. Other nations alike to Malaysia and Thailand were also investing heavily in education, with 23 per cent and 20 per cent of government spending being spent, respectively.

1.3 China's Global Game Change: From Emerging Economy to Global Player?

According to Reem Heakal, an emerging market economy (EME) is defined as being an economy with a low to medium per capita income. Such countries constitute approximately 80 per cent of the global population, and represent about 20 per cent of the world's economies. The term was coined in 1981 by Antoine W. Van Agtmael of the International Finance Corporation of the World Bank. However, the term "emerging market" is loosely defined, countries that fall into this category, varying from very big to very small, are usually considered emerging because of their developments and reforms. Hence, even though China is deemed to be one of the world's economic powerhouses, she too is regarded as being an emerging economy; alongside much smaller economies with significantly less resources, like Tunisia. Both China and Tunisia belong to this category because both have embarked on economic development and reform programs, and have begun to open up their markets and "emerge" onto the global scene. EMEs are considered to be fast-growing economies (Heakal). A growth in investment in a country often indicates that the country has been able to build confidence in the local economy. Moreover, foreign investment is a signal that the world has begun to take notice of the emerging market, and when international capital flows are directed towards an EME, the injection of foreign currency into the local economy adds volume to the country's stock market and long-term investment to the infrastructure.

The rise of China from a poor, stagnant country to a major economic power within a short time is often described by analysts and commentators as being one of the greatest economic success stories in modern times (Elwell and Labonte 2007). Prior to 1979, China maintained a Soviet-style command economy under which the state controlled most aspects of the economy. These policies kept the economy relatively stagnant and living standards were further significantly low. However, beginning in 1979, the government began a series of free market reforms and began opening up to the world in terms of trade and investment. These reforms have produced dramatic results. From 1979 to 2005, China's real gross domestic product (GDP) grew at an average annual rate of 9.7 per cent, the size of its economy increased over 11-fold, its real per capita GDP grew over 8-fold, and its world ranking for total trade rose from 27th to 3rd. China's economic reforms and growth have benefitted (or could benefit) the US economy in a number of ways: Over the past few years, China has been the fastest growing US export market among its major trading partners. For example, US exports to China in 2006 increased by an estimated 33 per cent. China's ranking as a US export market rose from 11th in 2000 to 4th in 2006, and overtook Japan in 2007 to become the third market for US industries. China's rapid economic growth, coupled with its large population and development needs, makes it a potentially huge market for the United States (Elwell and Labonte 2007).

The most impressive growth was in four of the biggest emerging economies: Brazil, Russia, India, and China, which Jim O'Neill of Goldman Sachs, an investment bank, acronymed into the BRICs in 2001. These economies have grown in different ways and for different reasons. But their size marked them out as being different on purchasing power terms, as they were the only $1 trillion economies outside the Organisation for Economic Cooperation and Development (OECD), a rich-world club, likewise with their growth rates. The Economist reckoned that they would, in a decade, become one of the foremost economies even when measured at market exchange rates. Today, they are four of the largest national economies in the world (The Economist 2013).

The remarkable growth of emerging markets in general and the BRIC nations in particular transformed the global economy in many ways; commodity prices soared and the cost of manufactures and labour sank, global poverty rates tumbled. The BRIC era arrived at the end of a century in which global living standards had diverged remarkably. Towards the end of the nineteenth century, America's economy overtook China's to become the largest on the planet. By 1992, China and India—home to 38 per cent of the world's population were producing just 7 per cent of the world's output, while six of the richest countries which accounted for just 12 per cent of the world's population produced half of it. In 1890, an average American was about six times better off than the average Chinese or Indian. By the early 1990s, s/he was around 25 times better off (The Economist 2013).

Significantly, from 1993 to 2007 China averaged growth of 10.5 per cent a year. India, with less reliance on trade, managed an average of 6.5 per cent, more than twice of America's average growth rate. The two countries' combined share of global output more than doubled to nearly 16 per cent. Global financial imbalances ballooned from 1999 as advanced economies ran a current account deficit which peaked at nearly 1.2 per cent of rich-world GDP in 2006. Emerging economies' combined current account surplus peaked in the same year at 4.9 per cent of GDP. Similarly, foreign exchange interventions made the export surge doubly tricky to manage. After the financial crises of the late 1990s, many emerging economies began accumulating dollar reserves to protect themselves against being caught short by big foreign exchange outflows. Building up reserves helped the growing economies to hold exchange rates below the levels they might otherwise have been able to attain, keeping exports relatively cheap. China was a particularly enthusiastic reserve accumulator, and now sits on top a $3.5 trillion hoard, the majority of it had been accumulated since 2000; BRICs have reserves of about $4.6 trillion (The Economist 2013). Currency adjustments have narrowed deficits. The Chinese Yuan has been appreciated by roughly 35 per cent against the dollar since 2005. Emerging world reserve accumulation has diminished along with current account imbalances. Since 2011, Chinese reserves have mostly been stagnant. Indeed, in recent years, reserve outflows have been a problem for some emerging markets (The Economist 2013).

Furthermore, in March 2015, Germany, France, Switzerland, and Italy joined a new China-led Asian investment bank after their close ally Britain defied the US pressures to become a founding member of a venture seen in Washington, as being a staunch rival to the World Bank. It was the $50 billion Asian Infrastructure Investment Bank (AIIB), a potential threat to the Washington-based World Bank. The concerted move to participate in Beijing's flagship economic outreach project was a diplomatic blow to the United States, and reflected Europe's eagerness to partner with China's fast-growing economy—the world's second largest after the USA (Parker 2015).

The Chinese military strategy underwent a major change in the mid-1980s. The threat of a Soviet land attack had diminished and the attention of the People's Liberation Army (PLA) turned to the threat of regional disputes.

Thus, the PLA started to focus on a strategy of limited war. However, with the downturn in relations with the West following the Tiananmen Square massacre, this strategy was revised. The Gulf War also had a significant impact on the Chinese leadership and thus the conflict was carefully studied. There has been a shift away from the philosophy that manpower is superior to machine power and that the offensive can be won by strength in numbers. Finally, there has been a decrease in reliance on the civilian population to fill the army's ranks as was required when the concept of the protracted people's war was in vogue. As a result of the major shifts in military strategy as described above, China has embarked on an ambitious military modernisation program. China's economic growth has been vital in determining the effective implementation of this program. However, due to the secrecy surrounding military matters, the actual size of the military spending is hard to determine. Officially, for example, China's 1996 defence budget was $8.7 billion. Independent estimates vary from $8 billion to $100 billion. Regardless of the independent estimates, the official Chinese defence budgets reveal a 200 per cent increase from 1988 (Par Hynes 2007).

Even in its present form, China has the world's largest military; the PLA consists of over two million men and is complemented by the world's third largest air force, consisting of 5300 aircraft, and the world's largest small ship navy. Although these figures look impressive, there are major problems with obsolete equipment, poor training, and the transition to the new doctrine. However, the future promises to be different. In an effort to modernise the People's Liberation Army Air Force (PLAAF), China is developing or acquiring the rights to produce six new tactical aircraft models (Par Hynes 2007).

China is equally expanding its military preponderance in Asia and Africa, respectively. To meet its oil and mineral needs, Beijing has consistently delivered arms to "Pariah States" in Africa, especially Sudan and Zimbabwe which have come under Western sanctions in the last decade. Beijing sold to Sudan alone, around $55 million worth of arms between 2003 and 2006, flouting the United Nations (UN) arms embargo (Fowale 2012). China deployed 700 soldiers to a UN peacekeeping force in South Sudan to help guard the country's embattled oil fields and protect Chinese workers and installations. While Beijing's troops will operate under UN command, their posting to South Sudan marks a sharp escalation in China's efforts to ensure the safety of its workers and assets in Africa and guarantee a steady flow of energy for domestic consumption. In addition, in March 2013, China sent some 300 peacekeepers to Mali to protect Chinese engineers building a UN camp in the town of Gao (Bariyo 2014; Abutu 2014).

1.4 The Impediments of Africa's Industrialisation in the Twenty-First Century

The current development situation in Africa is paradoxical. Although it is arguably one of the richest continents in terms of natural resources, Africa remains the poorest and the least developed region in the world (Tankeu 2007). While each case is certainly unique, there are some clear threads running through the situations of these LDCs. Alike to the NICs, there has been no shortage of desire for development and growth among the LDCs in Africa. Sunil Kukreja (1996) notes that

> It is quite hazardous to talk of development strategies in Africa…because it is not in the least clear that many African countries have a strategy which is identifiable.

For example, Nigeria overtook South Africa as the largest economy in Africa after rebasing her GDP in April 2014 (BBC 2014) in the same year; the new data makes Nigeria the 26th largest economy in the world. Although Nigeria is largely an import dependent economy which accepts virtually anything from anywhere in the world, (Finintell 2015) Crude oil remains the major export product while virtually everything else is further imported. Similarly, South Africa has a more diversified economy, and highly developed financial institutions, infrastructure, and expertise that are more entrenched. South Africa's spot as the only G-20 member from Africa facilitated the continent's entry into BRICS. The stage has been set for accelerated investment from both the BRICS and the advanced economies. In 2007, the Industrial and Commercial Bank of China bought a

20 per cent stake in South Africa's Standard Bank for R36 billion ($5.4 billion), making it China's largest foreign investment to date. In 2009, Beijing announced that the African headquarters of the China-Africa Development Fund would be in Johannesburg (Gordhan 2007). The question facing Africa's 54 countries is if China managed to lift 400 million people out of poverty in the space of three decades, what is hampering Africa's industrialisation prospects in the twenty-first century?

This may largely be due to a case of extreme characterisation, but the non-existence of consistency or an "identifiable" strategy can be traced to the absence of established and legitimate political institutions in many of these LDCs capable of promoting sustained policies. In the words of Kukreja (1996), "*the most pressing problems in Africa today are economic in nature, most governments on the continent are more concerned about their re-elections or political survival.*"

One fundamental indicator of this is the enormous resources that have been diverted to arms expenditures and other repressive state efforts. More so, political survival has consistently competed with economic development priorities. In the continent hard pressed to make available the basic amenities for its citizens, this diversion of resources indeed comes at a very high price (Kukreja 1996). For instance, the Niger Delta region of Nigeria, several militant armed groups, under the collective name of Movement for the Emancipation of the Niger Delta (MEND), have been waging a war against the Government, fighting for a greater share of Nigeria's oil revenues to go to the impoverished oil producing regions. Another terrorist group, Boko-Haram emerged in the northern parts of Nigeria, and have been active since 1999, killing thousands of people and have been demanding an Islamic state. Côte d'Ivoire and Guinea Bissau have also experienced armed conflicts; these upheavals are some of the major factors that have been hampering the African industrialisation process (Akukwe 2013). Moreover, Sudan has historically been marred with religious, ethnic, and tribal tensions. The Sudanese people have since struggled to maintain a fragile balance between their largely subsistence agriculture system and the delicate ecology of the region. Regardless, the inappropriate use of imported technology and the intensification of goods production for export (as advised by the International Monetary Fund [IMF]) have damaged the subsistence economy and the productive capacity of arable land (Balaam and Veseth 1996).

More importantly, Anna K. Dickson (1997) asserts that historical connections that African countries have had with the international economy continue to influence the fate of these LDCs. Since the colonial era, the African economies have been deeply entrenched in agriculture and primary commodity production (essentially directed for external consumption). However, this "comparative advantage" is not intrinsically detrimental; the almost exclusive dependence on primary product exports has left the LDCs constantly vulnerable to price volatility and terms of trade for these products in the international market (Dickson 1997). Furthermore, on aggregate, agriculture in Africa made up 47 per cent of GDP in 1965 and this had been reduced to 38 per cent by 1984. Again, industry's share of GDP during the same era augmented from 15 to 16 per cent. For example, in Asia, agriculture dropped from 42 to 36 per cent of GDP as industry's share grew from 28 to 36 per cent over the same period. As a result, diversification remains a chief priority to the development agenda for most countries in Africa (Balaam and Veseth 1996).

Similarly, since the oil disaster in the 1970s, LDCs in Africa have seen their debt burden progressively and sharply increase from 25 per cent in 1975 to 76 per cent in 1987. Regardless, the debt crisis is not exclusive to Africa's less developed countries. However, the burden has been especially crippling, since many LDCs were witnessing reductions in export revenue. The IMF has attempted to steer these economies out of this circumstance by insisting that extraordinary government spending, agriculture subsidies, and artificial currency controls be eradicated. While there is some movement in this direction, sceptics insist that unless primary product prices in the international market rebound, the financial situation for these economies will not improve appreciably (Balaam and Veseth 1996).

Climate change has been a significant cause of concern among African countries, with the major concern being how one can obtain an effective balance between economic development and environmental sustainability. Developing countries have argued in many environmental summits that developed countries reached their level of development at the expense of developing countries in what was called the brown way of economic growth (Aka 1996). Developing countries have argued that they need to follow the same path for them to industrialise and reach their desired levels of development. With regard to the debate on reducing emissions, developing countries have demanded four aspects to be met for them to comply with the demands of the West. First, they want the sufficient finances for adaptation, mitigation, capacity building and technology transfer—demands that the West, until now have been reluctant to fulfil. Within the emerging economies—the BRICS in particular, there is likely to be no improvements or agreements reached unless they can compromise and mediate effectively. Thus, it is up to the developing countries to efficiently utilise forums such as the G77 and China to push for a more favourable deal when it comes to climate change negotiations (Farah et al. 2011). This particular issue is another challenge facing Africa's industrialisation and development in the twenty-first century.

1.5 Conclusion

For more than 50 years, the development modus operandi for developing countries has been their foremost challenge. A complex mix of conditions both internal and external to these countries will continue to affect the result of their development endeavours. The East–West disagreement was a powerful international constraint that shaped the political economy of development. Alongside this, the developed world's domination of technology, capital and the institutional structures of the global economy facilitated strong political momentum among the LDCs to change the rules of the game and address the imbalance in global, political and economic power, and wealth.

In addition, as the global economy continues to undergo restructuring, the world should expect changes in development prospects for the Least Developed Countries. Although the implications are far from being clear, the propensity towards trading alliances in Europe, North America, and a more integrated Pacific Rim-East Asia will most certainly shift national and international priorities. For over five decades, the Least Developed Countries have forged alliances like the G-77 and the UNCTAD to help mobilise support for their economic agendas. The competence of the third-world countries to sustain such collective measures (to tilt the dominance of the developed countries) will certainly affect their regional ties in forthcoming years (Kukreja 1996). The export-led growth of East Asian

NICs has also vindicated proponents of the liberal model. Mercantilist trade policies in South Korea, Taiwan, and other Asian countries drive home the strategic role of an aggressive state in the development process.

Similarly, incongruent development trends in recent decades add to the potential weakening of a third-world alliance. Already, the East Asian NICs are increasingly resembling the developed countries economically, and have less in common with the Least Developed Countries of Latin America or Africa. This trend where some developing countries grow faster than others will definitely continue. Perhaps, the gap between the NICs and other LDCs may grow wider as desperately poor countries like South Sudan, Chad, Rwanda, and Somalia are trapped in a state of economic paralysis (Dickson 1997).

Thus, it is clear that the transformation of the world economy has resulted in the redistribution of the world industry away from the older industrialised countries: Western Europe, the United States of America and, to a lesser extent, Japan-towards Pacific Asia, Latin America, and other industrialising economies. The four Asian tigers employed an export-oriented strategy to achieve significant rates of growth. For example, by the late 1960s, South Korea and Taiwan began to ease into the next phase of restructuring. Hong Kong and Singapore seized the advantage of their ports to export their goods abroad. Specifically, these countries increased their international market shares by promoting the export of domestically manufactured durable products.

One of the biggest changes in the past decade has been China's emergence as a global economic power. In the face of the financial crisis, China has been making efforts to sustain its economic momentum and contribute to global stability (Yang 2013). The Economist in 2004 dedicated its survey of the world economy to the United States and China. It affirmed that China was the world's largest consumer of cement, steel, coal, and cooper; the world's second largest consumer of oil after the United States, and that in the year 2003, China consumed 40 per cent of the world's coal and 30 per cent of its steel. The Economist also projected that China's energy requirements would quadruple but its per capita use of energy would remain half of that of the United States (Dellios Rosita 2005). Moreover, the global economy is vehemently tilting towards Asia, as shown by the launching of the AIIB—which was formally launched by Chinese President Xi Jinping in 2014. The AIIB serves as one element of a broader Chinese push to create a new financial and economic institution that will increase its international influence. It has become a central issue in the growing contest between Beijing and Washington over who will define the economic and trade rules in Asia over the coming decades (Parker 2015).

Finally, the development dilemma facing Africa's industrialisation process has an inherent underpinning from historical records. Millions of Africans are still caught in the poverty trap, largely because of the failures to diversify their sources of growth, alongside the continued over-reliance on primary commodity exports. Africa's economic growth is currently largely driven by commodity exports, especially oil and metals. In contrast, the growth patterns of other developing regions, especially in Asia, where growth has been driven by a solid industrialisation agenda, places greater emphasis on manufacturing, which has resulted in rapid industrial growth in these countries. However, increased demand from Asia has played a significant role in the rise in the international prices of Africa's resource exports (Kaplinsky 2007; Sandrey and Edinger 2011). Thus, as a whole, Chinese export expansion has benefited African firms and consumers by reducing the price and increasing the availability of manufactures. At the same time, competition from Chinese manufactures in both domestic and third markets has reduced the demand for African manufactures and perhaps undermined Africa's manufacturing capacity.

Implementing sustainable structural transformations in Africa will not be easy, and there is no "one size fits all" approach. Each African country will have to design individual strategies and policies based on its own sectoral and resource priorities, environmental challenges, initial conditions, and domestic capabilities. Among other areas, focus should be placed on efficient, sustainable resources used to generate energy, industry, and agriculture (UNCTAD 2012). The planning and industrial acceleration process in Africa needs to define strong industrialisation strategies, identify priority sectors to focus on in the short term, as well as strategies for the medium and long terms, and it further needs to identify the key enablers to kick-start and sustain industrial development. This raises five key issues for massive industrialisation in Africa: leadership, strategy and policy, investments, business environment and policy implementation and coordination (United Nations Economic Commission for Africa 2013). These all call for a genuine partnership with the United States, Europe and with other key global players; partnerships that are not based on colonial history or competition over resources: perhaps a plan like that of the Marshall plan for Europe and in a way that synthesises with African norms and complies with their cultural ethos.

References

Abutu, L. O. (2014). *From non-interference to preponderance: China's future grand strategy in Africa*. Stellenbosch: African East-Asian Affairs, Centre for Chinese Studies, Stellenbosch University.

Aka, C. (1996). *Democracy and development in Africa*. Ibadan: Spectrum Books Limited, Spectrum House.

Akukwe, C. (2013). Africa's challenges for 2013: What political and developmental challenges are likely to confront Africa over the next 12 months? See online http://thinkafricapress.com/development/africa-2013-development-challenges. 29 Jan.

Bai, Y. (2013). China: An emerging economic power. Retrieved from http://english.cntv.cn/program/china24/20130306/106603.shtml. 23 Mar 2015.

Balaam, D. N., & Veseth, M. (1996). *Introduction to international political economy*. Upper Saddle River: Prentice Hall.

Bariyo, N. (2014). China deploys troops in South Sudan to defend oil fields, workers: Deployment marks sharp escalation in Beijing's efforts to protect interests in Africa. See more http://www.wsj.com/articles/china-deploys-troops-in-south-sudan-to-defend-oil-fields-workers-1410275041#. 18 Mar 2015.

BBC. (2014). Nigeria becomes Africa's biggest economy. See http://www.bbc.com/news/business-26913497. 10 Apr 2015.

Corden, W. M. (1971). The effects of trade on the rate of growth. In J. Bhagwati, R. W. Jones, R. A. Mundell, & J. Vanek (Eds.), *In Trade, the balance of payments, and growth*. Amsterdam: North-Holland.

Dellios, R. (2005). *The rise of China as a global power*. Gold Coast: The Centre for East-West Cultural and Economic Studies, The School of Humanities and Social Sciences.

Dickson, A. K. (1997). *Development and international relations: A critical introduction*. Cambridge: Polity Press.

Elwell, C. K., & Labonte, M. (2007). Is China a threat to the U.S. economy? Retrieved from http://congressionalresearch.com/RL33604/document.php. 15 Mar 2015.

Farah, I., Kiamba, S., & Mazongo, M. (2011). Major challenges facing Africa in the 21st century: A few provocative remarks, at the international symposium on cultural diplomacy in Africa – Strategies to confront the challenges of the 21st century: Does Africa has what is required? Berlin.

Finintell. (2015). Nigeria's trade relations: New landscape between the West and the Chinese. See online http://www.myfinancialintelligence.com/banking-and-finance/nigeria%E2%80 %99 s-trade-relations-new-landscape--between-west-and-chinese. 11 Apr 2015.

Fowale, T. J. (2012). China's military presence in Africa: How has this trade evolved since the cold war? Retrieved from https://suite.io/tongkeh-joseph-fowale/1szq26r. 18 Mar 2015.

Frank, C. R., Kim, K. S., & Westphal, L. (1975). *Foreign trade regimes and economic development: South Korea*. New York: NBER.

Gilpin, R. (2000). *The challenge of global capitalism in the 21st century*. Princeton: Princeton University Press.

Gilpin, R. (2001). Global Political Economy: Understanding the International Economic Order, Princeton: Princeton University Press.

Gordhan, P. (2007). An emerging new world order. See online http://www.aucegypt.edu/gapp/cairoreview/Pages/articleDetails.aspx?aid=75. 17–18 Mar 2015.

Heakal, R. What is an emerging market economy? See online http://www.investopedia.com/articles/03/073003.asp. 15 Mar 2015.

Heakal, R. (2009).What is an emerging market economy? Retrieved 15 March, 2015. See https://www.scribd.com/document/130170836/India-Factors-that-Made-it-an-Emerging-Economy

Hong, W. (1979). *Trade, distortions and employment growth in Korea*. Seoul: Korean Development Institute Press.

Hong, W. (1987). *Export-oriented growth and trade patterns of Korea*. Chicago: University of Chicago Press.

Kaplinsky, R. and M. Morris (2006b), "The Asian Drivers and SSA; MFA quota removal and the portents for African industrialisation?", paper prepared for Asian and Other Drivers of Change Workshop, St. Petersburg, mimeo, Brighton: Institute of Development Studies.

Krueger, A. O. (1977). *Growth, distortions and patterns of trade among many countries* (Vol. 40). Princeton: Princeton Studies in International Finance.

Par Hynes, M. H. A. (2007). China: The emerging superpower. Retrieved from http://fas.org/nuke/guide/china/doctrine/0046.htm. 17 Mar 2015.

Parker, G. (2015). 'Germany, Italy and France Defy US to Join China-Led Development Bank': A growing economy and trillions in reserves make China the new popular kid on the block. See online http://russia-insider.com/en/2015/03/17/4599. 23 Mar 2015.

Sandrey, R., & Edinger, H. (2011). *China's manufacturing and industrial tion in Africa* (Vol. 128). Tunis: African Development Bank.

Tankeu, E. (2007). From Commodities to Higher Value Products: Africa's Challenge for Sustainable Growth and Development in the 21st Century. Retrieved from http://www.unido.org/fileadmin/import/83887_070924_DGstatement_ExtraordinaryCAMI.pdf

The Economist. (2013). When giants slow down: The most dramatic, and disruptive, period of emerging-market growth the world has ever seen is coming to its close. Retrieved from http://www.economist.com/news/briefing/21582257-most-dramatic-and-disruptive-period-emerging-market-growth-world-has-ever-seen. 16 Mar 2015.

United Nations Conference on Trade And Development (2012). Statistics: UNCTAD.org. Retrieved June 15, 2015, https://unctadstat.unctad.org/TableViewer/tableview.aspx?Reportid=88

United Nations Economic Commission for Africa. (2013). *Industrialization for an emerging Africa*. Abidjan

Part I

Chinese Perspective in Africa

2

'Safari Tour' and Zhou's Dream of Mao's Land in Africa

Young-Chan Kim

2.1 Introduction

When President Xi Jinping chose Africa as the first continent to visit as the head of state on 25 March 2013, it essentially validated Derk Bodde's observation that 'In China more perhaps than in any other country, knowledge of the past is essential for an understanding of the present' (Derk Bodde, requoted from Salisbury 1993). Alike to his predecessors, Xi regarded Africa as potential strategic partners in sustaining the manufacturing side of his new global plan, known as the 'New Silk Road' initiative. Furthermore, to support his global project—he designed a new financial hub, 'the Asian Infrastructure and Investment Bank (hereafter AIIB)' which endeavoured to replicate the role of the IMF and the World Bank.

Y. C. Kim (✉)
University of Greenwich, London, UK
e-mail: y.kim@gre.ac.uk

Y. C. Kim (ed.), *China and Africa*, The Palgrave Macmillan Asian Business Series, DOI 10.1007/978-3-319-47030-6_2

Since Zhou Enlai's first visit to Africa in 1963 and 1964, China perceived Africa not only as strategic partners in economic and political terms—but as 'little brothers'.[1] However, the amount of amassed research on 'why one of the most powerful men in new-China, Zhou, chose Africa as the idyllic place in the midst of the emergence of subsequent super powers?' Thus, what was the main reason Zhou endeavoured to visit an impoverished continent plagued with poverty as well as being politically 'inferior' to the Zhongnanhai?

Hence, the purpose of this chapter is to consider China's African policy within Zhongnanhai's internal investigation during Mao Zedong's regime, with a focus on Mao's misconception of Zhou's pragmatic policy implementation and Zhou's unchangeable loyalty to Mao. Furthermore, Mao's counter offensive towards Zhou during the Geneva and Bandung Conference, illustrated his worries towards Zhou's power challenge. In addition, Zhou's surging appearance on the international stage and brewing conflict during the Sino-Soviet foreign relation was further analysed in line with the radical political movement (Ultra-Leftist) in China, alongside the Great Leap Forward Movement. Did Mao regard Zhou as a potential threat to his rule? Was Mao therefore attempting to remove him as he did with Liu Shaoqi—thus was Zhou attempting to illustrate his loyalty to Mao by trying to implement Maoism in Africa? Ultimately, what does Zhou's dream tell us about Xi's 'New Silk Road' project, and the intricacies behind it?

2.2 From Pragmatic to Maoism Diplomacy

As far as the Chinese foreign policy is concerned, Joseph Nye's 'soft power'[2] concept was deemed to serve as the theoretical foundation, and hence, his four primary initiative notion was to be pursued with

[1] In Chinese culture, 'brotherhood' is the foundation for a Guanxi relation. Post-independence, China used to refer to the Soviet Union as being their 'Big Brother'.

[2] Under the Beijing Consensus, Chinese 'Soft Power' foreign policy followed Nye's view, which stated that a country's culture, political values, foreign policies, and economic attraction are essential components of national strength, as those values provide the capacity to persuade other nations to willingly adopt the same goals and adhere to the same principles (Nye 2005).

regard to China's international status as an emerging country and this included the political element for regional security, especially Asia; the economic element for mutual growth, which has mainly blossomed since Deng; the international element for supporting (including voting at international institutions such as United Nations [UN]); and finally, the cultural element through human exchange programmes. As far as the political element was concerned, Mao relied on reports from the People's Liberation Army's (hereafter PLA) general chief of staffs, who were working on the front lines of the international military engagements. Although this was Zhou's main task, Mao did not entirely rely on Zhou's reports, especially prior to the Cultural Revolution. Therefore, Zhou endeavoured to focus on the international element to bolster China's international prestige to initiate the human capital exchange program with ease. Zhou Enlai, who was a well-known 'anti-imperialist and anti-colonialist' diplomat[3] who actively pursued the 'Five Peace Agreement' among the newly independent countries in Asia and Africa, further tried to cement China's status as the leader of the 'Third World' against the duopolistic nature[4] of the world political system.

It was difficult to understand why Zhou experienced such a volatile norm of foreign relations during Mao's first ten years. There was an important quotation from archive documents concerning the Chinese foreign policy until the Cultural Revolution which was 'Foreign policy is formulated by me and implemented by Premier Zhou' (Chinese Communist Affairs 1967).[5] In synthesis with the Chinese sociopolitical literature, the Chinese foreign policy was claimed to be drawn up by Mao who drew the international picture and then this framework often acted as a blueprint for Zhou's pragmatic foreign affairs yet, there were moments when there were ideological conflicts between the soft power foreign diplomacy (pursued by Zhou) and the hard power diplomacy (pursued by Mao) and

[3] According to Kissinger, Zhou was a compelling figure with short, elegant and expressive face—with luminous eyes dominated by exceptional intelligence and the capacity to intuit the intangible of the psychology of his counterpart. (Kissinger 2012, 241)

[4] The US and Soviet political manifestations could be described as a duopoly of political systems at that stage.

[5] Mao stated this was the reason behind appointing Chen Yi as the foreign minister to replace Zhou from the international theatre.

hence there were several unreasonable incidents which stained Zhou's skilful diplomatic achievements. The hard power diplomacy which aimed to enforce ideologies towards neighbouring countries were generally met with hostile receptions and became a key contributor to the isolation of China during the beginning of Mao's rule; in contrast, Zhou wanted to implement a form of soft power diplomacy which encouraged engagement from nearby countries. Hence, it seems rational that most of the effective foreign policy initiatives were managed in synthesis with Zhou's idea of 'soft power' politics; Geneva conference was a successful debut in imprinting China as a foreign power in the global scheme of things but then the first Strait Crisis, which caused hostile reactions from neighbouring countries, and the Bandung Agreement for organising Asian-African-led Third World and Great Leap Forward Movement (hereafter GLFM), brought dire consequences and economic and industrial setbacks in China. Was Mao worried of Zhou who could now challenge his authority with support from overseas, especially Moscow? In comparison to other leaders, Mao was one of the few who had very limited foreign knowledge and had been unable to study abroad;[6] this consequently limited his foreign diplomacy capabilities and due to this, he became more reliant on the actions of Zhou; yet, due to his personal insecurities, he did not wholly sympathise with the actions of Zhou on international affairs.

After just two visits to Moscow, Mao relied on Zhou as the key person to negotiate foreign affairs; however, it was understandable that Zhou's successful appearance in international field troubled Mao in governing domestic matters. Therefore, Mao tried to intertwine Zhou's international success with the domestic chaos and reduce Zhou's achievements in the international scale. This exemplifies the childish, yet, intricate psychological condition of Mao. According to Lucian Pye,

> 'at each stage of his life, Mao came into conflict with those in authority over him: his father, the school headmaster, other leaders of the Chinese Communist Party (hereafter CCP), Stalin, and Khrushchev. In each case, Mao drew his rival into conflict and focused his psychic energy on defeating

---

[6] Since 1918, most of intellectuals in China left for Europe for 'Work & Study program'. Mao decided to go to France, but dropped out at the last minute.

> that enemy. While idealising comradely love within revolutionary ranks, Mao seems to have been incapable of such feelings, and was prone to anger when he felt that his voice was being ignored. Mao's personal physician, with many years of attending to Mao, also noted that Mao was subject to bouts of "irrational suspicion" of plots directed against him, and that these bouts coincided with insomnia, headaches, anxiety, depression, and bad temper' (Garver 2016, 129)

His psychological turbulence made several last minute changes on the Chinese international affairs and it was Zhou who had to seal them.[7]

Mao's worries concerning Zhou emerged at the burgeoning stage of Chinese communism. Before the CCP was founded, there were three main groups supporting the CCP. The first group was the Beijing- and Shanghai-based workers who were working on foreign companies and was mutually supported by the Soviet intelligence, and was regarded as the main power houses for Liu Shaoqi between 1925 and 1932 before his trip to the Soviet Union. This group was considered to be the engine of Chinese revolution in terms of intellectual capacity, which bore similarities to that of the Bolsheviks in the Russian Revolution. Hence, Mao perceived this group with great hostility as they symphasised with the Russian communist groups. The second group was comprised of peasants mainly from Hunan province, who were led by a small number of intellectuals, one of whom was Mao. As a home-grown leader, Mao paid extra attention to this group and this division was continuously used by him during his regime. Lin Biao emphasised the second group on his 'Long Live the Victory of Peoples' War!' speech by stating that 'The countryside, and the countryside alone, can provide the broad areas in which the revolutionaries can manoeuvre freely. The countryside, and the countryside alone, can provide the revolutionary bases from which the revolutionaries can go forward to find victory' (Marxist Archive 2016). This is Mao's view on international peasants' revolution and Zhou try to implant this idea in several countries in Africa. The third group was labelled as the 'Work & Study' members, such as Zhou, Deng Xiaoping, and 'Father of the Red Army' Zhu De, who went Western

[7] Mao trusted the foreign affairs information from PLA field marshals, who were, he believed, front line soldiers that represented Mao style Chinese revolution.

Europe, especially Paris and Berlin. They were ready to serve China and demonstrated the pragmatic ideals that were necessary to enable China to pursue her independent manifesto with ease. From Mao's view, they were to be treated as valuable technocrats when the 'new' state of China was to be established. Nevertheless, much like the first denomination, their political ideology was a key concern to Mao. Especially due to their affiliations with the Soviets, Mao was cautious when there was the Sino-Soviet conflict. This was another reason why Mao was so sceptical in placing great responsibility and power to Zhou. Hence, the appointment of Chen Yi from Marshall to foreign minister was a political intervention from Mao to monitor Zhou's intentions and his foreign relation dealings. During the well-known 'ping-pong' diplomacy, furthermore, Mao appointed two translators (Nancy Tang and Hanzhi Zhang[8]) while Zhou was meeting with US delegates and received reports from them. Based on their reports, Mao made the simple conclusion about Zhou's foreign policy, which as illustrated by Brezhnev's visit to the USA, was essentially 'joint domination of the world'.[9]

On Zhou's international affairs, Mao had rather idealistic thoughts, he stated,

> Those who wish to move the world must move the world's hearts and minds, (and). … to move people's heart one must have great ultimate principles. Today's reforms all begin with minor details such as the parliament, the constitution, the presidency, the cabinet, military affairs, business and education—these are all side issues... Without ultimate principles, such details are merely superfluous... For the ultimate principles are the truths of universes… Today, if we appeal to the hearts of all under heaven on the basis of great ultimate principles, can any of them fail to be moved? And if all the hearts in the realm are moved is there anything that cannot be achieved? (Short 1999, 80).

[8] They were members of 'five golden flowers' and engaged in several issues on Chinese foreign affairs. Mao refused to read or to listen to what Zhou made, and enjoyed listening to the reports of the interpreters instead.

[9] It was rare case that Zhou was praised, as Mao strongly criticised him as being a surrender of US imperialism.

He knew the hearts will be a common agreement among people and it will come from the mass population, the peasants. His belief in peasants revolution remained unchanged until his death even when Lin Biao, Mao's favourite successor, was murdered in a plane crash on 13 September 1971.[10] Mao's view on revolution was highly reliant on quantity rather than quality, and thus he believed that every country would be able to achieve revolution from the bottom upwards. This view was opposed to that of Liu and Zhou's beliefs on revolution and that of Russian intelligentsia which stated that gradual revolution was the most coherent solution.

Similar to other first-generation Chinese leaders, Zhou was educated in Confucianism, and was then converted to Russian Marxism. However, Chinese centralism and Sinology remained his prime philosophy.

> According to its (Confucius) teachings, the first task of a learned person is to establish order and harmony and to serve his country and its people. The push to achieving this (*ren*) is to learn kindness and love for others, beginning with one's family. Self-cultivation, the raising of a decent family, the administration of the country, and the search for peace in the world (*xiushen, qijia, zhiguo, ping tianxia*) were basic principles that Zhou aimed to put into practice during his entire life. Closely linked to these principles was the promotion of the doctrine of the mean: the avoidance of excess and the tendency toward moderation as crystallised in the Confucius maxim, 'to go beyond is as wrong as to fall short'. Zhou, like many traditional intellectuals, was strongly influenced by these concepts. Even as a fervent revolutionary Zhou never allowed himself to go beyond what he considered appropriate. Loyalty to the king was another essential element of Confucius teaching, one that Zhou employed in his relations with the modern Chinese emperor, Mao Zedong, to whom he was the very picture of devotion (Barnouin and Yu 2006, 12).

After his short stay in prison in Nankai, Zhou and close friend Li Fujing were selected to receive Sino-French Educational Commission grant and headed to France on 7 November 1920. Unlike the members of Work

[10] One of the most symbolic figures from this group was Ji Dengkui, who followed Mao since Hunan and was one of the 'old and trusted friends' for Mao and Mao discussed Lin's issue with him before he died. (Salisbury 1993, 300)

& Study group, Zhou was financially safe and thus he spent most of his time travelling to England, Germany, and France and devoted himself to revolutionary activities. Moreover, he started to contemplate the ideal path China had to take to become independent from Japan. In his letter to his cousin, he stressed that there were '... two possible paths for China. Either China's ills had to be cured by violent means, like October Revolution in Russia, or "by gradual reform", as practised in England. I do not have a preference for either the Russian or the British way.' Zhou continued 'I would prefer something in-between rather than either one of these two extremes.' (Ibid, 26). As a pragmatic reformer, his political picture followed what he learned from the Confucius Gold Rule—gradual pragmatism through intelligentsia. And this was opposite to that of Mao's views and hence Mao thought Zhou was a quasi-Soviet idealist.

During the second CCP meeting on 1–19 January 1926 in Guangzhou, Mao met Zhou for the first time in Li Huchuen's house, who was disguised as a bearded Catholic priest.

> Mao was a rebel by nature, much less give to Party discipline and much less ready to compromise than Zhou. Mao was frequently at odds with the Comintern and much of the CCP leadership. In his famous report on the agrarian movement in Hunan published on 20 March 1927, he presented the unorthodox thesis regarding the vital importance of the peasantry—more vital than the proletariat—for the revolution in China. Because he was thoroughly acquainted with the countryside, he was capable of appreciating the vast revolutionary potential of the peasants... The countryside was remote from the national government, yet, in his view, it was the ideal location for maintaining and developing "separate armed soviet bases", with the potential to be self-sufficient and defensible by a strong and disciplined Red Army. Mao disagreed more or less openly with most of the central leadership's revolutionary strategies—largely inspired by the Comintern (Ibid, 53).

This viewpoint was disparate to that of Zhou; however, until 'Long March' Zhou was at a greater position than Mao, so it was only a minor issue during this period. At the beginning of 1932, Mao and Zhou came to tug-of-war about the military strategy for the Red Army due to the anti and pro-Comintern-led military strategy. Mao was still advocating mobile guerrilla tactics, including the device of luring the nationalist deep into the base camp; in contrast, Zhou thought that a strong defence at home was necessary in fighting positional warfare and carrying the offensive to the enemy territory instead of allowing the enemy behind the camp. Although there were disagreements between the two, mutual respect between Mao and Zhou was demonstrated during the Ningdu conference as Zhou defended Mao's mistake and made the formal request for him to keep his post; however, the conference appointed him to take over Mao's post as general political commissar of the First Field Army. 'Mao never forgot the humiliation that he had suffered, but he also remembered Zhou's defence of his policies, and recalled that during the Ningdu conference, Lo Fu (Zhang Wentian) wanted to expel me, but Zhou and Zhu De did not agree' (Ibid, 55). This was what Zhou learned from his past experience and he had the inherent belief that Mao would be a successful revolutionary when the time came about.

After the 'Long March', the political leadership in the CCP was controlled by Mao. On his arrival in Yan'an in July 1943 after his Chongqing life, Zhou showed strong loyalty to Mao and committed himself to Mao. The inherent value Zhou had was that the success of the People's Party superseded that of any other individual, including his ambitions. However, Mao criticised Zhou by stating that although 'only five (Mao Zedong, Zhou Enlai, Xiang Ying, Ren Bishi and Liu Shaoqi) had survived. Only two of them (Mao himself and Liu Shaoqi) had been clearly opposed to the Wang Ming line, while the other three had supported it' (Ibid, 93). Mao's suspicion lasted until the death of Zhou. During the 'Long March', Mao's ideological and political belief became rapidly nationalised; therefore, he wanted his successor to serve the new country with nationalistic beliefs he had come to embrace. Zhou, in Mao's eyes, was not a pure nationalist. However, Mao trusted Zhou as a faithful colleague to work with and a loyal servant in formalising a new China.

As a left hand man,[11] Zhou was put in charge of the Ministry of Foreign Affairs, the Ministry of the Interior, the Commission of the Overseas Chinese Emigrants, and the Secretariat. Needless to say, the Ministry of

[11] When China declared the independent Mao as their leader, Liu was considered as his right-hand man and Zhou was considered third in command.

Foreign Affairs was his main job and he stayed true to his role until his death despite it being transferred to Marshal Chen Yi in 1958.

Although he started his official diplomatic job in line with the establishment of China, his diplomatic career began in the early 1920s, when he was working as a representative of the CCP. He dealt with the Comintern and Soviet relations and he was in charge of the International Information Section in the Wuhan Office of the CCP-led Eighth Route Army during the anti-Japanese War. Since the Wuhan office moved to Chongqing, he had various relations with not only diplomats and military leaders but also journalists including Hemingway.[12]

Since 1 October 1949, the new Chinese government had to establish a 'new paradigm of international relationship' or 'make a fresh start' with not only the Asian neighbourhood but all over the world, with Kuomintang no longer representing China. On 1 October 1949, Zhou as foreign minister notified that any country who wished to have a diplomatic relationship with the People's Republic of China (hereafter China) had to first break diplomatic relations with the Republic of China (hereafter Taiwan) and express support for China's claim to Taiwan's seat at the Security Council at the UN.

This announcement clearly demonstrated that the Chinese foreign policy, even during their primary stages of independence, will be highly reliant on international support for acknowledging China in the international society and removing Taiwan from it. Within a day, Moscow was the first country to establish foreign relations and consequently, 11 Communist countries opened their diplomatic channels within two months. Between December 1949 and January 1950, 13 countries from the non-communist bloc established diplomatic links: Burma, India, Pakistan, Great Britain, Ceylon (later renamed Sri Lanka), Norway, Denmark, Israel, Indonesia, Afghanistan, Finland, Sweden, and Switzerland. While discussing with Burmese government, the Burmese foreign minister cabled to Zhou on 16 December 1949 that they were ready to cancel her obligations towards Taiwan, demand the expulsion of her representatives from the UN, and

[12] Ernest and his wife Martha met three key figures while they were in China, H.H. Kung, Chiang Kai-shek with their wives, and Zhou made very critical comments of both leaders and predicted that 'the communists would take over China after the war' (Barnouin and Yu, 89).

transfer ownership of Taiwanese property in Burma to China. Zhou took this agreement as a model for further negotiations on the establishment of diplomatic relation (Garver, 32).

Although Moscow was important for implementation of the Chinese international policy, Zhou thought nationalistic foreign policy was required post the disappointing visit in Moscow in 1950, and thus, he developed inherent nationalist tendencies in their efforts to achieve world power status and they insisted on stressing the role of the peasantry. He claimed that 'our form of communism is very different from that of the Soviet Union' (Hollingworth 1987, 76–77). However, Zhou at the same time emphasised to his staff 'to learn from the Soviet big brothers' (Barnouin and Yu, 200). To avoid international isolation, Zhou thought Moscow's support was essential not only diplomatically and in the military but also economically. Zhou's diplomatic adventure was forced to stop when the Korean War broke out on 25 June 1950.

The Chinese view on the Korean War was that it was the US-led imperialists attacking the proletarian internationalism regime and it was the first 'struggle for liberation' in Asia. It was Liu Shaoqi who provided theoretical reasoning in joining the war. He emphasised that 'when and where possible it is necessary to establish a national People's Liberation Army, powerful and good for fighting and led by the Communist Party... and the armed struggle is the main form of struggle for many colonial and semi-colonial peoples. These are the basic roads taken by the Chinese people in achieving victory inside the country... These roads can also be the pattern … for peoples of other colonial and semi-colonial countries' (Clubb 1964, 336). Mao had the fundamental expectation that China following the Russian Revolution of 1917 with the consequential CCP victory would be followed by similar upheavals in other parts of Asia, so participating in the Korean War was beyond question. Therefore, even Chinese leaders who had previously been unaware of North Korea sent forces to General Peng Dehuai. Mao reiterated in his party meeting that 'What you have said sounds reasonable. But it would be shameful for us to stand by seeing our neighbours in perilous danger without offering any help' (Hao and Zhai 1990).

However, this unexpected military intervention in the Korean peninsula caused serious concerns from neighbouring countries in Asia. Condemned by the UN as an invader, unable to obtain Taiwan's position in the Security Council in the UN and being diplomatically cut off from the majority of UN member states, Zhou faced a great crisis in his mission. The isolation that was caused by the involvement in the Korean War was having dire effects and Zhou needed to break through this crisis through various channels. 'His new diplomacy was highly pragmatic and guided by geopolitical rather than ideological consideration... Flexibility, negotiation, and personal diplomacy were the tools that Zhou employed to achieve his goals' (Barnouin and Yu, 152). When the war ended, the Chinese foreign office had to recover pre-war diplomatic relations, and Zhou's consolidation effort with neighbouring countries was supported by Moscow and the Geneva Conference came into substance under the Russian proposition to the United States, the United Kingdom, France, and China in formulating pragmatic solutions for the future of the Korean peninsula. It was the last piece of diplomatic support given by Moscow; nevertheless, this support triggered the suspicions from Mao to think of Zhou's pro-Russian tendency.

In preparation for his first appearance at an international conference as the head of a new country, Zhou took great care and made three visits to Moscow, and under the stewardship of Krushchev and Molotov, he was able to compose a pragmatic speech which encompassed the values and beliefs of the new China. A notable achievement of Zhou in the Geneva conference was laying the foundations in building bilateral relations with the British. A British representative recalled that 'Zhou is poised and firm in negotiations. He works for the fine points, even by the standard of his country' (Eden 1960, 138).

After the Geneva Conference in 8 May 1954, Zhou devised the famous 'Five Principles of Peaceful Coexistence'[13] which must be respected by newly independent countries from the Asian and African continent and that became the groundwork for China's Third World foreign policy. His appearance in international stage made a huge impact not only globally

[13] The Five Principles was initially designed by Mao during the Yan'an period, however it was implemented by Zhou in line with the Third World foreign policy.

but also domestically. *The New York Times* reported Zhou with the long featured headline: 'BEHIND THE BAMBOO CURTAIN AT GENEVA, and sub-headlined 'CLANNISH AND CLOSE-MOUTHED, RED CHINA'S DELEGATES ... PLAY FROM STRENGTH AND DEMAND BIG POWER STATE' (Ji 2008, originally emphasised). On 22 July 1954, People's Daily report Zhou's international appearance in length of report:

> For the first time as one of the Big Powers, the People's Republic of China joined the other major powers in negotiations on vital international problems and made a contribution of its own that won the acclaim of wide sections of world opinion. The international status of the People's Republic of China as one of the big world powers has gained universal recognition. Its international prestige has been greatly enhanced. The Chinese people take the greatest joy and pride in the efforts and achievements of their delegation at Geneva.

In 11 August 1954, few days after People's Daily report on Zhou's great achievement in Geneva, PLA attacked Kinmen and Matsu islands and it was labelled the first Formosa Crisis. It mainly comprised of bombardment, but its impact was much greater than it was forecasted. Since the Korean War and the Taiwan Strait Crisis,[14] Chinese-style 'shake-up' policy, which implemented aggressive foreign policy at times even local war, had the fundamental aim to divert attention from domestic problems, to compensate for domestic failures, or to recreate domestic unity, which was applied not only in mainland China but also in Taiwan via regional warfare. Domestic complaints in the two Chinas was reduced by the Strait Crisis—both leaders (Mao and Chiang Kai-sheck) knew that war was not viable unless the USA intervened; therefore, both leaders frequently used this idea as an instrument of their propaganda. In addition, Mao used 'shake-up' domestic strategy to regulate Zhou-led foreign policy.

[14] According to James and Zhang (2005), the notion of crisis in China embeds two levels of meanings; threat/danger as well as opportunity. In dealing with international crises, four bimodal attitude pairs provide mental readiness and useful heuristics for management of long-term Chinese foreign policy 'strategies' as well as short-term 'tactics' regarding immediate actions. (p. 36)

This Mao's 'shake-up' strategy, which correlates with 'hard power foreign policy' caused internal conflict and Zhou was replaced by former marshal Chen Yi's.[15] According to Yahuda, (1996), 'In 1958, when Chinese foreign policy shifted away from the moderation of Bandung towards a more militant revolutionary line, these misgivings about China intensified'. It was rather Mao's hard power foreign policy and Zhou's attempts to dilute it into 'soft power foreign relations' since the Geneva Conference.[16]

Regarding Zhou's 'soft power foreign policy',

> Mao could hardly tolerate that Zhou, and not he himself, was widely considered as the architect of the new Chinese foreign policy thus overshadowing him in international stature. In July 1973, Mao began to criticise the Foreign Ministry, whose appraisal of the world situation he did not appreciate. He complained that the Foreign Ministry was sending "incomplete documents" that he refused to read. He would not read the premier's speeches either, he said. In Mao's view, the ministry failed to discuss 'important matters' with him while producing reports on 'minor matters'. He warned that 'if the situation did not improve, revisionism was bound to occur. Mao's criticism threw Zhou into panic' (Barnouin and Yu 295).

Since Korea and the Indochina Wars, Washington's main diplomatic goal in Asia was Chinese isolation. Massive military invasion in Korean War, and diplomatic support to revolt groups in Indochina substantially hindered the US Army, 'Red China' was the main strategic goal from Washington, and therefore the isolation of China was the main diplomatic objective from the State. At the same time, Mao designed the goal of 'anti-imperialism', which had an underlying aim of claiming independence from Russia, led to the cut-off of relations between Beijing and Moscow. The aim of the Bandung conference was the opportunity for

[15] With Marshal Zhu De, Chen Yi was one of the most important generals for Mao before Lin Biao. During the Cultural Revolution, Chen tried to balance Chinese foreign policy between the 'Ultra-Leftists' and the 'pragmatic way' which was led by Zhou. (Short 1999)

[16] Although it was an appropriate choice in international relation's perspective, the pragmatic soft power diplomacy was criticised and Zhou made self-personal critics on Chinese foreign policy between the years 1954–58 in the Chengdu conference in 1958 and then stepped down from the position of foreign minister.

China to implant their foreign policy while stepping out of the Soviet Union's shadows. Zhou's approach to the Third World in line with India was highly pragmatic and was designed with various objectives dependent on different regions. According to Garver,

> After Nehru strongly endorsed Zhou's speech, opposition to 'peaceful coexistence' faded away. Zhou's personal demeanour—modest but self-confident, firm on principle but flexible in negotiation, treatment of others as equals open to reasonable argument and persuasion—impressed many delegates. Zhou expended considerable effort meeting and talking with delegates, both during and outside of conference sessions. As Huang Hua pointed out, 'China's role at the Bandung conference opened the door to increased contacts with many Asian and African countries' (p. 108).

It was diplomatic success from the Chinese foreign office to the Third World, and a personal triumph for Zhou himself; however, it was continuously criticised by the 'Ultra-Leftist' including Mao as the pragmatist. As a result, Zhou eyed African foreign policy to avoid critics and to implant Mao's 'peasant's communism' message in this continent.

According to Gillespie (2004), 'In many of these Asian countries, independence was accompanies by well-developed social and economic infrastructure. By contrast, many newly independent Africans states were open to new social and economic models. Thus, African decolonisation contributed to China's revolutionary zeal in that it provided a rare opportunity for China to put its new revolutionary-based policy into practice.' Not only geopolitical advantage, but exporting Mao's communism in Africa as fresh model, Chinese diplomatic effort in Africa was kicked off at the Bandung Conference in 1955 and then blossomed during Zhou's famous 'Safari Tour' in 1963–64.

The Bandung Conference, which led to the formation of a new strategic alliance among the Third World countries, especially Africa countries, launched the famous 'Five Principles of Peaceful Coexistence'. The 'Five Principles of Peaceful Coexistence' which was crafted in 1949 appeared as a cornerstone in this adventure. The statement was delivered by Premier Zhou in his visit to India and Myanmar. These principles reinforced mutual respect for sovereignty and territorial integrity; mutual non-aggression; non-interference in each other's internal affairs, equality and mutual benefit; and peaceful coexistence. In April 1955, the Bandung Conference, the Foreign Minister[17] Zhou met several African leaders and expressed the value of 'Five Principles of Peaceful Coexistence'.

'Zhou stated that Chinese farmers and miners had been sent to Africa when China suffered from European Powers' colonial rule. They were treated as slaves like African people. Zhou emphasised this during the meeting between Zhou and African leaders. It made the Chinese looked different from the Europeans who had been immersed in imperialism. That made cultural elements on Chinese foreign policy successful in a short period of time'. (Author's interview at the Conference in Jinan)

In addition, during the Bandung Conference, the first diplomatic appearance from China with Third World countries, Zhou tried to distinguish the pro-Soviets from the pro-Chinese in Africa. China displayed the notion of independence in the international stage, claiming that they were not Russian's followers, but they had their own ideal in the form of 'Maoism'. It was Mao's first independent and self-reliant form of diplomacy from China in the international stage after Stalin's failure to keep promises for the third times during the Korean War.[18]

Zhou believed that the Bandung conference emphasised the potential benefit for not only China but also her neighbourhoods including African countries to stand up against the two super powers. Therefore, he designed the international relations from Chinese perspective and it was delivered by Deng Xiaoping at the UN in April 1974. This is called Maoism foreign policy to emphasise people's power and their independence from foreign intervention. For enhancing Chinese role in the Third World, Zhou visited Cambodia, India, Burma, Pakistan, Afghanistan, Nepal, and Ceylon as a goodwill mission from November 1956 to February 1957. The main aim for this trip was to convince

[17] It is his last official engagement as Foreign Minister. After the 11th Plenum of the Central Committee meeting in 1957, Marshal Chen Yi had the job till 1972; therefore, most of Zhou's international roles till his death in 1976 were working alongside the Premier.

[18] According to Short (1999), at Xian in 1936 and in Manchuria in 1945, all that had been at stake were the political interests of a Chinese Party still struggling for power. But now (during the Korean War) China was a sovereign state, and Russia a treaty ally. 'Lean to one side' or not, the Soviet Union, Mao concluded, would never be a partner Chinese could trust (p. 430).

Chinese effort to keep 'Five Principles of Peaceful Coexistence' under Beijing's leadership and reassure the fact that China is the only reliable country without imperialist ambitions.

In the Third World foreign relations, diplomatic gesture and political implementation is quite often moved into different directions. It was the main concern from Asian neighbourhoods that how to reconcile Chinese official confirmation of non-interference in other countries' domestic issues while China provided economic aids. Zhou argued that 'the Chinese government had always differentiated between foreign affairs, on one hand, and revolution in a given country, on the other. The former was a matter of state-to-state relations while the latter is an internal matter. Echoing Mao, Zhou stressed that revolution was not for export' (Barnouin and Yu, 160). It was Zhou-led foreign office's perspective, and other committees in the CCP thought other way round, especially the PLA, which was led by Ultra-Leftist and even Mao himself.

These 'anti-pragmatic' opinions from other departments had been properly managed by Foreign Ministry when Zhou maintained power, however these people had not been controlled since the GLFM and the Cultural Revolution where Zhou was in a minor position and it led to troubles between Mao's 'hard power' diplomacy and her neighbouring countries especially Asian countries. Furthermore because of the continues wars against India, Russia and Vietnam that followed many Asian countries thought Maoist foreign policy was another type of existing imperialism. This doubt made Ultra-Left PLA continually bring about military intervention in neighbouring countries in an aggressive manner.

In the midst of extreme Maoism, the death of Stalin triggered the transformation of the relations between China and Russia from 'Big Brother' to that of hostility much like the 'Anglo-French' foreign relations. Stalin's failure to keep promises during the Korean War started to brew the role of communist leadership issues between Beijing and Moscow and this peaked when Khrushchev made critics on Stalin on February 1956 and announced his 'secret report', which was criticised by Mao that 'the Soviet leader had "disclosed (Stalin's) mistake" but, at the same time, had "made a mess of things"' (Barnouin and Yu, 200).

The first stage of Sin-Soviet diplomatic war was occurred in Africa, where Soviet Union and China increased their efforts to enlarge their own geopolitical stake on the international stage. Immediately after the Sino-Indian War in 1962, Moscow and Beijing competed for the allegiance of the various liberation movements and newly independent countries in the Third World, especially Africa. Therefore, Chinese engagement in Africa was the outcome of diplomatic hegemony between two Communists leaders. However, it was different from the diplomacy war in Africa between China and Taiwan. Because diplomatic competition in Africa between China and Russia was not in synthesis, but pretext that China is the country from which Stalin-Lenin's communism has originated.

> According to Chen (2005), Mao proposed an alternative version, a Chinese version of socialist internationalism, which was more radical, revolutionary and militant as well as being in line with Mao's view of Chinese nationalism. In 1963, the People's Daily unveiled this Chinese socialist internationalism: 'Workers of all countries, unite; workers of the world, unite with the oppressed peoples and oppressed nations; oppose imperialism and reactionaries in all countries; strive for world peace, national liberation, people's democracy and socialism; consolidate and expand the socialist camp; bring the proletarian world revolution step by step to complete victory; and establish a new world without imperialism, without capitalism and without the exploitation of man by man. This, in our view, is the general line of the international communist movement at the present stage.

Zhou's appointment of Wang Jiaxiang as Deputy vice minister[19] led to the arousal of Mao's suspicion on Zhou's Moscow connection. After GLFM, on a Mao's request, the Central Committee meeting, Wang as a head of the Party's International Liaison Department blamed the Beijing foreign policy by stating that 'China should try as much as possible to avoid international complications. … The spring brought faint signs of an easing of tension with India and the Soviet Union,

[19] Wang is lifelong friend of Zhou, who served as the ambassador to the Soviet Union and helped to convince Stalin of Mao's claims to the leadership. Although he left Wang Min and converted to Mao, he was categorised as being a pro-Soviet at the first stage of his job as Deputy Foreign Minister. Later, he was purged in the Cultural Revolution, and re-emerged at the tenth Party Congress in 1973.

and in June an understanding was reached with the Americans to avoid renewed conflict over Taiwan.' Although it was agreed by Liu and Deng, Mao thought it was betrayal. Mao took a counter offensive viewpoint at the annual summer work conference at Beidaihe that 'the responsibility systems were incompatible with the collective economy. The Party, therefore, faced a stark choice: "Are we going to take the socialist road or the capitalist road? Do we want rural cooperativisation or do not we?"' (Short, 514).

As far as policy implementation is concerned, there was no third way from Mao's view. Since Wang's comment, Mao carefully observed the relations between Zhou and Wang. In addition, Chinese five years development plan was initially designed between Moscow and Zhou after the Korean War, and thus Zhou tried to follow gradual industrial progress in China. On June 1956, Zhou's economic plan, which was opposite of what Mao wants, was severely attacked by Mao and other local party leaders. As Ke Qingshi, who is the Party secretary in Shanghai, as submitted report on 'Braving the Storm and Accelerating the Process of Construction of a Socialist New Shanghai', which demonstrated Mao's rapid industrial reform was worked in Shanghai, Zhou's gradualism was proven wrong. During this meeting, therefore Mao blamed Zhou's slow progress on industrialisation progress several times and triggered his vision on industrialisation program called 'GLFM', which was first major industrial set back in China since her independence. On self-criticism, Zhou emphasised the necessity of learning from Chairman Mao that 'On the one hand my errors have shown that if one departs from or goes against his guidance and instructions, one always goes astray and commit mistakes. On the other hand, if we do things correctly, it is due to Chairman Mao's leadership and thought' (Barnouin and Yu, 173). It was a fundamental change not only due to his diplomatic favours with Moscow, but the removal of all Soviet systems from Chinese politics. Nevertheless, as a new country, which had limited resources for an economically expanding country, departures from Moscow was politically dangerous and economically hazardous regardless of Mao's suspicions.

2.3 Safari Tour and End of Two Chinas Competition in Africa

China's move into Africa led them to encounter one enemy and a former ally, Taiwan and Soviet Union, and hence their foreign policy required skilful representation and the mixture of three main elements: political, international as well as cultural elements. Without the economic element,[20] which is a key area of interest from African countries, these elements required personal engagement and it was Zhou who went to Africa with the dream of a Mao's peasants' revolution in African countries.

As the Chinese leaders' view on Taiwan was that it should be considered as a state within their own country, all leaders thought the unification is vital. Although the relations between Beijing and Taipei would be similar to that of Hong Kong and Macao, the unification idea would be a historical process and that of great significance since the Han dynasty. However, from Taiwan's perspective as an independent country, it is a revised form of international intervention, not a domestic issue; therefore, the two 'liberation efforts' from Chinese attacks were inevitable. On 1958, the second crisis was the last physical confrontation between Taiwan and China and then the dispute got moved to international stage. In contrary to Beijing, the second attack seemed to provide Taiwan with a safety net and they appeared to be considered as an independent country in the global stage. Since the attack, US provided US$ 90 million in military enforcements alone as well as direct and indirect economic aid which allowed Taiwan to industrialise rapidly. Except territorial loss, which two islands were neutralised by US pressure, Taiwan secured military support from the USA and quickly diversified her main policy into industrialisation and this economic power was the reserve for extending diplomatic relations with the newly independent countries from Africa. Zhou, who believed unification was the process of Chinese history, did not allow the Taiwanese international recognition efforts to gain coverage in Africa and drove himself to visit Africa under the cultural element with the implementation of massive human exchange programs.

[20] In comparison to Taiwan and Russia, China's aid in Africa was relatively small and thus it was difficult to persuade leaders to support China among the African countries.

As far as diplomatic competition between Taiwan and China in Africa was concerned, there was a strategic mistake from Taiwan and it was opportunity for Zhou before the Bandung conference. On route to Hong Kong to Jakarta, Taiwan intelligence attempted to assassinate Zhou and the plane crashed into the sea, killing 11 passengers on board. There was little doubt that Zhou had been aware of the plot beforehand; however, he used this plot to curb diplomatic negotiation with Britain, which was relatively friendly towards Chinese foreign affairs at Geneva conference the year before. It was not only an accomplishment in terms of diplomatic success with Britain but also one of symbolic gesture regarding Chinese competition to Taiwan during the conference. This incident had a short-term effect on breaking off diplomatic relations with Britain and showing Taiwan's belligerence to the Commonwealth of Nations.[21] Furthermore, the relationship between Taiwan and the UK got diminished; hence, Taiwan lost a key global ally, which hindered their claims for independence.

One of the major political and diplomatic objectives in her relationship with Africa was to end Taiwan's diplomatic presence in Africa. This is as it was a matter of fundamental regime legitimacy that African countries grasped the notion of the 'One China' policy and accepted Beijing rather than Taipei as the only lawful representative of China. This 'One China' policy was initiated from the outset of China's establishment in 1949 and still stands as one of the primary diplomatic objectives from the Chinese global perspective. Chinese traditional revolutionists, such as Mao and Zhou, thought strongly that Chinese reunification was their important historical mission. The US-led Taiwan was a potential problem that could weaken Chinese political endeavours to secure regional policy.

In Africa, the 'Two Chinas' shared lots of similar strategies to penetrate the continent. Any new independent country will, on the day of her independence, be assured of receiving almost identical messages from the foreign officers of the two Chinas, to be recognised as an only China from this country. Both Chinas have sent and received delegations to and from various African countries, both have had African leaders on official state visits, both have given scholarships to African young generations for training in their

[21] Author's interview with several participants from 'The Chinese in Africa/Africans in China Conference' in Jinan University, Guangzhou, China 12–14 December 2014.

respective areas, and both are involved in aid projects in Africa. According to James and Zhang (2005), 'it is important to note that most of the activities that have expanded and improved Chinese diplomatic relations around the world have also been effective means to isolate Taiwan, which seeks international recognition as an independent state.' That was rapidly diluted when Deng came to power and pursue 'open and development' policy. Since Deng came,[22] there was no military involvement between strait.

After the Korean War, Mao's suspicions concerning Moscow's role as the head of international communism peaked. Stalinism which was highly criticised and graved by his successor Khrushchev took Mao's view on the Communist bloc into his own blue print. Especially, the Maoism, which represented peasants and rural-led revolution, was highly appreciated by the Middle and South American nations by ideological choice, even though only a few countries implemented his idea into practice. Within international relations, Mao and Zhou believed Sinocentric logic was key to foreign relations, as

> restatement in modern terms of the fundamental postulates of the old Chinese view of the world: that China was the centre of civilization... The Chinese view of the world has not fundamentally changed: it has been adjusted to take account of the modern world, but only so far as to permit China to occupy, still, the central place in the picture. To do this, it was necessary to accept from the West a new doctrine (but) it was inevitable that Chinese Marxism should be found to be purer than that of Russia, that Mao should be hailed as the greatest prophet, and that 'some people' should be shown to be in error. There cannot be two suns in the sky (Fitzgerald, requoted from Ford 2010, 233–234).

Due to the continuous regional wars in Asia, Sinocentric revival was hindered and simultaneously, domestic pressure was rife—which was a fundamental reason for Zhou's decision to enter Africa. Domestically, the failures of the GLFM, meant that a scapegoat was needed which incurred the famous '7000-cadre big conference', called by Mao on the 11 January 1962.

---

[22] Deng's personal acknowledgment about Chiang Ching-kuo during his stay in France where he tried to avoid direct war between the two countries.

> As a result, the notion that a bourgeoisie might emerge within the Party, which Mao had first raised at Lushan in August 1959, was once again placed centre stage, now explicitly linked to a rejection of degenerate Soviet communism in a simple, four-character slogan: *Fan xiu, fang xiu*—'Oppose revisionism (abroad), prevent revisionism (at home)'. That fatal nexus would inform Mao's thinking, and dominate the politics of China, for the last fourteen years of his life (Short, 515).

As a leading figure in the pragmatist movement from Mao's perspective, Zhou needed a breakthrough for political survival, therefore he chose Africa—as the ideal plain for Mao's peasant revolution as per his proclaimed 'Five Principles of Peaceful Coexistence' initiative.

The principle was emphasised by the former Premier Wen Jiabao during the 50 years Anniversary of the 'Five Principles of Peaceful Coexistence' that

> First, they provide a set of right guidelines for the establishment and development of relations among countries with similar or different social systems. Second, they point out an effective way to peacefully address the issues left over by history between countries or other international disputes. Third, they give a strong protection to the interests of developing countries and serve the improvement and expansion of North-South relations. Fourth, they have provided an important philosophical basis for the establishment of a new international political and economic order that is just and rational. (*China Daily*, 29 June 2004)

The original 'Five Principles of Peaceful Coexistence' values were replaced on the 15 January 1964 by the 'Eight Principles of Economic and Technical Aid' initiative during his visit to 14 African countries which occurred within the period of seven weeks (Dec. 1963–Feb. 1964). The additional principles were the following: Chinese technical assistance should build upon local capacities, and Chinese experts working in Africa should have the same standard of living as the local experts; economic cooperation should promote self-reliance and not dependency; and respect for the recipient's sovereignty should mean imposing no political or economic conditions' on recipient governments. These principles form the basis of China's present day emphasis on 'friendly relationships' devoid of political conditions or interference in the internal affairs of African countries.

During his visit, Zhou's promised that six million Chinese people could help the African revolution and give hope to African countries that were inhibited from growing due to their meagre population levels. These cultural elements illustrated through human exchange between China and Africa, implied that China, when compared to the USA or Russia, had relatively weaker foreign currency holdings and that they were still in the midst of industrialisation. Liu Shaoqi further emphasised during his speech in Moscow on July 1949 that the Chinese Revolution was uniquely suited to serve as a model for future revolutions throughout the backward, agricultural, and colonialist-dominated areas of Asia and Africa (requoted from Neuhauser 1970). As a new regime, Africa, where anti-colonialist agitation was becoming more common and more acute was the right place to demonstrate China's status as a global leader.

A unique instance during this period, however, was the strong Chinese intervention in Africa through technical, medical, and agricultural aids rather than capital or financial support. China needed a great deal of foreign currency to develop their domestic economy. Furthermore, when compared to financial support, which was bound to be dispersed among a small number of government technocrats—these investments demonstrated direct Chinese engagement with the African public rather than the people at the top. In addition, these investments allowed the Chinese government to implant the so-called Beijing model in Africa; through mutual visits from government technocrats who taught them the manner in which China embarked upon her development experiences. This was an exemplary instance of 'soft power' diplomacy which was pursued by Zhou since China's independence.

Compared to technical investments, which were mainly managed by state-owned enterprises, medical investment was a collaboration project between a university laboratory and pharmaceutical/traditional Chinese medical institutions. With regard to medical aid, the chance of it meeting ordinary citizens was far higher than that of monetary aid. Thus, many Africans perceived that Chinese medical treatment was good, and found the Chinese people to be intelligent, as they were willing to serve them—a relatively rare circumstance in their countries. The President of Maskara Hospital in Algeria said, 'Frankly speaking, Maskara Hospital's reputation came with the arrival of Chinese doctors' (Health Dept. report from

Hubei Province, 1993). Also, from the Chinese perspective, by sending highly educated (before the Cultural Revolution) manpower to foreign countries, especially to countries in Africa; China could carry out their policy of human-based investment, compared to the American alternative of injecting cash in the form of aid and investment, which they preferred at that time. These medical services were greatly increased during Zhou's visit to Africa in 1965. When Zhou visited Zanzibar in 1965, he told the Chinese medical team that 'the teams would sooner or later return home. It was therefore necessary that Zanzibar's doctors should be trained and helped to work independently. In this way, China would leave a medical team which would never go away' (Li 2011).

It was thus relatively easy for Chinese medical treatment to make inroads in Africa because Chinese traditional treatments like acupuncture and herbal medicines were similar to African traditional treatment. The Hubei province had been in charge of dispatching medical aid in January 1963 to Algeria (Hubei province), followed by Congo in 1967 (Tianjin province), Botswana (Fujian province) in 1981, and Ghana in 2009. Forty-six countries were the recipients of Chinese medical aid since 1963, and China's medical aid to Africa has further made significant contributions to the healthcare sector of Africa, which is further aided by the fact that they endeavoured to issue aid without any political attachment or conditions[23] (Wang and Sun 2014).

Furthermore, the university educational exchange programme has consistently been continued by constantly letting competent African students study in China and by helping them become central forces in Africa in the long term. From the Chinese perspective, the 'China-African Education Cooperation' is often divided into three phases. The initial phase was triggered with the first diplomatic relations that China started with Kenya, Egypt, Uganda, and Cameroon in 1956. At the same time, 24 exchange students travelled to the other side. The second phase consisted of a period of implementation: from the 1970s to the 1980s the number of exchange students increased, and an official document from the Chinese government recorded that 4570 Africans had studied in China by the end of

[23] However, China suspended the medical aid and support and even withdrew them completely when the recipient countries proceeded to form diplomatic relations with Taiwan.

1996. Moreover, during this phase, China began to provide educational equipment to build research laboratories all over the continent. Finally, by the turn of the millennium, phase three started with the 'Declaration of 2000': it was a programme for the China-African cooperation in economic and social development which included human resources development and education. China then drew up a list of measures regarding African personnel training, academic cooperation projects (such as joint laboratories and research institutes), and scholarship opportunities (Kaiyu requoted from Ferdjani 2012). Beyond this, here was the continuation of the scholarship mechanism for longer-term training, mostly at the degree level, and there was also the sending of teachers to Africa to facilitate channels of communication between universities of both sides. Hence, in this case, the seeds were sowed by Zhou and were eventually harvested by Xi.

2.4 Xi's New Diplomatic Paradigm on African

On his first visit to Africa as the head of state, he emphasised the fact that 'in the nearly five decades since we established diplomatic relations, we have built up trust and constantly supported each other. Our political, economic and cultural cooperation has yielded fruitful achievements' (*China Daily*, 25 March 2013). It was the first announcement that claimed all three main diplomatic objectives (political, economic, and cultural elements) in line with the policy of 'soft power', but failed to achieve the international element, which was eventually achieved in 1971 when China joined UN and the Security Council. There is thus no need to talk about the two China's issue in Africa, as rapid economic development in Africa demands equal diplomatic status. As a global superpower, China endeavoured to embrace the resource affluent African countries in line with her global dream, the 'New Silk Road'.

Xi's diplomatic stance, since he came to power was referred to as being 'smart power'.[24] This 'smart power' was a key issue when China was working with Africa in terms of the UN and international institutions'

[24] Nye J. and Wilson E. (2008) developed a new concept of 'smart power' which combines elements of soft power and hard power to achieve a nation's foreign policy goal. From Chinese view, it is relatively different view that of Zhou's 'soft power', since China became a super power.

voting related processes. With 54 countries, Africa is the largest voting bloc in the UN and subsequent global organisations. China's effort in Africa under Xi was more heavily aimed at political and economic elements on 'smart power', such as the UN Human Rights Commission and the international negotiation for the birth of the AIIB and the New Silk Road Project. At every turn, African countries have given China strong support in foiling anti-China motions introduced by some Western countries at the UN Human Rights Commission including the Tibet issue.

When Xi visited Africa in 2013, he proclaimed that 'Africa', which is generally friendly towards China, became the top choice for China's 'Going-Out' strategy (*Xinwha* 26 March 2013). Since the introduction of the 'Going-Out' strategy from Jiang Zemin, there were a collection of critics on 'China in Africa', who stated that China has pursued mercantilist policies in the region for pure economic benefits without respecting human rights or environmental concerns. Officially, Beijing rejected the criticisms and cited two main arguments. As then Premier Wen stated, 'We believe that people in different regions and countries including those in Africa, have their right and ability to handle their own issues. The second reason China emphasised, was that its involvement in Africa is different from the colonialism of the past, and that an affluent China is now putting money back into the local African economy. As Chinese leaders like to say, it is a win-win situation' (Jiang 2006). Under Xi, therefore Chinese foreign policy will be high dependent on the three Es, economic growth, energy security, and environmental protection—to avoid further conflicts with not only developed countries but emerging countries also. In line with handling these critics in the right way, he proposed the global Sinocentric development model, which essentially was the new version of the Beijing Model including the AIIB for financial services and the New Silk Road plan for mutual manufacturing development between China and emerging countries including Sub-Saharan countries.

The 'New Silk Road' initiative, which Xi' government designed and led in an endeavour to achieve their global development policy—political, economic, international, and cultural elements, which had been pursued as the main four diplomatic goals since the independent of China in 1949, were integrated into a new single world order that was development-oriented with mutual prosperity. This was not only an infrastructure investment plan but also a plan that aimed to integrate the global infrastructure network connecting all sub-regions in Asia, Europe, and Africa including natural resources, intra-transportation, and communications. This plan could further be integrated into the development plans of many different African countries, and could further be used to condense Africa into a single large region which has not only free trade but financial integration also. In terms of the financial process, China started to expand their currency trading schemes with several Asian neighbours and will aim to continue that through the AIIB. One of main influences which led to the establishment of the AIIB under Xi was the Chinese currency swap agreement—with more than 31 countries (Data till January 2016). As the People's Bank of China stated,[25] this swap agreement clearly provides an opportunity for stealth reform of the global financial market for Chinese interests, which is one of China's long-term global financial objectives. The success of the rapid swap agreement allowed the Chinese government to establish the AIIB. Hereafter, the Chinese government recognised the *yuan*'s current position in terms of economies of scale and scope in the global financial market and the openness of the Chinese financial market, which was one of the main problems that led them to constantly pursue the swap agreement. The establishment of the AIIB was another solution to avoid this kind of domestic problem in the financial market.

Regarding the African–Chinese relationships, Yun's interview result made clear that '(I) n absolute terms, China's investment and trade with Africa has grown significantly when compared with the past. However, China's total global investment and trade levels have also grown exponentially since the reform process. The whole pie is bigger, and so is the African piece. But this does not mean that Africa is occupying a larger share of the pie. In relative terms, compared with China's investment and trade with other areas—Africa is still far behind' (Yun 2014).

[25] PBOC stated that those swap agreements were intended not only to 'stabilise the international financial market', but to facilitate bilateral trade and investment deals (PBOC news released Dec. 2014).

2.5 Conclusion

As a statesman, 'He (Zhou) preferred to risk being seen as being scared of such martyrdom than to allow the whole structure of government, which he had personally and so painstakingly built up. … to be completely destroyed' (Wilson 1998, 29). In the midst of establishing and sustaining a new country, China's role in international affairs was crucial. Not only to avoid domestic critics on his pragmatic gradualism but also to challenge 'Isolation on the Red China Diplomacy' from the USA and other countries internationally; Zhou's choice was to liaise with Africa in order to build the Sinocentric brotherhood, which was the only available option, and he was right in doing so.

When Mao met Wang Hongwen and Zhang Chunqiao in the summer of 1973, he grumbled that 'the Foreign Ministry was not discussing "important matters" with him, and that if this continued, "revisionism in bound to occur". The Ministry was Zhou's responsibility. It was there, a year earlier that the Premier had spoken out against ultra-Leftism. Mao had not forgotten. The anti-Confucius campaign was his way of warning Zhou' (Short, 612). Under this suspicion, Zhou needed to implement what Mao's wanted to do in international affairs, therefore he moved his attention to Africa, where he endeavoured to build the Sinocentric peasants' country. Due to several domestic obstacles, he only just managed to gain an international foothold (to secure a seat on the UN Security Council) and cultural elements (through human exchange programs) from Africa, and the economic elements formally commenced when Deng came to power.

In February 2007, President Hu Jintao visited Zambia and emphasised the fact that, 'in China, we say that when you are drinking water, you should not forget the people who dug the well, so we cannot forget the birth of our friendship' (*Xinhua*, 4 Feb. 2007). It was indeed Zhou Enlai, who dug the well that allowed the Chinese government to come and drink from it—which paved the way for Chinese–African relations, despite him being criticised on 22 December 1973 in the Politburo for his 'rightist capitulationist' diplomacy. Alike to his last words, 'I am loyal to the party and the people. I am not a capitulationist' (Barnouin and Yu 311), he was indeed the nucleus behind China's eventual development into a globally integrated power.

References

Alden, C., Daniel, L., Oliveira, D., & Soares, R. (Eds.). (2008). *China returns to Africa: A rising power and a continent embrace*. New York: Columbia University Press.

Barnouin, B., & Yu, C. (1998). *Chinese foreign policy during the cultural revolution*. London: Kegan Paul International.

Barnouin, B., & Yu, C. (2006). *Zhou Enlai: A political life*. Hong Kong: The Chinese University Press.

Chang, Chen-pang. (1979). Tough knots in piping's four modernisation. In *Chinese communist modernisation problems*. China Publishing Company.

Chang, Kuo-tao. (1972). *The rise of the Chinese Communist Party 1928–1938*, vol II (pp. 497). Lawrence Pub.

Chen, Z. (2005). Nationalism, internationalism and Chinese foreign policy. *Journal of Contemporary China, 14*, 47.

Chi, Yun-sheng. (1984). Communist China's aid to South Africa 1956 – 1980'. Thesis, University of the Witwatersrand, Johannesburg.

Clubb, O. E. (1964). *Twentieth century China*. New York: Columbia University Press.

Cumings, B. (1979). The political economy of Chinese foreign policy. *Morden China, 5*(4), 411–461.

d'Hooghe, I. (2015). *China's public diplomacy*. Leiden: Brill Nijhoff.

Eden, Anthony. (1960). *Full circle*. Collins.

Fatile, J. O., Afegbua, I. S. & Ejalonibu, G. I. (2016). *New global financial order and promotion of Asian infrastructural investment bank: Opportunities and challenges for Africa*. Mimeo.

Ferdjani, H. (2012). African students in China: An exploration of increasing numbers and their motivations in Beijing. *Research Paper from Centre for Chinese Studies*. Open Society Foundation.

Ford, C. A. (2010). *The mind of empire: China's history and modern foreign relations*. Lexington: The University Press of Kentucky.

Garver, J. W. (2016). *China's quest: The history of the foreign relations of the People's Republic of China*. New York: Oxford University Press.

Gavshon, A. L. (1981). *Crisis in Africa: Battleground of East and West*. London: Penguin.

George, A. L. (1980). *Presidential decisionmaking in foreign policy*. Boulder: Westview Press.

Gillespie, S. (2004). Diplomacy on a south-south dimension: The legacy of Mao's Three-Worlds theory and the revolution of Sino-African relationship. In H. Slavik (Ed.), *Intercultural communication and diplomacy*. Malta: Diplo Foundation.

Gurtov, M. (1969). The foreign ministry and foreign affairs during the cultural revolution. *The China Quarterly, 40*(1), 65–102.

Hao, Y., & Zhai, Z. (1990), China's decision to enter the Korean war: History revisited. *The China Quarterly*, (121), 94–115.

Hollingworth, C. (1987). *Mao*. London: Paladin.

James, P., & Zhang, E. (2005). Chinese choices: A poliheuristic analysis of foreign policy crises, 1950-1996. *Foreign Policy Analysis, 1*, 31–54.

Ji, C. (2008). *The man on Mao's right: From Harvard Yard to Tiananmen Square, my life inside China's Foreign Ministry*. New York: Random House.

Jiang, W. (2006, June 21). China's booming energy relations with Africa. *China Brief, 6*(13), 1.

Khun, R. L. (2010). *How China's leaders think: The inside story of China's reform and what this means for the future*. Singapore: Wiley.

Kissinger, H. (2012). *On China*. London: Penguin.

Kotze, D. J. (1979). *Communism and South Africa*. Cape Town: Tafelberg Publisher.

Lam, W. W.-L. (2008). China's petroleum diplomacy: Hu Jintao's biggest challenge in foreign and security policy. In G. Wu & H. Ladsdowne (Eds.), *China turns to multilateralism: Foreign policy and regional security*. London: Routledge.

Lawrance, A. (1975). *China's foreign relations since 1949*. London: Routledge.

Li, A. (2015). African diaspora in China: Reality, research and reflection. *The Journal of Pan African Studies, 7*(1), 10–43.

Mark, C.-k. (2012). *China and the world since 1945: An international history*. London: Routledge.

Neuhauser, C. (1970). *Third world politics: China and the Afro-Asian people's solidarity organisation 1957 – 1967*. Cambridge, MA: Harvard University Press.

Nye, J. S. Jr (2005, December 29). The rise of China's soft power. *Wall Street Journal Asia*. Last accessed 12 Apr 2016. http://www.belfercenter.hks.harvard.edu/publication/1499/rise_of_chinas_soft_power.html

People's Daily Online. (2007, October 21). CPC Central Committee report. http://www.china.org.cn/english/congress/229158.htm. Last access 31 May 2016.

Raine, S. (2009). *China's African challenges*. London: IISS, Routledge.

Salisbury, H. E. (1993). *The new emperors: Mao and Deng a dual biography*. London: Harper Collins.

Short, P. (1999). *Mao a life*. London: Hodder & Stoughton.

Wang, X. & Sun, T. (2014, June). China's engagement in global health governance: A critical analysis of China's assistance to the health sector of Africa. *Journal of Global Health, 4*(1), 14.

Whiting, A. S. (1959, January). Dynamics of the Moscow-peking axis. *Annals of the American Academy of Political and Social Science, 321*, 100–111.

Whiting, A. S. (1972). The use of force in foreign policy by the People's Republic of China. *Annals of the American Academy of Political and Social Science, 402*, 55–66.

Wilson, D. (1979). *Mao The people's emperor*. London: Hutchinson.

Wilson, D. (1998). Zhou Enlai: The man and his work. *World Affairs*, (2), 79–91.

Wu, G., & Ladsdowne, H. (Eds.). (2008). *China turns to multilateralism: Foreign policy and regional security*. London: Routledge.

Yahuda, M. (1996). *The international politics of the Asia-Pacific, 1945-1995*. London: Routledge.

Yu, G. T. (1977). China's role in Africa. *Annals of the American Academy of Politics and Social Science, 432*, 96–109.

Zhai, Q. (1992). China and the Geneva conference of 1954. *The China Quarterly, 129*, 180–183.

Zhao, S. (Ed.). (2015). *China in Africa: Strategic motives and economic interests*. Oxon: Routledge.

Zhao, J., & Chen, Z. (Eds.). (2014). *China and the international society: Adaptation and self-consciousness*. Singapore: World Century Publishing Corporation.

Zheng, Y. (2014). Multinational Asian Bank plans capital of $100b. *China Daily*, 30 June.

Several Quotations from These Internet News Archive Resources

China Daily. http://www.en.people.cn/

South China Morning Post. http://www.scmp.com/frontpage/hk

Xinwha. http://www.xinhuanet.com/english/

3

From White Elephants to Flying Geese: China in Africa a New Model for Development or More of the Same

Marina Thorborg

3.1 Introduction: Searching for New and Functioning Development Models

After World War II and de-colonisation, the newly independent states were exposed to its former motherlands, and a number of institutions and experts were all officially intent on helping them to find a shortcut to modernisation. Half a century later, it is possible not only to look at the ebb and flow of different development theories but also at the practical results.

Focusing on former colonies, including those achieving their independence during the nineteenth century, is it possible to find any common features for those managing to catch up with the most developed countries and for those falling hopelessly behind?

M. Thorborg (✉)
Soderton University, Stockholm, Sweden
e-mail: marinathorborg@hotmail.com

Y. C. Kim (ed.), *China and Africa*, The Palgrave Macmillan Asian Business Series, DOI 10.1007/978-3-319-47030-6_3

The first part of that question was discussed in a study for the World Bank led by Michael Spence, a Nobel laureate in economics. Since 1950, 13 developing economies were identified to experience rapid growth, 7 % or more annually, for a prolonged period of time of at least 25 years. From these 13 economies, five can be dismissed because of very special circumstances. Hong Kong, Singapore, and Malta are offshore financial centres and ports strategically located, while two with small populations—Botswana sits on a diamond mine and Oman on an oil field—are exceptions. Of the eight remaining countries, half of them experienced rapid growth in the short run which later petered out Indonesia, Malaysia, Thailand, and also Brazil.

Of the remaining four, China is still questionable, more about it below, while Japan, South Korea, and Taiwan are the clearest examples of latecomers catching up. * These three countries had some crucial, common features in their agricultural, industrial, and financial policies in addition to having access to the US market at critical periods during their catch-up periods. A common defining feature was the active role of the state in development, another being the high savings ratio turned into high investments ratio, strong investment in education and an industrial policy creating jobs as well as pragmatic provision of social services for those already educated.

Most important according to a new study by Eric Reinert, professor of Technology, Governance and Development Strategies, is the fact that successful latecomers all had tariffs and different types of protectionism—imposed by their own governments—for their emerging industries during the first development stages, that is, reinterpreting the dependency school industrialisation model combined with Schumpeterian imperfect competition. To develop an industrial base was crucial, because industries generate increasing returns on investment while more nations prioritising agriculture, the consequences were not positive. For this reason, all countries needed their own manufacturing and the Ricardian doctrine of comparative advantage had to be scrapped, where countries are supposed to concentrate on developing what they can do best. For example, the intentions of the Morgenthau Plan of 1943—making post-war, defeated Germany totally agricultural—had to be discarded within two years of application because when de-industrialisation sets in not only did unemployment and poverty rise but agricultural productivity also plummeted.

Instead, the Marshall Plan of 1947 was devised to reindustrialise, thereby increasing overall productivity including that of agriculture through inter-sectorial synergies. Therefore, countries concentrating on their comparative advantage in activities with diminishing returns such as agriculture or extraction of raw materials will eventually end up with permanent underdevelopment, while building an industrial base is a sine qua non for economic development.

When the first industrialisation period of import substitution behind tariff walls was over and export production began, low wages and low overhead contributed to both higher employment and exports. In a later stage in order to be less exposed to the vagaries of the world market, the solution was domestic, demand-led growth. However, sustaining it requires higher wages. In order to achieve higher wages as well as more equal income distribution, most research points to the importance of independent trade unions.

Hence, countries that so far have an intensive export of raw materials have less developed manufacturing and processed goods industries, implying a connection between being resource rich and underdeveloped.

The second part of that question of why countries fail was eminently answered by Paul Collier, professor of Economics Oxford University, in his book *The Bottom Billion*. He showed that being landlocked with bad neighbours, having bad governance in a small country, recently having experienced civil strife and war, and being exposed to the "resource trap" was a recipe for disaster.**

After 30 years of a planned economy, China was in 1980 still a poor, developing country, worse off than the average for all of South Asia, Latin America, and Sub-Saharan Africa in relation to GDP per capita per annum. However, by 2000, China had outperformed them all (see Table 3.1). When China started its rapid growth period in 1978, it followed in the footsteps of the successful latecomers but has neither reached this later stage of domestic, demand-led growth nor of development towards a more equal income distribution.

The question is can China repeat its own successes in Africa while avoiding its mistakes? This chapter approaches first China's internal development and then how it relates to cooperation with African states.

Table 3.1 Comparisons of key variables China, South Asia, sub-Saharan Africa, and Latin America and the Caribbean

Change between				
	1980	1990	2000	1980 and 2000
GDP per capita per annum (constant 2000$)				
China	186	392	949	+763
South Asia	235	328	450	+214
Sub-Saharan Africa	590	531	515	−75
Latin America and the Caribbean	3566	3258	3852	+287
Share of agriculture in GDP (%)				
China	30	27	15	−15
South Asia	37	31	24	−13
Sub-Saharan Africa	19	20	19	0
Latin America and the Caribbean	10	9	7	−3
Population growth per annum (%)				
China	1.3	1.5	0.7	−0.5
South Asia	2.5	2.1	1.8	−0.6
Sub-Saharan Africa	3.1	2.9	2.5	−0.6
Latin America and the Caribbean	2.3	1.8	1.5	−0.8
Average years of schooling over age 15 (year)				
China	4.8	5.9	6.4	1.6
South Asia	2.5	3.2	3.8	1.3
Sub-Saharan Africa	2.2	2.9	3.4	1.2
Latin America and the Caribbean	4.9	5.5	6.2	1.3

Sources: World Bank, World Development Indicators, various years

Subsequently, it explores different development models employed by China and finally relates them to the Chinese development policy in Africa, particularly looking at the employment effect.

3.2 Background to Chinese Development Models

The Soviet development plan by Preobrasjenskij, also called the Stalin model—made for a resource rich country with a sparse population and low population growth—was extra ill-suited for China with the opposite resource set up in 1953 when it officially began its first five-year plan after the Communist armies won over the Nationalists in 1949. With extensive Soviet help, 156 projects were put into practice for laying the foundation for modern capital-intensive industry. China learnt the importance of knowledge and technology transfer the hard way when the Soviet Union abruptly turned off its aid and left its turn-key projects in 1960. The collectivisation of agriculture in China eventually driven to its extreme during the ill-fated Great Leap in 1958–1961 led to the worst famine recorded in human history with 45–70 million dying from preventable causes.

Hence, when reviving the economy after this human disaster, pragmatism prevailed among some Chinese communist leaders, among them Deng Xiaoping. Using his experience from the first base area in Southern China in the 1930s—when Communist guerillas were dependent on good relations with the surrounding peasant population—Deng introduced tenancy agriculture and "small freedoms" with free markets for farmer's surplus produce in the early 1960s. The ensuing rapid recovery of agriculture in the early 1960s came later to serve as a model. After the death of the leader Mao Zedong in 1976, this development policy was launched in China in 1978. In agriculture, the Household Responsibility System (HRS) reintroduced tenancy farming permitting families to retain everything produced above a certain quota, leading to a rapid increase in agricultural production. After the HRS was a success at that time encompassing the majority of the population, limited experiments were introduced with the de-centralisation of State Owned Enterprises (SOE) in the early 1980s.

A radical, experimental banking reform in the early 1980s initiated from the highest levels of authority tolerated a variety of loan forms and policies particularly geared towards the poorest parts and provinces in China. This policy was meant to encourage private entrepreneurs often with the local authorities as partners to start small-scale businesses either developing along family lines or as Township and Village Enterprises (TVE) soaking up a large part of the underemployed in Chinese agriculture. As long as these types of businesses got equal treatment with SOEs, they developed rapidly. However, after the Tiananmen massacre and the ensuing boycott by the West in 1989, banking policies became altered by actively discriminating them and favouring SOEs.

Therefore, the promising development of the 1980s of getting a huge number of impoverished peasants to become either their own undertakers or co-developers of local cooperatives stalled. Instead, they eventually became migrants working in sweatshop assembly lines in world market factories in China's Special Economic Zones (SEZs) after China opened up for foreign investment. Thereby, China created the largest difference in the world between urban and rural areas, as the urban registration system, the "hukuo", hindered rural migrants from enjoying the full fruits of industrialisation. It made them into both second-class citizens in their own country and an exploited labour force thus, indirectly favouring and subsidising the urban population.

In retrospect, China since 1978 experienced more of muddling through, ad hoc policies, experiments, pragmatism, flexibility, and feedback, and theoretical adjustments than clear-cut plans and visions. However, the contrary is usually stressed from the Chinese side. Nevertheless, these policies resulted in a prolonged, rapid growth period for China, thereby surpassing most other developing countries and regions (see Table 3.1).

China's current growth model characterised as extensive export-led growth with unbalanced regional, economic development shows many similarities to policies earlier executed in Japan, Taiwan, and South Korea. China has labelled it "feeling the stones when crossing the river". To counterbalance this lopsided development, China has eventually attempted to "Go West" by furthering industrialisation in its Western parts. When China was turning towards Africa, it could use its own development experiences.

3.3 From Political to Economic Cooperation in Africa

China in its encounters with Africa in the 1950–1970s stressed mainly the political aspects especially after the break with the Soviet Union after 1960. After re-approaching the West in the 1980s—followed by the debacle of Tiananmen in 1989 and the Western boycott of China—Africa again came into the Chinese limelight in the 1990s. In 1998, Chinese President Jiang ZeMin proclaimed, "Economic 'globalisation' is an objective tendency in world economic development. Nobody can avoid it, and we must all participate in it".

When China turned from a reactive, ad hoc foreign policy to an active one after the 1990s, it could draw on its experience of different development models.

Economic transactions became dominated with imports of raw materials to China and exports of cheap, light manufactured goods from China to Africa resembling Western trade patterns with Africa. In the West, a debate ensued with regard to the Chinese involvement in Africa. Some Chinese reports have also been released.

In Africa, some of China's development models have been used such as the White Elephant Model, the SEZs Model, Development Hubs, the Hong Kong Model, the Flying Goose Model, and the new international Land Lease Model.

3.3.1 The White Elephant Model

During the early era of Western and Soviet development aid to African countries in the 1960s and 1970s, there was heavy reliance on infrastructure development and sometimes on showcase constructions such as football stadiums and congress halls, while the antecedents in China were considered as "pet-projects" by local ministers. In Africa, the lack of funding for maintenance, combined with a hard, tropical climate and often coupled with local corruption, resulted in many of these "White Elephants" as they were called, decaying after a couple of years, standing there as monuments of ill-conceived aid. However, when the Chinese experienced the same phenomena, they began by repairing many of their old "White Elephants" from the 1960s, thereby demonstrating that they did not want to waste their resources. With so much of other infrastructure in disrepair, particularly in conflict-ridden countries, such as Angola, Sudan, Zimbabwe, and DR Congo, China began in the 1990s with massive infrastructure development in Africa.

This type of development was in tandem with the demands of Jeffrey Sachs who proclaimed that the West should build these large-scale infrastructure projects in Africa in order to "jump-start" economic development. The difference was that China repaired many of its old "White Elephants". They were criticised for acting just like the West, by placing the large-scale infrastructure projects in geographically advantageous areas which could be useful in the future for the Chinese. To counteract this critique, China could refer to the 1960s when despite the fact that they were still very poor, much poorer than the countries she was helping, it did build the TAZARA railway from Zambia to Tanzania for shipping Zambian copper to avoid its dependence on railways controlled by a white colonial regime in Rhodesia (see Table 3.1).

However, much of this investment was wasted because of lack of functioning locomotives leading to grave underutilisation.

Some sources claim up to 60 % of all Chinese development aid went to this railway. At that time and also later, China mainly was using its own manpower—15,000 labourers—to a degree not seen before in Africa. This has been criticised as preventing local employment, transfer of knowledge and technology. China has delivered "turn-key" projects to African countries where planning, construction, and handling of the material were done by the Chinese, thereby achieving quicker implementation and simultaneously avoiding too much local siphoning off of resources. In the 1950s, Soviet "turn-key" projects had helped China to re-erect an industrial base after a generation of civil war and strife.

Hence, a Chinese "White Elephant" model would mean maintenance of old infrastructure combined with new turn-key projects with a heavy involvement of Chinese labour. This means that the development impact frequently remains limited, because of restricted use of African labour, local suppliers, and subcontracting to Africans firms leading to limited transfer of knowledge and technology, but results in rapid implementation of projects. After the uprisings against dictatorial regimes in North Africa and the Middle East, with more than 36,000 Chinese evacuating from Libya, China might have to reconsider its policy of investing in countries shunned by the West.

3.3.2 The Special Economic Zones Model

At the moment, China is busily erecting SEZs in Africa. So far, zones have been set up in Zambia, Mauritius, Nigeria, Ethiopia, and Egypt. In erecting these zones, China is doing what was usually earlier a success in China. The first zone supposedly endorsed by Chou Enlai in 1968 to the 1978 creation of larger zones opposite Taiwan, (Xiamen*)*, bordering Hong Kong, (Shenzhen*)*, and Macao, (Zhuhai*)*, and finally *(*Shantou*)* in Guangdong province where most Chinese living in Thailand originate were eventually successful. These zones were closely modelled on those in Taiwan and South Korea at that time, viewed by the Chinese authorities as a shortcut to industrialisation by inviting foreign capital, modern technology, and management while guaranteeing favourable treatment in relation to taxation, land lease and "peaceful" and low-paid labour.

Visiting all the SEZs in Taiwan and South Korea while working for the United Nations in 1990 and 1991, I could see them being either moved to China or being integrated into local society. Hence, they could be regarded as a step towards more mature industrialisation.

Seeing China as the potentially largest consumer market in the world and investment in the SEZs as a way of getting access to this future market were major motives for foreign investment during the 1980s.

However, the Tiananmen massacre in 1989, with the ensuing Western economic boycott, showed China how fragile the dependence on export production to the West was as Chinese exports to the West fell dramatically in 1989 and 1990. Because of this, China began to redirect its attention towards Africa. After more than a month-long stay in Shenzhen, the main economic zone, Chinese leader Deng Xiaoping with his "Southern Tour" in 1992 tried to again jump-start the Chinese economy on to the path of continued modernisation and globalisation. In this, he succeeded so well that China eventually attracted more foreign capital than any other country except until lately the USA. Though Africa might be important for raw materials, new technology and capital are an indispensable aspect which could only come from the most industrially advanced countries; hence, China needed a dual approach, both the West and Africa. China encounters many obstacles in repeating its own success with setting up SEZs in Africa. Because China since the Bandung conference of non-aligned states in 1955 has stressed non-interference, it cannot push other African countries to change their laws in their SEZs in Africa. Can China forbid African trade unions, though it has tried to, as this is not only interference but also resembles old Western colonialism.

Using mainly Chinese labour as a way out of this dilemma, which has often been the case for a number of reasons, normally invites heavy local criticism in African countries with high unemployment, especially of unskilled labour. The main attractions of China's zones for the West was the future, large consumer market, which in most African countries does not exist or lies far into the future. Hence, for the SEZ model to work in Africa, China would need concentrated investment in infrastructure synchronised with compatible laws and a stable enough regime for at least the medium term in order to get something back on its investment.

3.3.3 Development Hubs

Currently, China is setting up a kind of logistics hub next to the port of Dar es Salaam in Tanzania. This hub is more than just an export processing zone as it is planned to concentrate on developing basic trade infrastructure, necessary for further economic growth and training of manpower to handle it. This maritime hub is planned to have five zones: a warehouse, an exhibition area for products, an area for technical training and one for service support and finally an import-export processing zone. First, the distribution facilities for imports from China will be built and later those ones for exports from Tanzania. This sequencing has already been criticised, but as China is the main financier its interests, naturally, are looked after first. This logistics hub is planned as well to serve neighbouring land-locked countries. This new hub and other infrastructure development, such as a natural gas pipeline and a power station also developed by China, are welcomed by the local authorities. Through this 150-acre hub, China could import more gas, minerals, and agricultural products from Tanzania. Land-locked markets and insufficient infrastructure are seen as major obstacles to economic growth in Africa according to a survey by the Africa Center of the Atlantic Council. Compared to other developing regions, transport cost is 63 % higher in Africa it stressed.

Since 2005, China has invested more in infrastructure in Africa than anywhere else.

In a similar way in Nigeria, China is helping to build another hub outside Lagos, the Lekki trade zone. This project will include a deep-water seaport, water plants, roads and power plants, and a new international airport close by.

China's own experience of developing trade infrastructure was the annual Canton trade fair, which functioned even during more autonomous, economic periods. As late as 1973, when I, as a PhD student, was interviewing and travelling within Southern China, in the month running up to the trade fair, only chicken skin and bones were served while, as, I was repeatedly told, the meat was preserved for the Canton fair.

This fair served China well as an important barometer of global textile trade.

Developing SEZs and hubs takes us one step further to the Hong Kong model.

3.3.4 The "Hong Kong Model"

Paul Romer, professor of economics, has been promoting the idea of a rich and modern country chartering a city in an un-industrialised country and then introducing a free-trade policy for that city running and developing it as a free-trade area. His model does not only concern Hong Kong but also Lybeck from the twelfth century since it got a free-trade charter, there were consequentially developments in the Baltic Sea area for a number of centuries. He maintains that physical capital including: the length of worktime, the labour force, and its education is important but what supersedes them are rules, regulations, and the ideas behind them. To further strengthen his argument, Romer puts an emphasis on the limits of geography, giving the example of Asia that in 1820 they stood for 56 % of the world economy, only 16 % in 1950 but 39 % in 2008 despite the fact that the geography of the place has not changed, but governing policy, rules, and laws did.

The ideal is how the British made Hong Kong into a free-trade area which led its rapid development. They introduced low taxation, a minimum of state regulation, and legal protection of property and contracts. In this way, economic productivity was eight-doubled between 1913 and 1980, making every Hong Kong inhabitant ten times as rich as every Chinese under the planned economy in the People's Republic just across the border. When China reformed from 1978 onwards it began by imitating, eventually making a number of Hong Kong "light" copies by developing different types of zones along its Southeastern seaboard and outside major cities.

China might be recreating enlarged Hong Kong copies with its new zones in Africa. The question is can this increase local employment and transfer of knowledge the way it has happened in China's zones? The problem is also which other country, given the sordid history of imperialism, would like to act as a modern colonialist by taking over the governance of such an area?

The recent controversy in Honduras where apparently the richest man in the country planned to create such a zone after the Romer model by introducing rules and regulation customs made for investors but not for its future workers demonstrates the pitfalls of this model. Since the Supreme Court made the development of special zones legal in May 2014, the battle for guaranteeing rights for its future workers began. Meanwhile, Romer himself has opposed the way in which his ideas are currently being understood and applied.

3.3.5 The "Flying Geese" Model

This notion of thought is not necessarily a model but an image by Kanema Akamatsu seeing Japan as the culturally leading nation, symbolised as the first flying goose to break into the air and this leading to the other nations to follow, hence the benefits trickling down gradually to all. Later, this vision was applied to economics. The Japanese Minister of Foreign Affairs, Saburo Okita, used this "Flying Geese" Model in the 1980s, proposing that poor countries should be enabled to upgrade their technology by switching from producing one type of goods to another each with an increasingly, higher skill content. Meanwhile, the leading goose, Japan, will constantly, through innovations and inventions, upgrade and produce more sophisticated products. Through sequential technological upgrading, modern technology and knowledge would spread downwards through a vertical, international production chain.

Not only East Asian economic growth and integration, but as well the economic development in China moving from the coast to inland with its "Go West" policy has basically followed this pattern. By beginning with manufacturing in Africa, such as buying the whole tobacco yield of Zimbabwe—earlier employing up to three-fourth million people during peak times—China has developed the tobacco manufacturing industry in Zimbabwe so as to improve the value added of its tobacco harvests and to increase local employment.

This model with sequential upgrading spreading along countries is also in line with the World System theories of Emanuel Wallerstein. In the Flying Geese Model, industrialisation is helped along from country to country increasing modern employment. With China's new concern being ways to increase the African manufacturing capacity, this could be beneficial to Africa as a whole, in line with what Reinert is recommending. According to him, the only way forward for Africa is through industrialisation initially sheltered from international competition. This has to be done in the East Asian way and not the Latin American way. But usually the institutions are sorely lacking when it comes to accomplishing this form of industrialisation. Particularly, crucial is the existence of a bureaucracy following a national agenda and becoming greater than the vested interests of belonging in a clan or class. This contributes not only to higher industrial growth and employment but also over time to a more stabilised society.

While the Flying Geese Model is focused on transforming a country through manufacturing, the Land Lease model is concerned with the basic human necessities; food and food security.

3.3.6 The Land Lease Model

The simple idea of the land lease model is that any country with a lack of land can lease an area from another country for producing its own inhabitants. This kind of land lease has already been accomplished by, for example, Saudi Arabia, Qatar, South Korea, Jordan, and China in Africa. The idea is that by leasing part of its land, the leasing country will get access to not only more resources but also modern technology and modern scientific, agricultural methods. However, the problem is of course, who is leasing? Is it a responsible elected government in agreement with the local population concerned or is it a neither responsible nor elected elite pocketing the proceeds from the leasing of land from people not at all consulted or knowing about the lease of their land? Many cases reported so far seem to be of the latter kind. To give a prime example, when Madagascar leased half of their arable land to a South Korean conglomerate, the president had to flee when the opposition got wind of it in 2009.

In Africa, land-lease is extra sensitive for a number of reasons. According to a recent report by the World Watch Institute, the leasing and even buying of land in Africa by rich countries does put local populations at risk of losing both land and work contributing to a deterioration of the hunger problems on this continent.

The International Food Policy Research Institute gives an approximation of 49 million acres of agricultural land that were negotiated for land lease 2006–2009.

A World Bank report leak to the Financial Times sums up, "investors in farmland are targeting countries with weak laws, buying arable land on the cheap and failing to deliver on promises of jobs and investment". Agriculture is important for Africa, more than any other continent. Up to two-third of Africa's employment, half of its export, and one-third of its Gross National Income were derived from agriculture in the early 2000s. In 2012, it still employed 60 % of its population but contributed only to 17 % of its GDP, showing the limited impact rapidly increased resource extraction and exports made on employment.

According to an analysis from the African Development Bank, 38 million people equivalent to 4 % of Africa's population are very highly vulnerable to hunger, malnutrition, and food insecurity, that is, Eritrea, Gambia, Djibouti, Zimbabwe, Mauritania, Niger, and San Tomé & Principe. Another 330 million people equivalent to 33 % of Africa's population in 11 countries are highly vulnerable; Congo Republic, Burkina Faso, Rwanda, Ghana, Nigeria, Kenya, Senegal, Cap Verde, Mozambique, Morocco, and Cameroon. In a similar vein, UNCTAD calculated that 300 million Africans are exposed to chronic hunger while 21 nations in Africa are facing crises of food security. The African Development Bank Group estimated that still 40 % of Africa's population was living in poverty in 2012.

In comparison, China in 2014 with 160 million out of 1356, just above 8 % of all, living in absolute poverty are not doing much better, on 1.25 USD/day. Aside from India, although it is predominantly due to the population dynamics, China has the greatest number of people living in absolute poverty. However, according to China's new poverty line from 2011 of living below 3.63 USD/day, only 6.1 % were poor.

Historically, just as earlier in China, famines were considered to be caused by natural catastrophes such as draughts and floods. Recent research by Professor Amartya Sen, Nobel Prize Laureate in Economics, has shown that bad governance coupled with an irresponsible elite of whom does not have to stand for the election is a main cause of famine.

Rising global prices for food since 2003—set in motion by price increases in agricultural inputs, combined with increased demand to a large part because of diversification of food to biofuel production, and export restrictions—have led to a deterioration of food security in Africa. Because of global warming 75–250 million Africans are likely to be affected by lack of water according to the UN Intergovernmental Panel on Climate Change. This means that food insecurity will increase as harvests from rain-fed agriculture could be halved and this type of agriculture is still the most prevalent form in Sub-Saharan Africa. Against this background, the official Forum on China-Africa Cooperation, (FOCAC), has developed on Action Plan for 2010–2012 promoting growth in agriculture through increased use of technology, by establishing centres for technology with technicians dispatched for transfer of scientific knowledge. In order to strengthen South–South cooperation, the need to put a higher skill content into African products was particularly emphasised at the FOCAC meeting in 2009 and again in its Beijing Action Plan, (2013–2015) at its fifth ministerial conference in 2012.

This makes sense considering the fact that in Africa one-third of the arable land is untilled. Seen from another angle, this makes up 60 % of the arable cultivable land in the world.

Therefore, Li Ruogu, head of China ExIm bank, could declare in Chongqing 2007 that his bank would help to resettle dislocated farmers, by dams and urbanisation, to Africa. "Chongqing is well experienced in agricultural mass production, while in Africa there is plenty of land.... Chongqing's labour exports have just started but they will take off once we convince the farmers to become landlords abroad". This statement was first officially toned down, but later reiterated in subdued forms, stressing China's need for food security.

In addition to labour exports, China is in the process of training Zimbabweans in irrigation and aiding smallholders developing their plots. Improving the conditions for local smallholders is considered far superior to the Land Lease Model leading to increased employment, improvements in livelihoods, better environmental care, increased yields, and food security.

Interpreted in a positive way, the land lease model could lead to a transfer of agricultural knowledge, investment in infrastructure, and modern technology. However, in contrast, it could be just an amended form of land grabbing or a new form of colonialism.

3.4 Chinese Development Policy in Africa

China has stressed sovereignty and non-interference. However, China takes part in multinational peacekeeping in Africa which can be seen as a softening of this principle along the lines of the African Union, (AU), stressing non-indifference***. China has emphasised political equality and consistently treated all African leaders with dignity. Although China and African countries remain economically asymmetrical, China nonetheless in its rhetoric focuses on mutual benefit and "win-win" cooperation. On a practical level, all of the Chinese workers in Africa are supposed to live on the same level as their African counterparts and likewise all Chinese in a project live on the same level, sharing the same facilities, in contrast to Westerners.

However, surveys from international organisations, NGOs, and media in African countries report that Chinese firms in their labour policies offer harsher working conditions, lower minimum wages, longer working hours, more overtime, and show less concern for safety of their workers than the local or other foreign-invested firms do and in addition prohibit trade unions and are not prepared to follow local rules and regulations. Chinese encounter most resentment from locals when they compete with Africans in the simplest types of unskilled work such as hawking in local markets, something not done by Westerners. Therefore, if not carefully prepared, mass resettlement of Chinese farmers in Africa, aided by Chinese banks, could lead to unrest among poor African farmers.

In their treatment of African labour, the large Chinese state companies do not seem to follow the original policy reserved for registered, urban employees in China, but instead lean more towards the minimum policies usually reserved for Chinese, rural migrants. In addition, being SOEs, they have a cavalier attitude towards laws and regulations just like in China.

However, in China out of a labour force of 772 million, 84 % of the total, in all 650 million, belong to the informal sector having no benefits and no protection. Because independent trade unions are not allowed, people can only vote with their feet and not organise legal, independent unions fighting for better conditions. In razor sharp competition for foreign investment, local Chinese governments are giving privileges to investors and circumventing costly formal regulations on protection of labour and environment resulting in both rapid growth and mounting social and environmental crises. This kind of "planned informality" is done "with the tacit approval of the central government".

Hence being used to riding roughshod over rules and regulations at home, it is no wonder Chinese SOEs behave in similar way abroad. For this reason, the only ones capable of modifying this would be either the Chinese state or outside actors. Many argue it is up to African governments to make stricter requirements and not only blame the Chinese. Some change is already on its way, for example, Nigeria and Angola have demanded increased local contents as a condition for foreign investment and more local enterprise participation and employment while Ethiopia has set up a Joint Committee on quality control for imports.

A contradiction is developing between ideal and reality. While the Chinese state is trying to transform its development vision into reality—by, for example, supporting manufacturing in Zimbabwe, or voluntarily introducing quota systems in South Africa in order not to wipe out their textile industry—their own SOEs are in practice sabotaging some of their actions. On the other hand, not accepting independent trade unions is a non-controversial issue for all official Chinese actors. Some argue there is no Chinese development model or "Beijing consensus", while others are more undecided. My point is that Chinese development model has evolved over time based on China's own experiences. The more Chinese actors that are involved over time, the harder it is for Chinese authorities to impose any consistent model.

3.5 Conclusions

In discussing if there is a distinct Chinese development model or if China employs its own mix of different models, it is fruitful to look at China's earlier experiences at home, which is distinguished by wide swings and a hefty dose of pragmatism at times. The Chinese development model since 1978 has been characterised as "feeling the stones when crossing the river" implying flexibility, ad hoc solutions, pragmatism, and productive feedback. However, in contrast to the West, the stress in China on a high level of government activism with cavalier interpretations of rules and regulations, might lead to quicker economic development in Africa, but this has come with failures and heavy criticism from the local population. From earlier stressing politics to later economics in its dealings with Africa, a parallel development inside China took place. When the AU changed its policy on non-interference so did China but with a time-lag. In regard to intervention in Libya, China changed as well.

When an overall contradiction developed between China's growing need for energy and raw material what Africa can supply in abundance and African countries own need for a sustainable development instead of only being exporters of primary goods, China modified its policies in order to aid and develop the manufacturing sector within the African continent.

In its dealings with Africa, China is replicating what China judges as successful traits in the developing strategies it copied from the world's most successful latecomers; Japan, South Korea, and Taiwan. China's own massive investment in infrastructure is mirrored in its engagement with African countries.

Various "pet-projects" by different ministers in China can be seen as antecedents of the *White Elephant* policy. In the 1950s, Soviet "turn-key" projects helped China to re-erect an industrial base and China is attempting to implement the same means in the current day and age with heavy involvement of Chinese labour.

China's own model with *SEZs* succeeded because of its allure as the future largest consumer market in the world. However, this is not now the case in any African country. Hence, China must use its own resources to get the necessary investment. With these heavy outlays, it could be relevant to question if the regime in the chosen country is stable enough to justify these outlays.

Similarly, the same questions can be asked about *Development Hubs* and the *Hong Kong model.*

If successful, the "*Flying Geese Model*" could create industrialisation and employment eventually contributing to limited transfer of technology. Not only East Asian economic growth and integration, but also the economic development in China from the coast towards the Western interior has basically followed this pattern.

The Chinese *Land Lease model* could be viable if carried out according to the FOCAC plan with transfer of resources and technology. However, by encouraging skill transfers to smallholders in agriculture and by developing manufacturing in Africa, the employment effect would be much greater than large-scale interventions by outsiders in agriculture or exports of only raw materials.

In summing up, this means that the externalisation of China's own development experiences has steered Africa towards a path of development, from White Elephants to Flying Geese.

References

Akorsu, D., & Fang, L. C. (2011). Labour standards applications among Chinese and Indian Firms in Ghana: Typical or atypical. *The International Journal of Human Resource Management*, 1–19.

Alden, C. (2006). Levering the dragon: Towards 'an Africa that can say no'. *South African Yearbook of International Affairs*, South African Institute of International Affairs.

Alden, C., & Christopher, R. H. (2009). Harmony and discord in China's Africa strategy: some implications for Foreign policy. In J. C. Strauss & M. Saavedra (Eds.), *China and Africa: Emerging patterns in globalization and development.* Cambridge: Cambridge University Press.

Alden, C., & Daniel, L. (2011). China's exceptionalism and the challenge of delivering difference in Africa. *Journal of Contemporary China, 20*(68).

Bech, J. (1987). *Unequal equals a study of China in Africa*. Harvard University.

Becker, J. (1996). *Hungry ghosts China's secret famine*. London: An Owl Book.

Björnelid, R. (2007, Sept 27). Tillväxtens bakgård (The backyard of development) *Veckans Affärer*, (Business Weekly).

Bräutigam, D. (2009). *The Dragon's gift the real story of China in Africa*. Oxford: Oxford University Press.

Broadman, H. S. (2007). *Africa's silk road: China and India's new economic frontier*. Washington, DC: World Bank.

Carasik, L. (2014). Bad role models–the embattled arrival of Honduras' Model Cities in website of *Foreign Affairs*, August 1st, translated into Danish in *Udvikling*, Danish Ministry of Foreign Affairs and DANIDA, October/November 2014, nr 5, pp. 46–49.

Chen, X., & Su, I. (2014, June-July). A different global power? Understanding China's role in the developing world. *The European Financial Review*.

Chen, C., Chiu, P.-C., Orr, J. R., Goldstein, A. (2007). "An empirical analysis of Chinese Construction Firms' entry into Africa", the CRIOM2007 International Symposium on advancement of Construction management and Real Estate, Sydney, Australia, 8–13 August.

Ching, K. L. (2009). Raw encounters: Chinese managers, African workers and the politics of casualization in Africa's Chinese enclaves. In S. Julia C. & S. Martha (Eds.), *China and Africa: Emerging patterns in globalization and development*. Cambridge: Cambridge University Press..

CIA (2014). *The world factbook*, China.

Collier, P. (2007). *The bottom billion why the poorest countries are failing what can be done about it*. Oxford/New York: Oxford University Press.

Davies, P. (2007). *China and the end of poverty in Africa—towards a mutual benefit?* Sweden: *Diakonia*.

Dikötter, F. (2010). *Mao's great famine the history of China's most devastating Catastrophe 1958–1962*. New York: Walker & Co.

Eisenman, J. (2005). Zimbabwe: China's African Ally. *China Brief, 5*(15).

Fantu, C. (2007). *Decoding the evolving China-Africa relations*. Uppsala: Nordic Africa Institute.

Fantu, C., & Cyril, O. (2010). *The rise of China & India in Africa*. London: Zed Books.

Feng, B. (2014, Sept 12). China expands investment in Tanzania. *The New York Times*.

Fravel, M. T. (2008). *Strong borders secure nation*. Princeton University Press
Gu, X. (2005). China's return to Africa. In: Hans-Dieter A., & Karin Moser von F. (Eds.), *China's new role in the International Community*. Peter Lang Europäisches Verlag.
Gu, J., & Richard, Schiere. (2011), April. Post-crises prospects for China-Africa relations. African Development Bank Group (Working Paper Series, No. 124).
Guenther, B. (2008). The Asian drivers and the resource curse in Sub-Saharan Africa: The potential impacts of rising commodity prices for conflict and governance in the DRC. *The European Journal of Development Research, 20*, 347–363.
Hanes, S. (2009, December 17). Africa: From famine to the world's next bread-basket? *The Christian Science Monitor.*
Hansen, K. (2014). Protest mot salg av jakt-terreng til Dubai-prinser, (Protest against sale of hunting ground to Dubai princes). *Aftenposten*, Norway, November 27, p. 20.
Huang, Y. (1998). *FDI in China an Asian perspective*. Hong Kong: The Chinese University Press.
Huang, Y. (2008). *Capitalism with Chinese characteristics: Entrepreneurship and the state*. Cambridge/New York: Cambridge University Press.
Huang, P. C. C. (2011). The theoretical and practical implications of China's development experience: The role of informal economic practices. *Modern China*, *37*(1).
Hutchinson, A. (1975). *China's African revolution*. London: Hutchinson & Co..
Jiang, W. (2009, 19 September). Fuelling the dragon: China's rise and its energy and resource extraction in Africa, *The China Quarterly.*
Johnson, S., Ostry D. Jonathan. and Subramanian, Arvid. (2007). The prospects for sustained growth in Africa: Benchmarking the constraints (IMF Working paper, WP/07/5).
Kennedy, S. (2010, June). The myth of the Beijing consensus. *Journal of Contemporary China*, *19*(65).
Klochko, M. (1964). *Soviet scientist in red China*. New York: Praeger.
Korhonen, P. (1994). The theory of flying geese pattern of development and its interpretation. *Journal of Peace Research*, *31*(1).
Lam, W. W.-L. (2006). *Chinese politics in the Hu Jintao era new leaders new challenges*. London: M.E. Sharpe.
Larkin, B. C. (1971). *China and Africa 1949–70 the foreign policy of the people's republic of China*. Los Angeles: University of California Press.
Li, A. (2007, Summer). China and Africa: policy and challenges. *China Security*, *3*(2).

Lin, J. Y., Fang C., & Zhou L. (1996). *The China miracle: Development strategy and economic reform*. Hong Kong Chinese University Press.

Lu, H.-P. (2001). *China transnational visuality global postmodernity.* Hong Kong Chinese University Press.

Ma, C. (2003). *On changes of economic position of coastal prosperous provinces*. Shenzhen, China No. 2: China Development Institute, CDI Review.

McGregor, R. (2010). *The party the secret world of china's communist rulers*. London: Penguin Books.

McMillan, J., & Barry, N. (1992). How to reform a planned economy: Lessons from China (Oxford Review of Economic Policy, No. 8).

Meng, G. (2003). *The theory and practice of free economic zones*. Peter Lang Verlag (Diss.).

Moyo, D. (2011). *How the West was lost fifty years of economic folly—and the stark choices ahead.* Penguin.

Naughton, B. (2007). *The Chinese economy: Transitions and growth*. Cambridge, MA: M.I.T Press.

Naughton, B. (2010, June). China's distinctive system: Can it be a model for others? *Journal of Contemporary China*, *19*(65).

Ncube, N. Africa coordinate agenda crucial to FOCAC Summit: Expert 2012/07/08. Interview: 29 June 2012, www.focac.org/eng/-2014.11.29

Ngai, P. (2004). The precarious employment and hidden costs of women workers in Shenzhen special economic zone, China. *Journal of Oxfam.*

Nierenber, D., & Ronit, R. (2011, August 3). Opinion: Corporate land grab threatens food security. WorldWatch Institute, at www.worldwatch.org/node/6523

OECD and African Development Bank. (2007). *African economic outlook*. Paris: OECD and African Development Bank.

Oxfam Hong Kong Briefing Paper. (2004). *Turning the garment industry inside out purchasing practises and workers' lives*. Oxfam: Hong Kong.

Palley, T. I. (2006, February). External contradictions of the Chinese development model: Export-led growth and the dangers of global economic contraction. *Journal of Contemporary China*. *15*(46).

Pereira, A. A. (2002, December). The suzhou industrial park project (1994–2001): The failure of a development strategy. *Asian Journal of Political Science, 10*(2).

Reine, S. (2009). *China's African challenges*. Abingdon/New York: Routledge.

Reinert, E. S. (2010). *How rich countries got rich and why poor countries stay poor*. London: Constable.

Renard, M.-F. (2011, April). China's trade and FDI in Africa (Working Paper Series, No. 126). African Development Bank Group.

Romer, P. (2011, July 23). www.chartercities.org

Sachs, J. (2005). *The end of poverty*. New York: Penguin.

Saidi, D. M., & Christina, Wolf. (2011). Recalibrating development co-operation: How can African Countries benefit from emerging partners. OECD Development Centre, (Dev/Doc, (2011)10) (Working Paper No. 302).

Sen, A. (1999). *Development as freedom*. Oxford University Press.

Serge, M., & Michel, B. (2009). *China's Safari on the trails of Beijing's expansion in Africa*. New York: Nation Books.

Shapi, S. (2007, November 19). Chinese labor policies mar African welcome, in *International Business Times*. www.ibtimes.com/articles/20060809/china-africa-mining-investment.htm

Snow, P. (1988). *The star raft: China's encounter with Africa*. New York: Weidenfeld & Nicholson.

Snow, P. (1995). China and Africa: Consensus and camouflage. In R. Thomas & S. David (Eds.), *Chinese foreign policy theory and practice*. New York: Oxford University Press.

So, A. (1991). *Social change and development, modernization dependency and World System Theories*. Newbury Park: SAGE.

Spence, M. (Ed.), (2008). The growth report: Strategies for sustained growth and inclusive development. World Bank, at http://www.growthcommission.org/index.php

Strauss, C. J. (2009). The past in the present: Historical and rhetorical lineages in China's relations with Africa. In C. S. Julia & S. Martha (Eds.), *China and Africa: Emerging patterns in globalization and development*. Cambridge: Cambridge University Press.

Studwell, J. (2002). *The China dream the elusive quest for the greatest untapped market on earth*. China Perspectives, at https://chinaperspectives.revues.org/398

Sung, Y.-W., Pak-Wai, L., Yue-Chim, R. W., & Piu-King, L. (2004). *The fifth dragon (the emergence of the pearl river delta)*. Singapore: Addison Wesley.

Sydsvenska, D. (2011, July 28). Landförvärv förvärrar svält, (Land acquisitions worsen hunger).

Tan, G. (2003). Pearl river delta: World Factory Coupled with contemporary logistics, (CDI Review, No. 3).

Taylor, I. (2006). China's oil diplomacy in Africa. *International Affairs, 82*, 5.

Taylor, I. (2010). *China's new role in Africa*. Boulder: Lynne Rienner Publishers.

The Economist (2014, August 23). Essay China, "What China wants", p. 40.

Thorborg, M. (1978). "Chinese Employment Policy in 1949–78 with special emphasis on women in rural production", *Chinese Economy Post-Mao*, Joint Economy Committee, Congress of the United States, Nov.1978, p. 535 ff, U.S: Government Printing Office, Washington, DC.

Thorborg, M. (1980). *Women in non-agricultural production in post-revolutionary China*. Uppsala University.

Thorborg, M. (1991a). Environmental occupational hazards in Asian Export Processing Zones. In: Takesumi Yoshimura et al. (Eds.), *Toxicology and industrial health an International Journal, 7*(5/6). Princeton Scientific Publishing Co.

Thorborg, M. (1991b). *Korea program on women*. Vienna: United Nations Industrial Development Association, UNIDO.

Thorborg, M. (2006). Chinese workers and labour conditions from state industry to globalised factories how to stop the race to the bottom? In Myron A. M., Morando S., Philip L., & Eula B., (Eds.) *Living in a chemical world framing the future in light of the past*. New York Academy of Sciences, 1076. pp. 893–910.

Thorborg, M. (2007, March). "China in Africa" paper presented at China-World Conference: "Made in China vs. Made by Chinese: Global Identities of Chinese business". Britain: University of Durham, pp. 19–20.

Thorborg, M. (2009). Business as usual or yellow man's burden. Collegium Ramazzini, Carpi, Internet publication.

Thorborg, M. (2014). *Kvinnor i Kina pirater, järn-flickor och finanslejon, (Women in China Pirates, Iron-girls, and Financial Wizzards)* (p. 358). Stockholm: Atlantis.

Tjönneland, E. N. with Brandtzaeg, B., & Garth, le P. (2006). China in Africa implications for norwegian foreign and development policies, Christian Michelsen Institute, R 2006:15, (CMI Report).

Tse, E. (2010). *The China strategy harnessing the power of the world's fastest growing economy*. New York: Basic Books.

Tull, D. (2006). China's engagement in Africa: Scope, significance and consequences. *Journal of Modern African Studies, 44*, 3.

United Nations Development Program. UNDP, *Human Development Report*, HDR, various years.

Vhumbunu, C. H (2014, October). Drawing lessons for African integration from accelerated development in China, Discussion Paper, (FOCAC) Stellenbosch.

Wang, F.-l. (2005). *Organising through division and exclusion China's "Hu-kou" system*. Stanford University Press.

Wang, D. (2006, December 8). Yearender: China-Africa relations advance to a new stage in 2006. *Xinhua.*
Wei, L. (2010). New Africa policy: China's quest for oil and influence. In S. Guo & B. Jean-Marc (Eds.), *'Harmonious World' and China's new foreign policy.* New York: Lexington Books.
Wild, L., & Mephan, D. (Eds.). (2006). *The new sinosphere China in Africa.* London: Institute of Public Policy Research.
World Bank. (2014). World development indicators, various years www.focac.org/eng/- 2014.1129
Yang, J. (2012). *Tombstone the great Chinese famine 1958–1962.* Allen: Lane.

4

Cyrildene Chinatown, Suburban Settlement, and Ethnic Economy in Post-Apartheid Johannesburg

Liang Xu

4.1 Introduction

Despite sporadic xenophobic attacks against foreigners, post-apartheid South Africa is an important destination country for immigrants in Africa. The reopening of its borders in 1994 has not only witnessed the massive influx of Africans from within the continent, but also attracted hundreds of thousands of immigrants from other parts of the world including Europe and Asia, which adds to its long-standing and already complicated racial and ethnic dynamics. The presence of Chinese population is not an entirely new phenomenon in South Africa, as people of Chinese descent have been an established minority in the country since as early as the seventeenth century. However, the scale and the potential socio-economic impact of the recent wave of Chinese immigration have been unprecedented. One of the most visible expressions of the vitality of the growing Chinese community

L. Xu (✉)
Harvard University, Cambridge, MA, USA
e-mail: xuliangpku@gmail.com

Y. C. Kim (ed.), *China and Africa*, The Palgrave Macmillan Asian Business Series, DOI 10.1007/978-3-319-47030-6_4

is the rapidly booming Chinatown in Cyrildene, a former Jewish settlement in the northern suburbs of Johannesburg, but now claiming itself as the youngest and fastest-growing Chinatown in the world.

In this chapter, I present Cyrildene Chinatown as a case study to illustrate the significance of new Chinese settlements in post-apartheid South Africa. By relying on ethnographical observations and drawing on scholarships of urban immigrant settlement and urban political economy, this chapter attempts to outline three major arguments. First, it contextualises the birth and growth of Cyrildene Chinatown within two broader developments. This chapter suggests that Cyrildene Chinatown must be examined with a full understanding of both the new waves of Chinese migration in Africa and the dramatic suburbanisation (or urban decentralisation) in post-apartheid South African cities. Second, it presents a critique to the notion of "ethnic enclave." This chapter will argue that Cyrildene Chinatown functions more as an integral part of Chinese "ethnoburb" in Johannesburg's eastern suburbs. Chinese residential and commercial structures in Cyrildene interact with host society and wider networks in complex and intimate ways that attest hybridised forms of socio-economic integration. Lastly, this chapter claims that the growth of Cyrildene Chinatown raises critical questions on city planning, town-keeping, and urban governance in post-apartheid South African cities. By revisiting the complications of both the achievements and challenges of the Chinese settlement in Cyrildene, this chapter argues that suburbanisation in post-apartheid South Africa has boosted the degrees of civic engagement amongst the country's suburbanites.

4.2 Putting Cyrildene Chinatown in its Contexts

As Daniel Large has reminded us recently, China is perhaps "the most important development for Africa in the twenty-first century" (Large 2013: 707). Similarly, in a response to Jean and John Comaroffs' *Theory from the South*, the prominent political philosopher Achille Mbembe argues that if "Euro-America is evolving toward Africa, Africa in turn is evolving toward China rather than toward Euro-America," and more importantly, he further suggests that Africa–China will become the most important material relations in global capitalism (Mbembe 2012). To some observers of China–Africa, such claims may sound a little exaggerating. However, China as a phenomenal economic force in Africa since 2000 is revealed more concretely in numbers.

In 2009, China emerged as Africa's largest trading partner. China–Africa trade increased from US$1 billion in 2000 to an astounding $221.88 billion in 2014 (Chinese Ministry of Commerce 2014). China reportedly gets a third of its oil and natural resources from Africa. By the end of 2014, Chinese investment (stock) in Africa was close to US$30 billion, and its commercial loans to Africa exceeded US$50 billion (FOCAC 2015). Meanwhile, physical infrastructure that had seen no significant expansion since the end of colonial rule has now been rehabilitated and expanded with Chinese capital and technology, and this is a dimension that other kinds of private foreign investment, often enclaved and closely focused on extraction, do not engage. In the area of development aid, a recent controversial report suggests that between 2000 and 2011, China had funded 1673 projects in 51 African countries with a total of $75 billion in commitments of official finance, whilst the USA had offered $90 billion official finance during this time (Strange et al. 2013; Brautigam 2013). A more moderate and better received study by the Rand Corporation suggests that between 2001 and 2011, "49 countries in Africa received approximately $175 billion dollars in pledged assistance which includes grants, interest-free loans and concessional loans," and that the actual "cumulative delivered aid increased from $52 million in 2001 to $18.4 billion in 2011" (Wolf et al. 2013).

By any standard, China's presence on the continent does seem "overwhelming." Scholars distinguish at least three qualitative "faces" of China in Africa, namely the Chinese state and the SOEs, private Chinese companies, and the grassroots Chinese immigrants (Akyeampong and Xu 2015). What really complicates the story and began to generate tensions in China–Africa relations is the "third face," Chinese migrants in Africa, which has thus far received inadequate scholarly attention.[1] Although the

[1] In the past several years, interest in the Chinese migrants in Africa has been growing. For instance, Yoon Jung Park in 2010 initiated a global research working group (Chinese in Africa/Africans in China), under which there are now (as of early 2016) over 600 researchers from across the world.

exact number is difficult to obtain, many China–Africa researchers and policymakers cite one million as a rough estimate for the size of Chinese migrants in Africa.

South Africa so far has the largest Chinese population on the continent. The earliest arrival of Chinese in South Africa, brought in as labourers by the Dutch, can be traced back to the seventeenth century. However, the first major wave of Chinese migrants came to South Africa in the early twentieth century as indentured gold miners. The second wave, mostly Taiwanese and Hong Kongese, came in the early 1980s under the apartheid government invitation as industrialists who helped set up labour-intensive industries within and near South Africa's black homelands ("bantustans") (Pickles and Woods 1989; Woods 1991; Lin 2001; Hart 2002; van der Watt and Visser 2008). The third wave commenced in the mid-/late 1990s and is still ongoing. In comparison with their predecessors, recent Chinese migrants who made their journey to Africa constitute the most diverse band, ranging from state-owned enterprises' managers to contract workers, from clothing factory owners to small retailers in black townships, from Chinese restaurant bosses to college students, and even prostitutes. As Chris Alden once remarked, numerous of them "are pursuing opportunities and have used migrant brokers, both legal and illegal, to obtain the necessary paperwork to immigrate" (Alden 2007: 52; for a detailed account of the third wave, Park 2009a: 14–15). Now, the estimated Chinese population in South Africa varies depending on sources, but is believed to be somewhere between 300,000 and 500,000 (Park 2009a). Many belong to the "third face" and are extremely active in trade and small businesses. Their presence and business conduct have generated profound implications, one of which is the birth and continuing proliferation of Chinese quarters in major South African cities. The growth of Cyrildene Chinatown in Johannesburg is a vivid manifestation of this rapid development.

The other context that needs to be highlighted as we try to understand the emergence of Cyrildene Chinatown is the economic stagnation and decline of Johannesburg's inner city in post-apartheid era, a phenomenon that Martin Murray described as "Johannesburg turned inside out" (Murray 2011: 87). We often associate the abandonment of the urban with high crime rates in the inner city and consider it as a post-apartheid development. Murray in his book traces the roots for such changes a generation earlier. He explains, since about the 1970s, "the introduction of new transportation technologies, the early start of real estate speculation on the urban fringe, suburban tract-housing developments, state subsidies promoting schemes along strict racial lines came together to accelerate the process of urban decentralisation" (Murray 2011: 105). Indeed, by the end of the 1970s, new "periphery" business centres such as Rosebank, Hyde Park, Parktown, and Sandton had already begun their competition with the central business districts. It is, however, safe to suggest that this process of urban decentralisation has splintered in the post-apartheid era.

Facing a declining inner city, a number of well-known private and public schemes were initiated to slow, if not able to reverse, the exodus of businesses. For instance, AMPROS, the corporate owner of the Carlton Centre, had once imagined transforming the hotel site into a multi-function business complex that would offer facilities such as a casino, entertainment, and convention centre. The municipality also initiated ambitious projects such as creating the Fashion District and Jewel City on the east side of the inner city, and the revitalisation of the Newtown Cultural precinct (Murray 2011: 98, 104). To the disappointment of many, none of these plans seem to have achieved their proclaimed goals. As a consequence, private investment and major business activities continued to flock into booming suburbs.

Under this context, it needs to be mentioned that prior to the existence of Cyrildene Chinatown, there was (and still is) an old inner-city Chinatown on the southwestern edge of the city, an area now bounded by Commissioner, Alexander, Ferreira and Frederick Streets, where the early Chinese first established their community life in the 1890s (for a brief history of the old Chinatown, Yap and Man 1996: 84–85). For almost a century, this tiny segment of the city was where Chinese would come for authentic Chinese groceries, seek cultural roots, and enjoy fellow affections. It was a home that once accommodated the new arrivals and provided them with communal and emotional support. It was also an important place where Chinese community led their anti-apartheid resistance in the heyday of racial segregation. Today, the area is only left with several shops along the very western end of the Commissioner Street. As Park has lamented,

> [the] first Chinatown's dwindling fortunes finally fell away in the 1990s decline of Johannesburg's inner city, due to white flight to the northern suburbs and increased crime, when even the lure of good cooking and large, boisterous gatherings of family and friends were not enough to entice any but the most intrepid Chinese into the central business district (CBD) or downtown area. (Park 2009b: 116)

An initiative to revitalise the old Chinatown was proposed by the shop and property owner's association in the area, but "no budget [was] allocated to the project for implementation" (Savage+Dodd Architects 2009: 2–3). After the new Chinatown Precinct plan came out in 2009, a reported eight million Rands have been set aside to regenerate the old Chinatown area (Park 2009b: 116). No further details regarding the actual use of the funds were provided. No concrete projects have been executed ever since either. Like the fate of many other downtown revitalisation schemes, it is probably safe to suggest that a real revival of the old Chinatown looks rather distant in the future.

4.3 Cyrildene and the Making of an "Ethnoburban" Chinatown

In the past 20 years or so, in correspondence to the gradual decline of the inner-city Chinatown, a new ethnic Chinese settlement, Cyrildene Chinatown, emerged on Derrick Avenue between Friedland and Marcia Streets. Oral evidence suggests that the first Chinese-operated shop in this area was a Chinese noodle restaurant owned by a Taiwanese businessman, Mr. Qin, who later moved back to Taiwan but is still affectionately remembered by some older Chinese residents as "Grandpa Qin" (Interview with D. Li 2012). The first mainland Chinese business that made its entry to Derrick Avenue in 1995 was a restaurant called "Northern Dumplings," which is still in business but now under a different owner, a family relative of the original owner (Interview with

Li 2012). Starting from the mid-1990s, other Chinese followed suit and accelerated their occupation of the area through purchasing properties, opening restaurants and supermarkets, and setting up novelty shops.

One would probably wonder: Why Cyrildene? It turns out that the choice was not that of pure coincidence. On the one hand, due to its proximity to the airport and the N3 Highway, Cyrildene occupies a "perfect" location for many Chinese businessmen. In particular, the N3 Highway is the major traffic artery between Johannesburg and Durban, South Africa's major port where all major imports from China are offloaded and then transported accordingly. Meanwhile, Cyrildene is only 15 minutes away by car from the O. R. Tambo International Airport, an important factor for these frequent travellers between Asia and Africa (Interview with M. Chen 2012).

On the other hand, the rise of Cyrildene also benefited from the growing Chinese population in its nearby areas, which predated the new Chinatown's birth. Historically, Chinese, once classified as "Coloured" under apartheid, had residential right mainly in the southern edges of the city, where the mining dumps were, whilst the northern suburbs were reserved for the white population. Due to the small numbers of Chinese, it was difficult for the apartheid state to accommodate them in formal apartheid structures. In fact, many Chinese found ways to navigate on the fringes of all racial groups. Later, because of privileges given to the Japanese in the 1960s and to Taiwanese investors in the 1980s, the Chinese community was exempted from the Group Areas Act in 1984 (Yap and Man 1996: 317–321, 374–379; Osada 2002: 145–164; Harris 2002: 107; van der Watt and Visser 2008: 122). As a result, in the 1980s, some wealthy Chinese began to make entries to the Bruma and Edenvale area (adjacent to where Cyrildene is situated), considered a more or less middle-class neighbourhood. Therefore, as Cyrildene started to emerge as a Chinese business cluster in the late 1990s, the relatively concentrated Chinese population in nearby residential areas also served as a crucial catalyst. Considering the limited financial means of early Chinese immigrants in the 1990s, Mr. Xinzhu Li, one of the most successful Chinese businessmen in South Africa confessed, even in the 1990s, to imagine starting a business in prime locations like Sandton and Rosebank would be "unrealistic" for a Chinese shop-owner at the time. The cost of opening a small business in Cyrildene seemed much more "reasonable" (Interview with X. Li 2012). Cyrildene, in Li's words, became a "natural option" for Chinese immigrants due to their dual consideration of convenience and affordability. The following depiction by Park best illustrates the vibrancy of Cyrildene Chinatown today.

> [this] new Chinatown is home to over 25 Chinese restaurants which offer up delicacies from various regions. The area also boasts at least 15 Chinese grocery stores and market garden stalls, and a half dozen specialty food shops including butcheries, seafood shops, a liquor store, and several rice wholesalers. There are also service providers who ensure that Chinese migrants as well as other daring Jo'burgers can look and feel their best on the cheap; these include a half dozen beauty and hair salons, 4-5 Chinese medicine practitioners (acupuncturists, doctors and herbalists), and three massage parlours. Several Chinese community organizations are also based in Cyrildene, including the Southern Africans Zhejiang Association, the Fujian Regional Association, the South Africa Chinese Community & Police Co-operation Centre, the All Africa Association for Peaceful Reunification of China, and the Chinese language newspaper African Times. (Park 2009b: 118)

For an outsider, what cannot be easily captured, perhaps, are the invisible economies camouflaged under the cover of normal businesses. On Derrick Avenue, for example, an assuming photocopy shop can where illegal paperwork such as fraud visas, passports, and driver's licenses get traded. A regular travel agency may in fact be an underground money-laundering service provider. Similarly, massage parlours or karaoke bars can be synonyms for brothels. Some of the gated buildings along Derrick Avenue, down on Hettie Street or up on Janelea Street in particular, are believed to be hiding places for drug dealers and usury/loan sharks (Personal communication with Ben, a police officer at the South Africa Chinese Community and Police Co-operation Centre 2012). Ironically, in the South African context, the proliferation of gated housing is designed in response to security challenges. But at the same time, these insulated and guarded spaces can in turn serve as protection and cover for illegalities and criminal activities. As Mingwei Huang has powerfully showed us, this nature of "business duplicity" is not only unique to Cyrildene Chinatown; it is a constitutive feature of all China malls that have concentrated in the south and east edge of the city, as Chinese traders try to escape state financial surveillance and hide from threat of black criminality (Huang 2015: 21–22).

Though we have witnessed segments of Johannesburg's inner-city neighbourhoods being taken over by mixed groups of African immigrants (Nigerians being the most prominent, Simone 2008), Cyrildene Chinatown appears to be the only suburban ethnic settlement in post-apartheid South Africa whose boom is by and large attributed to one single immigrant group. Shall we then call Cyrildene Chinese settlement a Chinese "ethnic enclave"? "Ethnic enclave" as an analytical term is widely used in immigrant settlement studies, especially amongst American scholars. As Professor Wei Li correctly points out, unlike a ghetto, which is "mainly an ethnic residential area without an internally functioning economic system controlled by the ethnic group," an ethnic enclave "operates as a social and economic complex within its boundaries" (Li 2009: 18). Traditionally, an ethnic enclave was regarded more as a liability to socio-economic assimilation, rather than an asset. Depictions of ethnic enclaves were often associated with internal conflicts, high crime rates, and exploitation and abuse of illegal immigrants by sweatshops.

Wilson and Portes' classic study of the Cuban immigrant enclave in Miami, however, suggests that ethnic enclave provides better apprenticeship and upward mobility potentials for newly arrived co-ethnics (Wilson and Portes 1980). Their finding later became known as "the ethnic enclave hypothesis" (Waldinger 1993: 444). Zhou Min's 1992 celebrated study of New York City's Chinatown came to similar conclusions with Wilson and Portes' work. She argues that temporary hardship in an ethnic enclave would benefit new immigrants in the medium- and long-term future, hence a reaffirmation of the ethnic enclave hypothesis (Zhou 1992: 119–151).

Although the positive socio-economic functions of the ethnic enclave are now well appreciated amongst scholars, the term itself still evokes a crowded inner-city settlement image and a lower socio-economic profile, and is thought as a shelter for ethnic groups of disadvantages or immigrants from much poorer nations and/or of illegal backgrounds. Dissatisfied with "ethnic enclave" as a concept to account for the Asian suburbanisation along the Pacific Rim in the USA, Wei Li introduced a new analytical concept, “ethnoburb,” to better capture the emerging urban ethnic settlement patterns in areas where a certain ethnic imprint is “significant but not overwhelmingly dominant” (often times around 30 per cent of the area’s total population) (Harrison et al. 2012: 902). Ethnoburbs, in other words, are suburban ethnic clusters of both residential and business districts within a larger geographical boundary, but of a lesser degree of concentration compared to traditional Chinatown settlement models.

To better define Cyrildene Chinatown, we need to have a better sense of the broader picture of Chinese settlement in Johannesburg. Harrison, Moyo, and Yang have observed five different patterns of Chinese settlement in Johannesburg (Harrison et al. 2012: 914–924). First is the inner-city cluster, the old Chinatown. As discussed earlier, due to the general inner-city decline and outwards exodus of business, the old Chinatown has become only a symbolic space, mainly for a small group of older generation South African-born Chinese. Second is the eastern ethnoburb, which consists of areas such as Edenvale, Bedfordview, and Observatory, where large numbers of Chinese reside but their presence is hidden and hard to map. Third is the Cyrildene Chinatown cluster. Fourth is the Chinese wholesale and retail shopping complexes (referred as “China malls” in South Africa) concentrated primarily around Crown Mines and Fordsburg. Lastly and the final settlement is the Sandton clusters where major Chinese state-owned enterprises, especially big banks, construction, and telecommunication companies, occupy office spaces and begin to showcase China as a major foreign investment source for South Africa.

It is difficult to define what type of settlement Cyrildene cluster represents. On the one hand, Cyrildene Chinatown is very different from traditional ethnic enclaves; on the other, it is not a typical ethnoburb either. Harrison et al. expressed this bewilderment very cogently.

> Cyrildene, with its origins in the 1990s, is however, not the archetypical Chinatown—which would generally have a long history going back to the waves of Chinese emigration from the late nineteenth century – and has a suburban, rather than an inner city location. It is also not an ‘ethnoburb’ as it is a space of petty entrepreneurialism that is overwhelmingly and very

> visibly Chinese, although it is embedded within the broader and more diffuse cluster of Chinese activity in the eastern part of Johannesburg...firms [in Cyrildene] are mainly involved in customary Chinese activities such as food and traditional medicine, whilst the precinct is visibly marked with Chinese symbols. (Harrison et al. 2012: 917)

However, a closer examination suggests that Cyrildene Chinatown does function more like an ethnoburb (or as part of an ethnoburb) rather than a traditional Chinatown, although it does share important characteristics with the latter, such as crowdedness, internal conflicts, and certain degree of business closedness. Three major features indicate that Cyrildene Chinatown represents something new from typical ethnic enclaves. First of all, a primary distinction between "ethnoburbs" and ethnic enclaves is that ethnoburbs are settlements of choice "through some form of deliberate efforts of that group," whereas ethnic enclaves or ghettos form largely "in response to social or economic discrimination and exclusion" (Li 2009: 28). The fact that Cyrildene Chinatown thrived after 1994 when formal racial/ethnic segregation had been removed suggests that this Chinatown is indeed formed out of deliberation. Although the majority of residents of Cyrildene Chinatown (the Fujianese) are disliked as less educated and with lower social status by their better-off compatriots, they are still for sure much richer than most of local black South Africans (and even many white South Africans). Therefore, it would be misleading to suspect a process of "ghettoisation" when we try to conceptualise the formation of Cyrildene Chinatown.

Second, Cyrildene Chinatown calls into question the economic and geopolitical restructuring of post-apartheid South Africa. On the one hand, it defies the commonly held neo-liberal predications that once the apartheid is abolished, class lines are supposed to replace racial/ethnic lines in social integration. Apartheid obviously has a resilient afterlife. As wealthy middle class relocate to the northern suburbs, ethnicities do not simply disappear but are reorganising themselves in different forms. On the other hand, Cyrildene Chinatown is also a natural expression of post-apartheid South Africa's trade and immigration policies. Under such policies, large-scale immigration is tolerated. Massive influx of Chinese immigrants could no longer be all housed in the crowded inner-city Chinatown. An alternative settlement was then pursued. These Chinese, thanks to their access to manufacturing powerhouses in China, found commerce extremely lucrative in South Africa under its liberal trade regulations, and they began to dominate the wholesale and retail sector in the country.

Lastly but perhaps most importantly, it is inappropriate to read Cyrildene Chinatown businesses as an ethnic enclave economy, which is traditionally understood as "a set of ethnic niche activities… [that] form a more or less self-contained economic system with relative weak ties to the dominant economy" (Li 2009: 24). From an economic point of view, although the majority of shops and firms on Derrick Avenue are customary Chinese businesses, they are much more integrated to the new and broader Chinese settlements in South Africa. Cyrildene not only emerges as a hub of retail networks with traders coming from afar to purchase wares or stocks from local supermarkets and wholesalers; it also occupies an important place for retail and wholesale businessmen in the China malls. Many still prefer Cyrildene as a better residential choice due to various conveniences it offers. And more crucially, as Huang's study shows, it serves as a crucial "pass-through" point for the moving of Chinese capital between the Crown Mines and China, and between "the official and unofficial" (Huang 2015: 22). Many of the shop owners and residents on Derrick Avenue are themselves involved in retail and wholesale business in the China malls.

To imagine or depict Cyrildene Chinatown as a closed ethnic economy is misleading. The growth of Cyrildene Chinatown, as Dittgen contends, is undergoing processes of "hybridization" (Dittgen 2013). Cyrildene Chinatown functions as a commercial as well as a residential hub for Chinese business people in and near Johannesburg. For newly arrived Chinese immigrants, Dittgen reminds us, Cyrildene provides as a stepping stone where new comers can find easy access to accommodation, network, and market information. For those already running a business in the country, be it in major China malls or in remote villages far from the city, Cyrildene means social and cultural life when they come for groceries, stock purchases, party gatherings, or even prostitute consumptions. A small place as it is, Cyrildene, however, links herself to much larger commercial and social webs.

Cyrildene Chinatown, though considered a semi-closed economy, and physically separated from the outside society both by the newly erected border gates, is a socio-economic space that interacts with the outside in multiple and intimate ways. Almost all shop helpers on Derrick Avenue are black Africans, mostly Zimbabweans, but there are also South Africans, Malawians, Congolese, Nigerians, Mozambicans, and Angolans. Every day, these African workers "commute" on foot between Cyrildene and their "homes" in Yeoville and Hillbrow. They have picked some colloquial Chinese, started to appreciate Chinese food, and some even have made Chinese friends through mundane contacts. Derrick Avenue is where these people place their hopes to earn remittances for families thousands miles away. They are paid at a modicum weekly wage around 500–700 Rands (roughly 30–50 USD). Their income, however, is not limited to wages. The employment in Cyrildene facilitates their "entrepreneurship" (or more realistically their survivalist skills) in the informal economy. I was informed that many make resale profit in their own inner-city neighbourhoods from goods that they have acquired at a discount price from their employers on Derrick Avenue (Interview with Trust 2013).

I also encountered a white South African taxi driver whose everyday job is to give rides to Chinese travelling between Cyrildene and various China malls. Understandably, he is extremely popular amongst his Chinese patrons due to the fact that a white driver is less likely to be stopped, harassed, and extorted by policemen on street (Interview with Ray 2013). I also met another white South African who married to a Chinese lady and comes to Cyrildene twice a week as a volunteer to teach Chinese residents English language (Interview with May 2013). Perhaps, another manifestation of this interconnectedness between Cyrildene Chinatown and the outside is that Cyrildene is a favourite target for armed robbers who would frequent Derrick Avenue to reap some cash.

The reason why it is difficult to tell whether Cyrildene is a traditional Chinatown or ethnoburb is perhaps the blurring boundaries between the "sub" and "urb" in contemporary cities. As Peter Muller once wisely pointed out,

> [since] the late 1980s…the outer city is no longer 'sub' to the 'urb'…[and] the suburbs clearly have become the essence of the contemporary city." "Today's metropolis is no longer a single evolving system, but is composed of distinct parts that have their own character, attitudes, and functions… In general the basis of metropolitan form and structure is no longer relative location with respect to, or distance from, the central city center. Instead we have today a world of urban realms; each of economic, social, and political significance and each contributing the main force in shaping itself. (Muller 1989: 41–43)

Instead of taking shape in spatial patterns that followed the "garden city model" proposed by Ebenezer Howard about a century ago, an ardent proponent for urban zoning and scientific separation of functional specialisations (Howard 1902, cited from Lindstrom and Bartling 2003: xvi–xvii), Johannesburg's suburban settlements represent more of what Murray would call "edge cities" that "have developed around a serial replication of identical work, residence, and shopping uses" (Murray 2011: 106). Suburbs are no longer simply residential areas serving the urban centres; they are increasingly evolving as "town centers in their own right" (Murray 2011: 106). An ethnoburb, therefore, should be better understood as something in between, or a hybridised combination of, "suburban" and "urban." The differences between Cyrildene Chinatown and other "edge cities" such as Parktown, Rosebank, and Sandton lie primarily in her salient ethnic imprint.

Cyrildene Chinatown may not be an ethnoburb itself, but it is part of an "ethnoburban" Chinese community that stretches a wider geographic area in the northern and eastern parts of Johannesburg. We can call it an "ethnic edge city," or an ethnoburban Chinatown (a Chinatown that grows out of the broader Chinese ethnoburb). However, it caters for people and immigrants of much diverse backgrounds, and takes unique advantage of transnational business networks and global capitalism. Cyrildene Chinatown is essentially a centre for the larger Chinese residents in the northern and eastern suburbs, and therefore an integrated part of the Chinese ethnoburb/s in Johannesburg. At the same time, Cyrildene Chinatown when compared to other premier edge cities is of a lower profile, less imposing, and relatively more accessible for the subaltern black Africans (especially immigrants from neighbouring African countries).

4.4 Self-Governing Chinatown: Achievements and Challenges

In this section, I would like to briefly turn to a recent dispute over the construction of border arches on each end of Derrick Avenue as a case to illustrate the dynamics between community formation and state. This section stresses that the whole debate around the arch project reflects fundamental challenges facing community-building as well as municipal governance in post-apartheid South African cities.

Chinese community leaders first brewed the idea of erecting two arches on Derrick Ave in 2004. They only started to implement the plan three years later. Almost immediately, the arch project was challenged by both the city council and local South African residents in neighbouring areas. The city councillors representing other non-Chinese Cyrildene residents put on the table five reasons that they thought Chinatown border gate project should be prevented. Firstly, Cyrildene Chinatown for a period of time had been regarded a messy, dirty, and overcrowded place with high rates of criminal activity. Therefore, allowing such arch project might be seen as legitimising the dark sides of the Chinese business conduct in this area. Secondly, local non-Chinese residents tend to think of the arches as an undesirable mutation of the original cityscape and architectural taste of this area, hence potentially causing severe damage to Cyrildene's cultural and historical tradition and legacy. For instance, some accused Chinese property owners of illegally building "ugly" extensions and subdivisions to accommodate ever-increasing tenants on their estates. Thirdly, the city council stresses the notion that South Africa is a rainbow nation. Any effort to create provincialism or to promote narrow/ethnic nationalism is viewed with reservation or careful scrutiny. Fourthly, the criminal activities in Cyrildene reached its peak around the year of 2005, which caused extremely negative coverage in media. For example, one Chinese community leader in Cyrildene recalled, shamefully, that prostitution was so notorious around that time even white and black South African clients would come in large numbers to the Chinese whorehouses in and near Cyrildene Chinatown, causing public outcry and condescending reports about the Chinese community in Johannesburg (Interview with

M. Chen 2012). Fifthly and finally, the majority of Chinese businesses on Derrick Avenue were believed to have cheated on taxation. Therefore, city councillors contend that the municipal administration is not obligated to allocate general revenue to develop this area and provide proper services (Interview with M. Chen 2012).

As journalist Ho summarised in 2013, other non-Chinese Cyrildene residents and local councillors "keep catalogues of all that is wrong with a booming Chinatown," ranging from "illegal construction, ignored court orders, traffic infringements, subdivided houses and rearing livestock in residential areas" (Ho 2013). Maure Chen, Chinese chief negotiator with the city council, admitted that such accusations were valid and that Chinese community leaders must come together to help tackle the problems with full effort. He emphasised, however, that the arch project was part of the broader initiative to build a better Chinatown and to make it a genuine tourist attraction for both the locals and foreign travellers. Whilst acknowledging many of the aforementioned problems, the Chinese community leadership in Cyrildene stressed that these problems speak precisely to the city council's regulatory inability and its profound failure in town-keeping and surveillance. For instance, the parking infringement issue, Chen suggested, reflected serious defects in town planning. He contended, "if land is designed for commercial use, parking lot should be pre-planned and reserved for that purpose" (Interview with M. Chen 2012). City planning must be more comprehensive and should anticipate and give consideration to future development.

However, in post-apartheid South Africa, to lay hope on the Municipality might be a wrong bet. Simone has warned us, urban restructuring and capacity building in South Africa now only "centers on developing proficient forms of codification" (Simone 2008: 86). The emphasis is "on the ability to locate and to define the built environment, specific populations, and activities so that they can be registered," because the prevailing wisdom is that, "once registered, these phenomena can be better administered and their specific energies, disciplines, and resources extracted" (Simone 2008: 86). The actual town-keeping, utility provision, and people's mundane survival are beyond city urban planners' purview of concerns and therefore should be decentralised. This had led to, especially within the confines of the suburban settlements, the emergence of a particular form of civic governance. Lack of confidence in the Municipality to perform in these areas has forced South African suburbanites to rely first on neighbourhood or homeowners' associations to regulate community life through private legal initiatives. What is being widely practised is to bind "all property owners to a corporation, the association, to which they pay dues, and which in turn discharges such municipal functions as garbage removal, landscaping of common areas, street maintenance, fire protection, traffic regulation, and security services" (Murray 2011: 288). What is striking about such practices is an "inversion of private and public functions" which essentially signals the drift towards a process that Murray coined "privatopia" (Murray 2011: 288).

Cyrildene Chinatown has witnessed precisely the same process of "privatopia." As mentioned earlier, the year of 2005 seemed to be a turning point for Cyrildene Chinatown. In that year, residents, tenants and business owners on and near Derrick Avenue came together and formed the Cyrildene Chinatown Community Association (CCCA), which was subsequently authorised to collect duty fees from shops for maintenance purposes (or "public works fee"). For instance, the Association "contracted an armed response security company to provide protection to businesses...[encouraged] regular clean-up activities, [helped] newcomers to understand the laws and regulations of their newly adopted home, and meet regularly to discuss and resolve issues that arise" (Park 2009b: 118). One of the greatest achievements has been the drop of crime rates in the area. Weak law enforcement and massive unemployment has made South Africa notorious for its high crime rates, which was a long-time headache for Chinese in Cyrildene who prefer cash transactions in their businesses. To make the business environment safer, the CCCA under former President Xinzhu Li, initiated a police contact point (the Chinese Community and Police Cooperation Center) in Cyrildene with the help from Johannesburg Police Department and the Chinese Embassy. This police contact point also collaborates with Chinese Ministry of Public Security to ensure that Chinese citizens who commit crimes in South Africa be put in due justice (Interview with X. Li 2012). Li further suggested the most efficient way forward for town-keeping in Cyrildene would be to outsource all maintenance work through private funds collected from community members. Another major achievement is of course the arch project, for which the CCCA managed to raise over three million Rands amongst its members. As Mr. Chen reiterated that, the Municipality has not distributed a single penny for the reconstruction and development of Cyrildene Chinatown (Interview with M. Chen 2012) it is evident that fund raising has met with difficulties as one of the two arches is still incomplete by early 2016.

Needless to say, self-governing is by no means an easy task. Like many other ethnic settlements around the world, Cyrildene Chinatown is also freighted with internal conflicts and tensions amongst sub-groups and prominent members. So far, Fujianese are the majority group in Cyrildene Chinatown, accounting for over half of the Chinese population in the area. Discords between Fujianese and immigrants from Northern China and those from wealthier Eastern China are numerous. As the Deputy Secretary of Fujianese Fellow Association once informed me, the rapid increase of associations in Chinatown was the most vivid expression of conflictive interests amongst community leaders. A cogent example would be the following: when one leader disagrees with another, what follows is a split of the existing association, and the one who quits will soon establish his own, because being an association leader implies irresistible economic and political benefits as it facilitates his access to the Chinese Embassy as well as to economic resources back in China (Personal communications with W. Chen 2012, 2013). Native place associations and networks have long been recognised as a key characteristic of the socio-economic life of the Chinese diaspora in history (McKeown 1999). What adds to the significance of such networks today is the presence of a strong Chinese state (and its embassies overseas) which has indirectly contributed to the proliferation of various associations amongst Chinese diaspora.

To sum, this section has argued that Cyrildene, under the absence of an effective state taking care of urban development challenges, has embarked on self-governing initiatives. The establishment of CCCA is a proactive response to the city council's inability to regulate, manage, and monitor rapid urban development, which parallels civic engagement patterns observed in many post-apartheid suburban settlements. A comparison to civic engagement in the American context offers us an interesting contradiction. The distinguished political scientist, Robert Putnam, in one of his classic works, implied that accelerated mobility and suburban sprawl contributed to the decline of social capital in twentieth-century America (Putnam 2000: 204–215). The experience of Cyrildene Chinatown, however, seems to point to the opposite: in the context of post-apartheid South Africa, suburbanisation has in fact boosted rather than hindered civic engagement from below. As a co-ethnic to many Cyrildene Chinatown residents, I share the same dream that the arches not only bear metaphorical significance but also attest to the community's long-term commitment to civic engagement.

4.5 Conclusion and a Note on Chinese Migration and Globalisation

Claiming itself as the youngest Chinatown in the world, Cyrildene's new Chinatown presents a critique to the notion of "ethnic enclave." This chapter has argued that Cyrildene Chinatown as deliberately formed ethnic settlement is better captured by using "ethnoburb" or "ethnic edge city" as an analytical term. This chapter has shown that Cyrildene Chinatown skilfully uses a whole range of "hybridised" strategies in opening itself to new and different worlds. Through business outreach, it weaves itself into a complicated web that enables itself to navigate opportunities between South Africa, China, and other African nations. On its twentieth birthday, Cyrildene Chinatown still faces some fundamental challenges, some of which have to be solved from within, whereas others need to be tackled with assistance from the Municipality. What the growth and expansion of Chinese settlement in Cyrildene helps illustrate is perhaps the degree to which this new Chinatown, unlike Chinatowns in the old days, is shaped by complex imbrications of global, national, and local forces. Nevertheless, whether Cyrildene Chinatown's experience corresponds with formations and settlements of other trading diasporas in African history, and whether it offers any insight about future Chinese communities in other major cities on the continent remain to be investigated.

Since Chinese transnational capitalism and Chinese migration in Africa have garnered enormous scholarly attention, I would like to end by returning to a couple of seemingly divergent views on globalisation propagated by two eminent anthropologists. James Ferguson, in his masterpiece, *Global Shadows*, audaciously claims that in the African contexts the global does not flow it only hops. Global capitalism in Africa has largely been "concentrated in spatially segregated enclaves," connecting only "the enclave points" whilst "excluding the spaces that lie between points" (Ferguson 2006: 38, 47). As a result, globalisation in Africa is socially "thin" rather than socially "thick." Nevertheless, Gordon Mathews, in an outstanding study of Chungking Mansions, a dilapidated building in the heart of Hong Kong's tourist district that accommodates traders, labourers, and asylum seekers from all over Asia and Africa, powerfully tells a story of "low-end globalization," which is "distinct from the gleaming headquarters of multinational corporations," and operates in ways that work for "the majority of the world's people" (Mathews 2011: 19–21).

The question then is: between Ferguson's "spatially segregated enclaves" created by global capitalism and Matthews' "low-end globalization," where do places like Cyrildene Chinatown stand? Whilst studying the Fujianese immigrants in Europe, Frank Pieke and his colleagues come up with a term "Chinese globalisation." This term, they suggest, is coined to look at the increasingly interconnected world through Chinese eyes. They argue that "Chinese globalisation has opened up a range of transnational social spaces" that combine both "transnationalism from above and transnationalism from below of a variety and scale that truly are unprecedented" (Pieke et al. 2004: 12). Indeed, Chinese global migration represents hybrid forms of both the high-end and low-end globalisation. Perhaps, that "unprecedentedness" is why we feel inadequate to define certain patterns created by Chinese migration, but that "unprecedentedness" is also where new theorisation of globalisation and of Chinese migration in Africa will emerge. The omnipresent flows of Chinese goods, Chinese people, Chinese capital, or the more broadly China in the world are becoming an important window through which observers and researchers contemplate and imagine what we call "globalisation." I hope this chapter will move beyond the myth of Chinese enclaves in Africa and open new possibilities and territories where more constructive discussions and debates can be pursued.

References

Akyeampong, E., & Xu, L. (2015). The three phases/faces of China in independent Africa: Re-conceptualizing China-Africa engagement. In J. Lin & C. Monga (Eds.), *Oxford handbook of Africa and economics, Policies and practices* (Vol. II, pp. 762–779). Oxford, UK: Oxford University Press.

Alden, C. (2007). *China in Africa*. London: Zed Books Ltd.

Brautigam, D. (2013). AidData: Why it is not Wikipedia, May 2. Link http://www.chinaafricarealstory.com/2013/05/aiddata-why-it-is-not-wikipedia.html. Last accessed on 5 July 2016.

Chinese Ministry of Commerce (2014). 2013年中国与非洲贸易首次突破2000亿美元. Link: http://www.mofcom.gov.cn/article/i/jyjl/k/201401/20140100475427.shtml. Last accessed on 5 July 2016.

Dittgen, R. (2013). Chinese malls in Johannesburg: Towards a process of spatial and commercial hybridization. Paper presented at the African Center for Migration and Society, Johannesburg, South Africa: WITS University, November 27. Link: http://urban-africa-china.angonet.org/content/chinese-malls-johannesburg-towards-process-spatial-and-commercial-hybridization. Last accessed on 5 July 2016.

Ferguson, J. (2006). *Global shadows: Africa in the neoliberal world order*. Durham: Duke University Press.

Field Interviews and Personal Communications:

Interview with D. Li (2012, August 16). Owner of Da Lao Li Restaurant on Cyrildene Avenue.

Interview with M. Chen (2012, August 18). Chief coordinator of the arch project.

Interview with Trust (2013, July 25). A Zimbabwean shop helper at a supermarket on Derrick Avenue.

Interview with X. Li (2012, August 19). A prominent businessman and owner of *African Times* (a major local Chinese newspaper).

Personal communication with Ben (2012, August 16). (Pseudonym), a Police Officer at the South Africa Chinese Community and Police Co-operation Centre.

Personal communications with May (2013, August 2013). A volunteer English teacher, two times.
Personal communications with Ray (2013, August 2013) (Taxi driver) in a tea-shop on Derrick Avenue, three times.
Personal communications with Wang Chen (2012) Deputy Secretary of Fujianese Fellow Association in South Africa, multiple conversations, August 2012 and July 2013.
FOCAC (Forum On China-Africa Cooperation) (2015). 中非关系: 务实合作走进新常态. Link: http://www.focac.org/chn/zfgx/zfgxrwjl/t1242090.htm. Last accessed on 5 July 2016.
Hart, G. (2002). *Disabling globalization: Places of power in post-apartheid South Africa*. Berkeley: University of California Press.
Harris, K. (2002). Whiteness, blackness, neitherness—the South African Chinese 1885–1991: A case study of identity politics. *Historia, 47*(1), 105–124.
Harrison, P., Moyo, K., & Yang, Y. (2012). Strategy and tactics: Chinese immigrants and diasporic spaces in Johannesburg, South Africa. *Journal of Southern African Studies, 38*(4), 899–925.
Ho, U. (2013, July 12). The arch angle on booming chinatown, *Mail & Guardian*.
Howard, E. (1902). *Garden cities of to-morrow*. London: Faber and Faber.
Huang, M. (2015, October 5). Hidden in plain sight: Everyday aesthetics and capital in Chinese Johannesburg. Paper presented at the WiSER seminar, Wits University, Johannesburg.
Large, D. (2013). China, Africa and beyond. *Journal of Modern African Studies, 51*(4), 707–714.
Li, W. (2009). *Ethnoburb: The new ethnic community in urban America*. Honolulu, Hawai'i: University of Hawai'i Press.
Lin, S.-H. (Gary). (2001). The relations between the republic of China and the republic of South Africa 1948–1998. Ph.D. dissertation, University of Pretoria.
Lindstrom, M. J., & Bartling, H. (Eds.). (2003). *Suburban sprawl: Cultural, theory, and politics*. New York: Rowman & Littlefield Publishers.
Mathews, G. (2011). *Ghetto at the center of the world: Chungking mansions*. Hong Kong/Chicago, IL: University of Chicago Press.
McKeown, A. (1999). Conceptualizing Chinese diaspora, 1842–1949. *Journal of Asian Studies, 58*(2), 306–337.
Mbembe, A. (2012). Theory from the antipodes: Notes on Jean & John Comaroffs TFS. *Cultural Anthropology*, February 25. Link: https://culanth.

org/fieldsights/272-theory-from-the-antipodes-notes-on-jean-john-comaroffs-tfs. Last accessed on 5 July 2016.

Muller, P. O. (1989). The transformation of bedroom suburbia into the outer city: An overview of metropolitan structural change since 1947. In B. M. Kelly (Ed.), *Suburbia re-examined* (pp. 39–44). New York: Greenwood Press.

Murray, M. (2011). *City of extremes: The spatial politics of Johannesburg*. Durham: Duke University Press.

Osada, M. (2002). *Sanctions and honorary whites: Diplomatic policies and economic realities in relations between Japan and South Africa*. Westport: Greenwood Press.

Park, Y.J. (2009a, January). *Migration in Africa* (SAIIA Occasional Paper, No. 24).

Park, Y. J. (2009b). Chinese enclave communities and their impact on South African Society. In S. Marks (Ed.), *Strengthening the civil society perspective: China's African Impact* (pp. 113–127). Nairobi: Fahamu.

Pickles, J., & Woods, J. (1989). Taiwanese investment in South Africa. *African Affairs, 88*(353), 514–515.

Pieke, F., Nyiri, P., Thuno, M., & Ceccagno, A. (2004). *Transnational Chinese: Fujianese migrants in Europe*. Standford: Stanford University Press.

Putnam, R. (2000). *Bowling alone*. New York: Simon & Schuster Paperbacks.

Savage+Dodd Architects (2009). *Chinatown precinct plan 2009*. Link: www.joburg-archive.co.za/2011/inner_city/chinatown_precinct_plan2009.pdf. Last accessed on 5 July 2016.

Simone, A. (2008). People as infrastructure. In A. Mbembe & S. Nuttall (Eds.), *Johannesburg: The elusive metropolis* (pp. 68–90). Durham, NC: Duke University Press.

Strange, A., Bradley, P., Michael, J. T., Andreas, F., Axel, D., & Vijaya, R. (2013, April). *China's development finance to Africa: A media-based approach to data collection* (Working Paper 323). Washington, DC: Center for Global Development.

Van der Watt, L. M., & Visser, W. P. (2008). Made in South Africa: A social history of the Chinese in bloemfontein, free state province, South Africa, ca. 1980–2005. *Journal of Contemporary History, 33*(1), 121–142.

Waldinger, R. (1993). The ethnic enclave debate revisited. *International Journal of Urban and Regional Research, 17*(3), 444–452.

Wilson, K., & Portes, A. (1980). Immigrant enclaves: An analysis of the labor market experiences of cubans in Miami. *American Journal of Sociology, 86*(2), 295–316.

Wolf, C., Xiao, W., & Eric, W. (2013). China's foreign aid and government-sponsored investment activities: Scale, content, destinations, and implications. The Rand National Defense Research Institute.

Woods, G.R. (1991). Taiwanese investment in the homelands of South Africa. Ph.D. Dissertation, Ohio University.

Yap, M., & Man, D. L. (1996). *Colour, confusion and concessions: The history of the Chinese in South Africa*. Hong Kong: Hong Kong University Press.

Zhou, M. (1992). *Chinatown: The socioeconomic potential of an urban enclave*. Philadelphia: Temple University Press.

5

China's Energy Diplomacy Towards Africa from the Perspective of Politics

Cheng Aiqin and Cai Jianhong

5.1 Introduction

Politics has always been a very important factor for China to establish and develop relations with Africa. Occasionally, it can be considered as the top factor. Many people attributed this situation to the Chinese government's political stand, which is not completely correct. Political relations between China and Africa are far closer than economic, cultural, and

This article is a stage result of A Regional Research About the Initial Stage of the Maritime Silk Road from the Social Science Fund of Hebei Province in 2016 (Project Number: HB16LS011) and A Study on Cultural Symbiosis Model of the Construction of the Maritime Silk Road in Twenty-first Century from the Social Science Development and Research Project of Hebei Province in 2015 (Project Number: 2015020312).

C. Aiqin (✉)
Hebei University, Henan, China
e-mail: xianzhai19610521@163.com

C. Jianhong
Graduate School of Chinese Academy of Social Science, Beijing, China

Y. C. Kim (ed.), *China and Africa*, The Palgrave Macmillan Asian Business Series, DOI 10.1007/978-3-319-47030-6_5

other relations. In fact, this shows the truth of the world's political revolution of the twentieth century. Especially after World War II, with the formation and strengthening of ideological opposition, political relations between the countries have become a top priority of international relations. Accordingly, the world is divided into the Soviet-led Eastern bloc and the US-led Western camp.

National independence movements against Western colonial and apartheid rule rose one after another on the African continent. The Eastern blocs that try to overthrow the global capitalist system get new joint forces. As a very important member of the Eastern bloc, when China develops relations with Africa, her first consideration is how to make these anti-Western forces to become their political allies or partners. In fact, during this period the African policy of the West camp is mainly out of political considerations, but they mostly focus on how to maintain political control in Africa. So, overall, back then on the political map of Africa, the Western camp is on the defensive, while the Eastern bloc is on the offensive. China was a relatively strong offensive member in the Eastern bloc.

In modern times, China and Africa establish and develop the relationship under two conditions. One is that China has established a stable and independent regime and ended a century-long war turmoil after getting rid of the Western political domination and economic slavery. The other one is that the related African countries gained state sovereignty to establish an independent regime from Western colonial rule. The similar historical fate, similar international status, and similar political demands are the important foundations of China–Africa relations. Under the oppression or threat of political survival of the West, China and Africa continue looking for common interests in a complex international environment, and eventually formed a strong international political dependence system mutually.

Throughout the 65 years of development of China–Africa relations, each period has its distinctive features. It developed from safeguarding the international political right to life to defending the right to maintain national economic development; from defending national sovereignty to safeguarding the national politics right to choose; from focus on the traditional security to non-traditional security; from focus on the political revolution to development and cooperation; from monistic diplomacy to pluralistic diplomacy; from pure economic assistance to multilateral economic cooperation. With the development of the current situation, the relationship between China and Africa is moving towards a comprehensive, stable, orderly, reciprocal, mutual benefit, and symbiotic state of 'community of destiny'. Energy is an important part in China's cooperation with Africa and is also one of the most important thing of the International Society. This article explains China's energy diplomacy with Africa from the international political perspective.

5.2 Africa of China's Political Diplomacy

China is a country of pan-politicisation that pays much attention to politics. China's 3500 years history is essentially a history of politics. It is different from most of the Western countries. In China, everyone has his political worth, and every action is a political action. China has the strongest political reversibility sense in the world. As the old saying goes, everybody is responsible for the rise and fall of the country. It is rooted in Chinese clan society, which originates from Chinese ethics. The Confucian thesis emphasises the Five Ethics, which are relations between rulers and subjects, fathers and sons, husbands and wives, brothers, and friends. All these human orders are in fact social orders. The Ten Righteousness in the Book of Rites has brought all acts or social relations of human society into social or social–political order. The Confucian thinks that human society is composed of individuals. Everybody is part of the basic social unit. Individuals and groups complement each other and depend on each other. Both cannot leave the other side. Chinese vividly call the relationship between the individual and the group the relationship of the skin and hair. With the skin gone, what can the hair adhere to? No one can survive separated from social groups. Social nature of human beings is valued extremely, while trying to suppress individuality of human. This 'Humanity' eventually becomes the basis of Chinese human nature of pan-social nature or pan-political nature. This close relationship between human and social and political life expands to relations of man and the nature. Humans and the nature fully integrate as a whole. Lao-Tzu said that Tao is big, the heaven is big, the earth is big, and the human is also big. The four are big and humans are one of them. This thought completely integrates man and the nature as one. This concept cannot be seen in the West.

In the special history background of pan-politicisation, the anti-Western Africa is important for the same anti-Western China, so Sino-Africa relations naturally become part of China's diplomacy. For China, Africa is almost a political unit, so its economic, cultural, and historical function is just part of its political structure. At least in the short time after the establishment of People's Republic of China (PRC), Africa has been regarded as playing an important role in China's politics.

5.2.1 Africa Has a Strong Role in China's Political Diplomacy

The PRC was founded on October 1, 1949, when the declining Western capitalist system and expanding non-capitalist system went towards a comprehensive confrontation. The Chinese Communist Party, the founder of China, has close relations with the sweeping global ideological confrontation from its very beginning. In other words, the Communist Party of China came into being from this confrontation and it ultimately founded China. In this sense, the success of the Communist Party of China is actually a result of the international political struggle.

Since the establishment of the PRC is an outcome of the international political struggle, and then it can be understood that its foreign philosophy has clear political orientation. Mao Zedong, Chinese Communist Party leader, clearly stressed on the opening of the first plenary session of the Chinese people's Political Consultative Conference, on the eve of formal establishment of Chinese regime, 'Internationally, we must unite with all peace-loving countries and peoples. Above all, uniting with the Soviet Union and the new democracies together, we can guarantee these fruits of victory of People's Revolution and we will not be isolated when fight against restoration conspiracy of internal and external enemies' (Mao 1994 pp 114).

During this period, Mao Zedong put forward a clear-cut diplomatic concept of leaning to one side, which is a fatal selection of modern Chinese history, but also the last resort of the Chinese Communist Party, because there was no other choice. It was caused by history but also by reality; in the meantime, it was made by the West but also by the East. In this regard, Mao explained, 'leaning to one sided policy is based on four decades of experience of Sun Yat-sen and 28 years of experience of the Communist Party. We know that to achieve and consolidate victory we must lean to one side. Forty years and twenty-eight years of experience taught Chinese people that we either lean to the side of imperialism or the side of socialism, without exception. Sitting on the fence is not enough, and there is no the third way' (Mao 1960b, pp 1477–1478).

In addition to historical reasons, the US-led Western bloc took the policy of 'isolation' and 'containment' on politics, policy of 'blockade' and 'embargo' on economy to the new regime of PRC. It promoted China to move closer to the former Soviet Union objectively (Wang 2013). On October 3, 1949, Truman told the State Department that we should not recognise this government in a hurry and thus, China had to wait 12 years to be recognised as a communist regime in synthesis with the Soviet Union (Tao 2003). The USA believed that it is obligated to 'foster and support the anti-Communist forces at home and abroad to boycott the Beijing regime' (DNSA 2016). The USA not only refused to recognise the new China, but also sent a note to Britain, France, the Netherlands, Belgium, India, Pakistan, Australia, and other countries asking them to maintain a concerted stance in tandem with the USA in refusing to recognise China under the communist leadership. Before 1954, for the USA, the stability of the Chinese Communist regime remained questionable. Rusk, the Chairman of the Rockefeller Foundation, once said that many of us did not believe that the Chinese regime would last long (DDE, NSC Staff paper 1953–1961).

In November 1949, 15 US-led Western countries sponsored the Coordinating Committee for Multilateral Export Controls (COCOM) to Communist Countries in Paris, which was specifically responsible for inspecting and controlling trade with the Soviet Union and other socialist countries. After the founding of the New China, the US government refused to recognise China politically and imposed a blockade policy on the Chinese economy in order to strain the economic capabilities of the Communist Party (The history of the Chinese Communist Party information, 1994).

After the outbreak of the Korean War, the USA escalated its blockade and embargo on China. On June 29, 1950, the USA issued the Output Control Law of 1950, according to which 11 kinds of goods including kerosene, rubber, copper, and lead could not be exported to mainland China and Macao without special export permit (Collection of Financial Records of the People's Republic of China 1949–1952, pp 447). On July 17, the US government officially announced that the trade restraint of the COCOM on the Soviet Union and Eastern bloc expanded to China and North Korea (The history of the Chinese Communist Party information, vol. 42 pp 202). On July 20, the US Department of Commerce announced the abolition of export licence of the American goods to China and the licence holders had to hand their licence over and have it re-examined. In August, the US government issued the Prohibition of Export Order of Special Goods in 1950, in which 16 kinds of special goods including metal machine tools, non-ferrous metals, chemicals, chemical application equipment, transportation equipment, telecommunications equipment, and navigation equipment were prohibited from being exported. In November, the US Commerce Department increased its control on strategic materials from around 600 objects to more than 2100 products for China. On December 2, the USA announced the Enhanced Command of the Control on Output of Strategic Goods that all exports to China, Hong Kong, and Macao were controlled, regardless of the fact that they were strategic goods or not. On December 8, the US government announced the Port Control Act, which not only prohibited American ships bound for China but also detained all foreign merchant ships transiting through the port of the USA carrying strategic materials without applying for approval from the port control mechanism. On December 16, the US government issued the Foreign Asset Control Act which froze all of China's private and public property in the USA (Collection of Financial Records of the PRC 1949–1952, 1994. Pp 448).

In May 1951, the United Nations (UN) passed an embargo to China under the manipulation of the USA (Collection of Financial Records of the People's Republic of China (1949–1952, 1994. pp 456).

In September 1952, the COCOM added the China Committee as the specialised actuators embargo against China (The history of the Chinese Communist Party information, 1994 pp 206). Until March 1953, a total of 45 countries participated in the embargo against China under immense pressure from the USA (Compilation of Sino-US Relations 1960 pp 352). During the period of the Republic of China (ROC), China mainly traded with Western countries. After the founding of PRC, facing comprehensive economic blockade of the Western Group, the Chinese government was forced to adjust the direction of its foreign trade and turned to the Soviet-led Eastern bloc. Mao Zedong said, 'Sino-Soviet treaties and agreements fixed the friendship of the two countries by the form of law, which get us a reliable ally, so we can launch out into domestic construction and deal with possible imperialist aggression and fight for world peace together' (Mao, The Significance of Sino-Soviet Treaties and Agreements, 1994c pp 131). In January 1951, it was submitted during the meeting of the National Trade Conference that China should expand trade with the Soviet Union and its allies actively. On June 16, 1951, Chen Yun, the Chinese leader who presided over the economic work, said in an interview with foreign reporters that under the current international situation, economic cooperation between China and Soviet-led bloc was important for China. This economic cooperation aided the formulation of the Chinese economy against the American blockade (*People's Daily,* June 22, 1951). Through the reliance on developing relations with Soviet-led Eastern bloc, China's foreign trade obtained certain development. It increased 1.5 times from $ 1.13 billion in 1950 to $ 1.94 billion in 1952, with an increase of exports from $550 million to $ 820 million and imports from $ 580 million to $ 1.12 billion, which, respectively, increased 1.5 times and 1.9 times (Collection of Financial Records of the PRC 1949–1952, 1994 pp 1022).

Many scholars, especially Western scholars, exaggerated China's dependence on the Soviet Union through the 'leaning to one side' policy, saying that China was almost entirely subordinated to the Soviet Union, which is inconsistent with historical facts. There was always a gap between the Communist Party of China under the leadership of Mao and the Soviet Union under Stalin. The gap existed since the Yanan period at least. Mao clearly pointed out that Yanan Rectification Movement actually criticised the error of Stalin and the Third International in guiding the Chinese Revolution (Mao, The Lessons of History, against Chauvinism, 1994t pp 254). After Mao came to power, this gap expanded step by step. In his speech in the meeting of the establishment of the Ministry of Foreign Affairs in November 1949, Zhou Enlai said, 'diplomatic work has two aspects. One is union and the other is struggle. There are difference between us and our fraternal countries. In other words, we should unite strategically with the brotherly countries, but not without criticism on tactics. We should struggle against imperialism countries strategically, but sometimes tactically on individual problems we can unite with them. We should understand it clearly, otherwise we will mix enemies with friends' (Zhou, 'On New China's diplomacy' 1990a pp 2–3). In August 1956, Mao Zedong stressed in the report of the Eighth National Congress of the Communist Party of China, 'China's revolution and construction are mainly relying on their own strength of Chinese people. Foreign aid is just the supplement. We must know it' (Mao, 'Solidarity with Fraternal Countries and Establish Friendly Relations with All Countries', 1994o pp 245). It is claimed that this rhetoric was aimed towards the Soviet Union.

When he proposed the 'Lean to One Side' policy, Mao never gave up independence. In December 1956, Mao Zedong stressed in a nationwide speech, 'we lean to one side to the Soviet Union but our relationship is equal. We have faith in Marxism-Leninism and combine it with the actual situation of our country, but not to copy the Soviet experience, which is wrong' (Mao, 'Is That Right to Lean to One Side?', 1994u pp 279). Mao convinced that it must be mutually beneficial while not harmful to any side, whether the cooperation was between people, parties, or countries. If either party compromised, cooperation could not be sustained. In December 1954, Mao Zedong said to the visiting Myanmar Prime Minister Nu U, 'it is rare that a country wins the revolution by foreign help or by other parties' help' (Mao, 'Countries Should Be Equal Regardless of The Size', 1994g pp 189). In May 1955, in a conversation with the Prime Minister of Indonesia he stressed, 'a nation not only survived but developed for centuries. It must have its advantage, or it cannot be understood' (Mao, 'Peace is above all', 1994k pp 209). In March 1960, Mao said to the visiting Prime Minister of the Kingdom of Nepal, 'our countries should rely primarily on our own efforts, meantime we should seek foreign aid as a supplemented. We need foreign aid, but what is the most important. Self-reliance is easy and initiative' (Mao, 'The Border of China and Nepal Would Be Always Peaceful And Friendly', 1994ab pp 393). For Chinese Communists led by Mao Zedong, due to the hostility faced by the Western forces the Chinese government leaned to the Soviets. However, despite the fact that there was the notion of 'leaning' towards the Soviet Union, China constantly maintained the stance that it was independent from foreign guidance or was at least attempting to gain independence. In January 1964, when Mao Zedong met the Japanese Communist Party Politburo member he said, 'We keep diplomatic relations with the Soviet Union and we are both in the socialist camp, but relations between the Soviet Union and China is not as good as the relationship of China and the Liberal Democratic Party of Japan, nor as good as relations with Ikeda faction. It is worth all of us to think about it. Because the US and Soviet Union have nuclear weapons and both would like to rule the world. The Liberal Democrat was controlled by American' (Mao, 'There Are Two Intermediate Zones', 1994v pp 507).

In the Ten Major Relationships, Mao Zedong once showed his dissatisfaction with Stalin. 'Stalin made some mistakes on China. Wang Ming left adventurism in the late of Second Revolutionary Civil War and Wang Ming Right opportunism in the early of Sino-Japanese War were both from Stalin. In the liberation war, at first he barred other people from revolution. He said that if civil war happened, the Chinese nation would at the risk of destruction. When came into the battle, he distrust us. When we won the war, he suspected it was a Tito-style victory. He gave us a lot of pressure in 1949 and in 1950' (Mao, 'On the Ten Major Relationships', 1986 pp 741). During his meeting with the Yugoslav Delegation, Mao Zedong said, 'Wang Ming route is actually the Stalin route. It ruined 90 percent of the strength of our base and ruined one hundred percent of the white area' (Mao, 'The Lessons of History, against Chauvinism', 1994t pp 252). Mao Zedong showed his dissatisfaction on many occasions. He thought that many Russians were too proud. In October 1955, when he met with Japanese guests Mao Zedong said, 'There is no one in the world should be always grateful to the other one unilaterally. If there were, it will not be good. Benefit should be mutual. Help should be Mutual. Appreciation should be Mutual' (Mao, 'The Sino-Japan Relations And the Problems of World War', 1994x pp 220). The naval base problem between China and the Soviet Union in 1958 was a typical example of this struggle of control and anti-control. When he described the quarrel with Khrushchev in the naval base, Mao Zedong said, 'I said to him, how about I gave you all Chinese coastline? He said what you can do then? I said that we went into the hills for guerrilla warfare. He said that guerrilla warfare was useless. I said what we can do except guerrilla warfare if you stuff our nostrils?' (Mao, 'Khrushchev's Life Is Not Easy', 1994i pp 516).

Mao was a nationalist. We can feel a strong nationalist ideology in the writings of Mao Zedong. His speech on opposition to US-led Western countries interfering in Asian affairs was actually said to the Soviets. Such as, he said, 'China, the center of gravity in Asia, is a large country with a population of 475 million; by seizing China, the US would possess all of Asia' (Mao, 'Farewell, Leighton Stuart' 1960a pp 1495).

'As the Eastern Pacific belongs to the eastern Pacific people, the Western Pacific belongs to Western Pacific people' (Mao, 'China and the US Did Not Go to War And There Is No Fire To Stop', 1994w pp 358). 'Chinese people have declared that the affairs of each country should be managed by its own people. Asian affairs should be managed by the Asian people, not by the American' (Mao, 'Defeat Any Provocation From Imperialism' 1994a pp 137).

In May 1959, when Mao Zedong met 11 delegates from socialist countries including Soviet Union, he said, 'Today, there are many ghosts in the world; There is a large group of ghosts in the western world, which are imperialism; In Asia, Africa, Latin America also has a large number of ghosts, which are the running dogs of imperialism and the reactionaries' (Mao, 'There Are Some One Afraid of Ghost But Some One Not In The World', 1994l pp 374). 'We Asians have a sense of inferiority that always feels we cannot, while Caucasian is stronger than we are. It is superstition need be overcome. Not only to get rid of superstition, but also learning from the West' (Mao, 'The Border of China and Nepal Would Be Always Peaceful And Friendly', 1994ab pp 393). 'I believe that we can do what white person can do, only better than they did. Because that they are less in number, only a few hundreds of millions' (Mao, 'Imperialism Is Not Terrible', 1994b pp 411).

Stalin who was eager to control East Asia or to gain access to East Asia through agents was very reluctant to see Mao Zedong publically announce this mode of regional and ethnic independence. In fact, Stalin had already felt the 'centrifugal force' of Mao Zedong and had regarded him as 'Oriental Tito'. After the death of Stalin, the split between the Soviet Union and China looked like a breakdown in relations between Khrushchev and Mao Zedong; however, the fragmentations within the relationship were evident even during the Stalin period. Sino-Soviet split was because of the outbreak between the two sides fighting for political leadership within the domestic and international political discourse.

It is no doubt that the US-led Western bloc was China's 'enemies' in the minds of the Chinese people at this period. Mao Zedong said, 'In front of us standing a formidable opponent, it is the United States. US will be mean to us once he has the chance, therefore we need friends' (Mao, 'Any Problem May Cause Suspicion or Impede Cooperation between Countries Should Be Solved', 1994h pp 175). Americans were hostile to China 'because it is the country ruled by Communist' (Mao, 'China and Pakistan Should Be Good Friends', 1994y pp 203). Zhou Enlai said in the meeting held by National Committee of the Chinese People's Political Consultative Conference in celebration of the first anniversary of the founding of the nation that the US government 'has proven it is the most dangerous enemy of PRC' (Zhou, 'Foreign Policy of the People's Republic of China', 1990c pp 23). According to Maoist thinking of with me or against me, 'whatever the enemy opposes, we have to support; whatever the enemy opposes, we have to support it; whatever the enemy supports, we have to oppose it.' (Mao, 'The Interview With Three Correspondents From the Central News Agency', 1952 pp 580). The African continent had important political significance because of their stance against Western colonialism, white supremacy and racism.

This political position was not formed in a single day, and nor was Mao's personal political philosophy. It was the consensus of the collective leadership of the Chinese Communist Party. The Bandung Asian–African Conference was an excellent opportunity to publicise China's diplomatic thoughts. Zhou Enlai, the implementer of the diplomatic philosophy of Mao Zedong, stated in Bandung Conference, 'It is a common requirement for the awakened Asian and African countries and people.

The requirement includes anti-discriminate, requiring for basic human rights, anti-colonial, asking for national independence, and safeguarding the sovereignty and territorial integrity of their country resolutely.' (Zhou, 'Speech In the plenary session of the Asia-African Conference', 1990b pp 117). He emphasised, 'All peoples regardless of race and color should enjoy basic human rights, should not suffer any abuse and discrimination' (Zhou, 'Speech In the plenary session of the Asia-African Conference', 1990b pp 116). China was spared to support Africa in opposition to the West. It was because the Chinese government believed that to defend the interests of Africa was to defend their own national interests. This support was not only on political philosophy but also on the political action. During the Bandung Conference, Zhou Enlai actively contributed to the Soviet arms' supplies to Egypt when China was unable to meet the needs of arms' supplies asked by Egypt Prime Minister Nasser (Nadine, *Nasser* 1976 pp 149–150).

Bandung Conference was a highly successful 'political show' of the Chinese government. It not only let the international community recognise the existence of China's new regime but also greatly enhanced the Chinese political discourse in developing countries. It was China's successful performance at the Bandung Conference that prompted Nasser to turn to pro-East 'positive neutralism' from pro-Western 'neutralism'. Chinese political support for Africa is long term, consistent, and stable. From the beginning of the 1950s, national independence movements flourished in the African continent from north to south, to the early 1990s, the last colony in Africa–Namibia's independence, it was China's basic foreign policy which supported national liberation movements across Africa against colonialism and racist rule. Zambian President Kenneth Kaunda said, 'Only China consistently defends Zambia against hostile neighbors' violations' (DeRoche 2007 pp 241)

It was specifically mentioned in the Central Intelligence Agency (CIA) report in 1967 that the Chinese assistance to African countries was different from the Soviet Union and the USA. Firstly, technical staff lived an extremely hard life there. They were consistent with the living standards in Africa (Mao, 'Our Relations with the People of All African Countries Are Good', 1994q pp 491). Secondly, they would not be in control of the assets through investment; they always left immediately after the completion of the task (DDRS, No. CK3100276982). Another report said that China's assistance in general was more favourable than the Soviet Union or the USA's aid. Most project aids by the Chinese would allow the recipient to obtain net income (DDRS, No. CK3100127315). This is because China in Mao's time has never regarded Africa as an object to obtain economic benefits. Politics was above all. Mao took Africa as an extension of the domestic politics. He needed the political support of the African continent, just as Zhou Enlai said, 'we will win more friendship by unselfish assistance' (He, 'The Decision Process of Aiding Tanzania Zambia Railway', 1993).

Of course, Mao Zedong also hoped that the Chinese revolutionary experience would be helpful to Africa's anti-Western political movements, because it was, after all, the essence of decades of revolutionary experience of the Chinese Communists led by Mao Zedong. In May 1960, when Mao Zedong met 12 visiting delegations of African countries, he said, 'I want to remind my friends that China has its own historical conditions and you have your historical conditions. China's experience can only be your reference' (Mao, 'Imperialism Is Not Terrible' 1994b pp 413). Within his rhetoric, the pride for a Chinese-style revolution is clearly evident.

Western governments believed that Mao Zedong had been trying to destroy Western influence, counter Soviet revisionism, and spread communist revolution of the Beijing Model (DDRS, No. CK3100572009). In fact, supporting all anti-Western forces in the world was Mao's consistent political stance. He never hid his views. 'Wherever revolution happens, we support it. The imperialists hate us and think we are warlike' (Mao, 'We Hope Arab Countries to Unite', 1994r pp 565). Mao said to Zambian President Kaunda that earlier independent states were obliged to help the latter independent countries. He stressed the difficulties of a newly independent state, but stated that China would offer as much assistance to ensure that states who wished to become liberated would become liberated. He further claimed that if aid was not of essence, no country could become liberated; if China could not liberate on its own, you cannot liberate yourself either. When Mao Zedong met the women delegation and economic delegation of the Government of Guinea, he said, 'All African friends were welcomed by Chinese people. Our relations with all African countries are good, whether independent or dependent people' (Mao, 'Our Relations with the People of All African Countries Are Good' 1994q pp 490).

The construction of the Tanzania–Zambia Railway (Tanzania–Zambia Railway Authority [TAZARA]) was an important manifestation of China's foreign policy in Africa during the Maoist period. It was also the most successful diplomatic case in Africa. Frankly, the economic value of the Tanzania–Zambia Railway was very limited. Before January 1965, Tanzania and Zambia had requested for aid from Britain, the USA, Germany, the World Bank, and other countries or organisations, but they were rejected. Reasons for the rejection were that, firstly, there were no obvious economic benefits. Secondly, the political prospects were uncertain. From an economic perspective, the construction of the Tanzania–Zambia Railway was unprofitable. The World Bank finally decided to refuse to provide loans after several visits. The US Agency for International Development said it was difficult to generate benefits (FRUS 1964b–1968 No. 465).

This was not second nature to the Chinese government. In the early 1950s, economic ties between China and Africa were minimal. They mainly involved green tea and a few other items to certain countries such as Egypt through indirect trade. The trade of the two sides amounted to only $ 12.14 million (China's State Council Information Office, 'China-Africa Economic and Trade Cooperation' 2010 pp 1). Aiding Tanzania–Zambia Railway had almost no economic interests at all for China. The purpose of the Chinese government to offer aid to TAZARA actively was never to pursue economic efficiency, but to seek international political interests and to improve the Chinese voice in international politics. Premier Zhou mentioned this clearly. "TAZARA not only has an economic sense, more importantly, it also has a sense of military and political for Tanzania and Zambia. The two sister countries were still surrounded by imperialism, colonialism, racism, and their followers. They had a common understanding that there would be no real independence of their own liberation without the independence and liberation of the countries around them. This steel transport line helped them to get rid of the control and blackmail of imperialism, colonialism, and racism. It helped in the transport of military supplies and living supplies that were provided by anti-imperialism and anti-colonialism nations to the hands of national freedom fighters in southern, central, and western Africa. Tanzania –Zambia railway must be built and there is no doubt.' (He 1993 pp 119).

Maybe Mao's macroeconomic knowledge was lacking, but his study of macroscopical political economics was very subtle. Mao's diplomatic thinking of politics superseding everything was consistent. In September 1956, Mao Zedong met the Egyptian Ambassador. He said, 'China is willing to help Egypt under no condition. No matter what you need, as long as we can, we must help you. Our assistance to you, you can give it back or not. We can give you help cost-free' (Mao, 'Chinese People Support Egypt's Recovery of the Suez Canal' 1994aa pp 249). Mao never had economic interests when it came to foreign relations. In this regard, Mao Zedong conducted a self-examination. In February 1972, Mao told the visiting US President Richard Nixon, 'We have bureaucracy in our work. You want personnel exchanges and small business. We deadly refuse. More than ten years, we insisted on that we will not go into small problems without solving big problems. And later found out you are right' (Mao, 'Now China and the US Are not at War with Each Other' 1994s pp 595).

The Chinese promised to aid Tanzania–Zambia Railway actively, but Tanzania and Zambia were sceptical at first. Firstly, they did not trust China's economic or technological strength. Secondly, they were worried that China's involvement would break the regional political balance and impact the regional political order. Tanzanian President Nyerere had asked the USA to provide assistance in order to maintain balance (Petterson 2002 pp 154), because he doubted China's intentions. After failing in searching for Western aid, Tanzania and Zambia began to actively cater to China's political propaganda to get China's support. They made the effort to politicise it. Zambian President Kaunda said, 'TAZARA is a free railway to strengthen African unity and independence … it is not intended to serve any imperialist forces' (President Kaunda's Speech 22 July 1973)

In spite of the limitations of national strength, China made the decision to aid TAZARA, which greatly shocked the USA. US intelligence agencies referred to it as the largest aid in sub-Saharan Africa by a single country (DDRS, No. CK3100127315). The American public also began to politicise TAZARA. They were worried that China would infiltrate into Africa and have an influence on the regional politics and even affect the development of the two countries. All American experts in Africa made urgent appeals to let the Communist Party of China get away from the heart of Africa (FRUS 1964a–1968, vol. 24). The US State Department issued a report and drew a similar conclusion with the assessment report of the CIA that the Chinese economic aid to Tanzania–Zambia was to support African national liberation (DDRS, No. CK3100295954). The US government began to worry that China's aid to Tanzania–Zambia Railway would undoubtedly strengthen the influence of communism on the sub-Saharan African region (DDRS, No. CK3100015295).

As for the project itself, the investment of TAZARA was not too much and it was not a large-scale project. Mao Zedong met Kaunda and said, 'This railway is only 1700 km. It is only 100 million pounds of investment. It is not a big deal' (He 1993). But it was a small project that became a symbol of political significance which affected the whole African political landscape after it had evolved into a political project. In fact, because of the huge differences in economic volume of this period, China's economic assistance to Africa was far less than that of the USA. Statistics showed that between 1960 and 1968 fiscal years, the US aid in sub-Saharan Africa was in total $ 2.1 billion, while China's aid was only $ 550 million and it was almost only in the form of aid for the Tanzania–Zambia Railway (DDRS, No. CK3100015295). In other words, China basically only aided this construction project. As some scholars pointed out, China's foreign aid was beyond its national strength at the given time. Like the construction of the Tanzania–Zambia Railway and assistance to Albania, China's foreign aid had reached up to 6–7 % of the Chinese national GDP, when Chinese national economy was actually very difficult. Even in the modern era, it is rare for foreign aid to be greater than 1 % of GDP in developed countries (Ye 2014 pp 84). There have been some researchers who have raised objections to the Maoist foreign economic policy, the notion of seeking discourse power within international politics via political and, at times, economic diplomacy. The idea of limited economic assistance bringing up huge international and political influence was an integral feature of Mao's political diplomacy.

In addition to financial assistance, China in the Mao Zedong era was more interested in supporting any form of anti-Western movement in Africa politically. In February 1959, Mao Zedong met an African delegation and said, 'Rely on Africans themselves to liberate Africa; African affairs should be run by themselves; Africans rely on their own strength but also need friends in the world, including China. As for China, we must support you' (Mao, 'Africa's Mission Is to Oppose Imperialism' 1994d pp 370). In May 1960, Mao Zedong met the delegations of Latin America and Africa and said, 'We need your assistance and support, meantime, we support your struggle. Let us stand together to support each other. Your struggle is our struggle and your victory is our victory; our struggle is your struggle and our victory is your victory. We do not have interest conflicts with you, but only unity and friendship.'

In May 1960, Mao Zedong met delegations of 12 African states and said, 'A struggle to anti-colonialism and anti-imperialism in Africa has more international sense. It is revolution of not only one country, but many countries; it is not just a few millions of people, but tens of millions or more people struggled for revolution of national liberation. We fully sympathize with you and fully support you. We also believe that your struggle supports us and helps us' (Mao, 'Imperialism Is Not Terrible', 1994b pp 407). In April 1961, Mao Zedong met foreign guests of seven African countries and said, 'You support our struggle; we support your struggle. We support the struggle of all peoples in the world, including your struggle. Unite all the friends fighting against imperialists and their lackeys. No matter which country and what political party' (Mao, 'Africa Is the Front Line of the Struggle', 1994e pp 467). China not only said so, but also did so.

In late October 1956, Britain, France, and Israel directly occupied the Suez Canal. The Chinese government immediately issued a statement that strongly condemned the conduct. The Chinese government also presented the Egyptian government immediately and unconditionally CHF 20 million in cash to support the struggle of Egypt against aggression. Mao even made recommendations of military deployment and strategic approach to the Government of Egypt against aggression. In August 1961, Nkrumah, the President of Ghana, became the second African Head of State to visit China. Consequently, Zhou Enlai scheduled a visit to Ghana on January 11–16, 1964. On the eve of the trip, the event of a possible assassination of Nkrumah was aborted. On January 8, in the morning, Nkrumah met with Ambassador Huang Hua. The Ghana government stated that they could fully control the situation and that the security of the Head of State was guaranteed. They hoped Zhou Enlai could visit on the scheduled time. Zhou Enlai promised to visit as planned. He said that we should not cancel the visit because they were experiencing temporary difficulties. It was lack of respect and a sign of weakness to those questioning their motives. He reiterated the idea that at times of need and difficulty, allies should remain closer together and that this visit would demonstrate the sincerity of their relations. Nkrumah had advocated the African Union and supported the African national liberation movement, which was to gain considerable influence on Africa, so the common rhetoric in China was that he required their support and assistance. On January 11, 1964, Zhou Enlai arrived in Ghana at the scheduled time. In the night, he went to the temporary residence of Nkrumah. Nkrumah was pleased and said, 'You are welcome, thank you very much for your coming!'

After the exile of Nkrumah, the Chinese leaders Liu Shaoqi and Zhou Enlai offered condolences by telegraph; Nkrumah had hoped that Mao Zedong would also send a letter of condolence. He believed that Mao's condolence had an important impact not only on Ghana but throughout Africa, which was kind of greatest support for him. Zhou Enlai handed the condolence letter of Mao Zedong to him. Nkrumah was very excited and instructed to publish the full letter. Ghana radio repeatedly played Mao's condolence letters. Nkrumah said to Zhou Enlai, 'I personally, the Government of Ghana and the people thank you for your visit. On behalf of all that I think your visit is the best one among all foreign leaders' visit' (Ding 2010 No. 5).

In 1970, when Zhou Enlai learned about the Portuguese mercenary's invasion of Conakry, the capital of Guinea from the sea, he immediately convened a meeting to discuss how to support Guinea against aggression. The meeting lasted until 3:00AM. Zhou Enlai repeatedly stressed that Guinea should do all in its power to prevent the invasion plot of the Portuguese mercenaries from succeeding, or a bad precedent would taint the notion of an independent Africa. Soon, the Chinese government issued a solemn statement that strongly condemned the invasion of the Portuguese mercenary. The Chinese government provided various forms of assistance, including military equipment. President Toure sent his regards thanking Mao Zedong and two ministers in China for their continued support and aid during times of national difficulty. During his meeting,

Zhou Enlai noted that Asian and African countries stood together in the struggle to safeguard state sovereignty and national independence.

5.2.2 Africa Is a Symbol of China's 'Independent Diplomacy'

The Communist Party of China was a product of the international communist movement. The establishment and development of the PRC was also inextricably linked to the international communist movement. But China has 3500 years of continuous culture and a very strong nationalist tradition. Wang Yi, the Chinese Foreign Minister, said, 'the characteristics of China's diplomacy originated in the profound Chinese civilization' (Wang 2014 pp 20). A hundred years of suffering oppression from Eastern and Western powers led the Chinese people to attach great importance to national independence and dignity. While Mao was forced to perform the diplomacy of 'leaning to one side', he had been seeking 'independent diplomacy'. Africa was the most pragmatic base in which Mao could achieve this goal. If saying that China's diplomacy in Mao's time was in synthesis with the practices of the former Soviet Union, then China's diplomacy in Africa was fully in compliance with the principle of independence.

Some researchers have said that one of the characteristics of Mao's diplomacy was insistent on independent diplomacy of the new China. When Mao Zedong thought about relations between China and foreign powers, a strong thought of a rising national autonomy was formed. With further changes in the international situation, such diplomatic relations gradually evolved into a prominent independent diplomatic imprint, which strengthened China's dominant position and self-awareness in the world system. The breakout of the Cold War brought China a new international situation. As a response to the new changes in the international situation, Mao developed the theory of the 'intermediate zones'. From that moment, Chinese Communists began to judge the international situation independently. Judgement on the situation of the Cold War was integral for Mao Zedong who was determined to take action on the global foreign policy front. The Korean War further strengthened the strategic thoughts of Mao's independent diplomacy and political will. His notion of independent diplomacy was highlighted in three aspects: Firstly, on the nature of war, in his view, China gained the support of the majority of the newly independent countries as well as became recognised as a major player in the field of foreign relations, and this strengthened his determination and will for the new China to be involved in wars independently. Secondly, he started to doubt Soviets mode of foreign policy due to their hesitant nature, which further strengthened the determination of implementing a form of independent diplomacy. Thirdly, he took the Korean War as the struggle of the forces of imperialism and the National Liberation Force. China's reason for entering the war was for the pursuit of independent diplomacy (Jiang 2013).

Richard Dowden, the President of the Royal African Society, had the fundamental thought that the Chinese people liked to deal with undemocratic governments. He saw the appearance, but did not thoroughly understand why the Chinese liked these so-called 'undemocratic governments'. It seems necessary to state that interests, common interests, are the underlying reasons behind China's dealings with these undemocratic and anti-Western governments. Under the great background that the world was controlled by US-led Western bloc and the Soviet-led Eastern bloc, Chinese leaders headed by Mao Zedong had been trying to find an international force that could compete with it. The African political power, which Westerners thought was undemocratic, happened to be China's main political ally and political fellow.

In the late 1950s, Mao Zedong put forward the notion that there was a third force of nationalist countries outside the two camps, also known as intermediate power, as mentioned previously. By the mid-1960s, Mao Zedong put forward the 'second intermediate zone' theory, mainly referring to the nation's discontent with the USA's control in the Western camp. In June 1973, Mao Zedong said, 'We are called the third world, or the developing countries.' In February 1974, Mao Zedong formally proposed the 'Three Worlds Theory' (Mao, 'About Three Worlds' Division Issue', 1994f pp 600–601). Africa was seen as an important part of the Third World by Mao. Actively engaging in yet more relations with Africa was conceived as the best way to get rid of the controls of the Soviet Union and the USA and to achieve large-scale independent diplomacy.

In September 1964, when Mao Zedong met with some French guests he said, 'The world is changing, not one or two countries can control it. National affairs of each country should be managed by its own people. It should not be interfered with by any foreign' (Mao, 'We Appreciate the Independent Policy of France Very Much', 1994p pp 542). China hoped to demonstrate this energy in the international political sphere through developing relations with Africa.

As such, Africa was seen as a unique political power by the Chinese leaders to balance the world political structure. China also stepped on independent diplomacy by developing diplomatic relations with Africa. On October 25, 1971, the 26th UN General Assembly adopted a proposal to restore China's legitimate rights in the UN by 76 votes in favour (of which African countries accounted for 26 votes), 35 votes against, and l7 abstentions. That 26 African votes in favour were great achievements of Mao's political diplomacy.

5.2.3 The Important Role of Africa in China's National Unification Strategy

Foreign policymaking of any country is based on the national leader's judgement of the national conditions and his understanding of the international situation. On the eve of the establishment of PRC, Mao Zedong made it clear that, 'Any foreign government, as long as it is willing to cut the relationship with the Chinese reactionaries and stop collusion with or aid Chinese reactionaries and take real but not hypocritical friendliness to China, we are willing to establish diplomatic relations with them in the principles of equality, mutual benefit and mutual respect for territorial integrity and sovereignty' (Mao, 'Address to the Preparatory Meeting of the New Political Consultative Conference', 1960c pp 1470). After the regime of the PRC was established, the Chinese government adhered to 'deny the old diplomatic relations of the Kuomintang government and other countries and to establish new diplomatic relations on a new basis' (Zhou, 'Our Foreign Policy And Guide Line', 1984b pp 85).

The importance of the Taiwan issue in China's politics cannot be realised or understood by Western political circles and academic circles. The concept of a national state in the Western mindset is very different to the traditional concept of a state in China. The concept of national unity is deep-rooted in China. The Taiwan issue is the most important issue that is listed in almost all Chinese diplomatic activities. Of course, it also involves the legal succession of the Chinese regime. In a sense, if the Taiwan authorities were to continually pursue a path of independence, the task of building governance from the perspectives of the Chinese government is not yet complete. Legally, the Government of the PRC is the successor to the ROC government. The political role of the ROC had to finish in order for the transition to the PRC to be completed. Many Western politicians and scholars do not understand the special nature of Chinese politics and Chinese culture, and thus are often puzzled, prone to opposition and condemnation on the Chinese government for its stubborn attitude on the Taiwan Strait.

In December 1953, Zhou Enlai proposed the five basic principles of mutual respect for territorial sovereignty: non-aggression, mutual non-interference in internal affairs, equality, mutual benefit, and peaceful coexistence (Zhou, 'Five principles of peaceful coexistence' 1984a pp 118). In June 1954, during his visit to Myanmar, Zhou Enlai and Myanmar jointly issued the initiatives of the implementation of the Five Principles in the world. Since then, the five principles of peaceful co-existence which were proposed by China, endorsed by India and Myanmar, and published to the world have become the basic principles of China's foreign relations. In the Asian–African Conference in 1955, Zhou Enlai urged to form 'Ten Principles' on the basis of five principles of peaceful co-existence. Mao Zedong said, 'What is mutual non-interference in internal affairs? It is to say that a country's domestic disputes should managed by itself. Other countries can not intervene, nor take advantage of this domestic dispute. we only recognize the government that chosen by its own people' (Mao, 'The Five Principle of Peaceful Coexistence Is A Long-term Policy', 1994j pp 181). The purpose of Zhou Enlai's proposition of 'five basic principles' was to defend national sovereignty and to oppose interference in internal affairs.

The Chinese government strongly emphasised that 'respect for national sovereignty' and 'noninterference in internal affairs' were key when it came to foreign relations. It is to resist the potential threat of international politics to the Chinese regime, but also to prevent international political forces from interfering in the China–Taiwan issue, which has been seen as a problem of internal affairs by the Chinese government and foreign forces are not allowed to interfere. On all official international occasions, the Chinese government has not allowed the emergence of the Taiwan authorities.

Africa used to be a relatively concentrated portion of Taiwan's 'allies'. With China's developing relations with Africa, out of the once 22 countries keeping 'diplomatic' relations with Taiwan, there are only three African countries remaining, namely Burkina Faso, the Republic of Sao Tome and Principe, and the Kingdom of Swaziland. After 2000, a number of countries cut off diplomatic relations with Taiwan. They are Macedonia (on June 18, 2001), Liberia (on October 13, 2003), Dominica (on March 30, 2004), Vanuatu (on November, 2004), Grenada (on January 20, 2005), Senegal (on October 25, 2005), Chad (on August 6, 2006), Costa Rica (on June 7, 2007), and Malawi (on January 14, 2008). The Taiwan issue was also very important when developing relations with Africa. The active promotion of the 'one China' policy in Africa is still an important part of China–Africa relations.

5.3 Africa in China's Economic Developing

After Mao Zedong, great changes have taken place in China. In the Deng Xiaoping era, China launched large-scale economic reforms. Meanwhile, China's foreign policy has developed dramatically. Deng Xiaoping said, 'There are a number of Third World countries that want China to take the lead but we do not take the lead, which is a fundamental national policy. We cannot afford enough strength to be a leader. There is no good to be a leader; lots of initiatives are lost. China will always stand on the side of the third world; China will never seek hegemony; China will never take the lead' (Deng 1993 pp 321). Major changes occurred in China's diplomatic philosophy. Overall, the political diplomacy retreated comprehensively and economic diplomacy and security diplomacy have risen sharply. China set diplomatic strategies according to its own interests and China's goal was to develop the economy. China also made its own foreign policy in accordance with its own ideas and cultural traditions. Chinese culture is basically introverted and China has become disinterested in the outside world. China does not like to expand. China's foreign relations mainly involved trade, surrounding regions' security, and security directly related to China.

With China's reform and opening up, from the late 1970s, China's economic relations with African countries have also changed. They developed from the single form of cooperation, that the Chinese government provide economic assistance to African countries unilaterally, to the cooperation of two-way, multiway system. China's diplomatic philosophy changed from being dominated by the international political ideology to economic cooperation led by national interests, from taking international political interests as the centre to the promotion of political and economic interests. In 1983, China proposed the new policy of 'equality and mutual benefit, stressing efficiency, diversity, common development', which formed a new model including the formation of project contracting, labour services, consulting and designing, joint investment, and other forms of two-way economic cooperation. China–Africa economic cooperation had greatly expanded, involving construction, irrigation, fisheries, textiles, electronics, steel, and catering industry. Sent personnel included varieties of senior experts such as construction personnel, medical personnel, sailors, mechanical maintenance workers, business management personnel, software developers, and education and training personnel.

China's economic assistance and economic cooperation did not attach any political conditions. It has welcomed many more African countries, and therefore they are now more willing to cooperate with the Chinese government. In July 1992, Chinese President Yang Shangkun visited Africa and published six principles of China to develop relations with African countries. The political principles inherited Mao's previous fivefold principles. They adhered to the traditional political philosophy and respected the country's sovereignty and political independence. Economically, China added a new concept of economic cooperation, stressing out the 'various forms of economic cooperation'. The Western countries usually attached political conditions to facilitate the politics going towards their model when they developed relations with Africa, especially in the provision of financial assistance and economic cooperation to African countries. This was what resulted in national ruling groups often unable or unwilling to accept these demands. China always adheres to the traditional diplomatic principles of 'non-interference in the internal affairs'. Even if these countries were going through civil unrest or so-called 'serious human rights crisis', China still regarded it as 'internal affairs' with no interference. And even pardons these countries or governments in the international community as a 'great power'; China's attitude on Sudan is a typical case.

Since 2009, China became Africa's largest trading partner for six consecutive years. In 2014, China–Africa trade volume exceeded $ 220 billion. China's investment stock in Africa was $ 25 billion in 2013. China has become an important impetus for African economic growth and even African revival. China still provides economic assistance to Africa. Fifty-three African countries now are all developing, but these countries are not identical in political and social system, history, level of development, and religious and cultural backgrounds. When China develops relations with Africa, it advocates equality of nations, adheres to the principle of 'non-interference in the internal affairs of African countries', and respects the social systems and political system of African countries. In this case, China's basic political principle of assistance to Africa is the same. China treats them equally regardless of the size of these countries. Sudan and Zimbabwe have been receiving unfavourable treatment from Western countries, but China still provides them with assistance and guidance. Unlike China, Western countries help other countries with political will as a precondition, which is often referred to as politicised or ideologised international aid.

China provided a large number of selfless aids to Guinea. China aided them with the construction of the radio and television centre, the People's Palace, Jinkang hydropower and Ding Jisuo hydropower, freedom cinema, cigarette match factory, the presidential palace, and the like, in which matches cigarette factory in Africa was China's first aid package projects. After being put into operation, under the guidance of Chinese experts, the quality and quantity of products continue to increase. It meets the needs of the domestic market of Guinea and has ended a history of long-term import dependence.

5.4 Africa in China's Energy Needs

5.4.1 African Energy

Most oil-rich regions were carved out by Western countries in the early twentieth century, but African oil was reserved for political reasons. It provided a rare opportunity for the Chinese to get overseas oil and improve the domestic oil energy tensions. Strengthening oil developmental cooperation with African countries and their governments has become the strategy of national energy security.

In the past two decades, China–Africa relations gained rapid, in-depth, and comprehensive development. There have been unprecedented levels of development in China–Africa cooperation from the perspective of either breadth and depth or the quantity and quality. Cooperation on oil exploitation with governments, that Western countries regard as 'authoritarian' or 'rogue state', often led to China being accused of 'losing principles' and being 'irresponsible', sometimes even accusations of 'neo-colonialism', 'economic plunder', 'resource plundering', and the like. Western countries pin four labels on China: The first one is 'new colonialism in Africa'; the second one is 'plundering resources'; the third is 'getting Africa into a debt crisis'; and the fourth one is 'assistance in and encouraging African tyranny'. China promotes and develops friendly relations with Africa on the basis of the 'five basic principles' to safeguard peace and common development. The relationships between China and Africa are based on political friendship and are comprehensive relations, which can be seen in a brotherly manner, rather than an economically exploitive manner often portrayed by the West.

Since the Mao era, China has always believed that Africa was a political force that should not be ignored. As claimed previously, during the Cold War at a time of East–West confrontation, China's international voice became louder through keeping friendly relations with Africa. In the twenty-first century, Africa's position continues to increase in the international political and economic arena due to rich mineral resources and agricultural resources. With the history of China–Africa friendship, it is imperative for China to speed up economic cooperation with Africa. However, great differences in history, religion, culture, political system, economic system, ideology, and ethnic customs may hinder further development of the China–Africa relations.

During the Maoist era, political demand was the basis of the friendly relations between China and Africa. Due to the prior blockades led by the US-based Western Group, Mao Zedong pursued the objectives of becoming idealistically common 'anti-imperialist', 'anti-colonialism', and 'anti-hegemony'. The pursuit of national equality was running through the main line of Mao Zedong's diplomatic philosophy. 'We should not treat people unequally we call it great power chauvinism. We openly educate Party members and the people that do not make the mistake of great-power chauvinism' (Mao, 'Talks with King Mahendra and Queen of Nepal', 1994n pp 479). In May 1963, when meeting with Guinean guests, Mao Zedong stressed once again, 'If our people do bad things in your country, you should tell us, like looking down upon you, arrogant, chauvinistic attitudes. Are there such person? If there are such people, we have to dispose of them. Are Chinese experts payed higher than yours in Guinea? Is there the case of specialisation? Maybe it is. Check it out. Treat them equally, or lower' (Mao, 'Our Relations with the People of All African Countries Are Good' 1994q pp 491). In the meeting with the Prime Minister of Somalia, Mao Zedong said, 'We get along well. We feel equal. We do not impose on you, and you do not impose on us. We help each other, support each other, and learn from each other's experience of struggle' (Mao, 'The Oppressed People Always Rise up' 1994m pp 497). As to the US-led Western bloc, China struggled to find their idea of 'equality' in tandem with theirs. As to the developing countries, small countries, and weak countries, China insisted upon 'equality' even at some expense of China's economic interests, and at times China's sovereignty. It was to set up an 'equal role' which would eliminate emotions of being 'alert' or 'fear' of China that may exist. When Mao Zedong met Tanzanian Vice President, he said, 'We are equal to each other. We speak the truth to each other. We do not have two faces.' When meeting with the Prime Minister of Somalia, he said, 'We not only oppose to imperialism in our country. We want to destroy imperialism in the world' (Mao, 'The Oppressed People Always Rise up', 1994m pp 497). 'We want to support the peoples against imperialist war. If we do not support, we will make mistakes, or we are not communists' (Ibid. 1994).

Many African countries still present China as a political and economic leader of the Third World and still hope to get political and economic support from China, while with the deepening of the globalisation process and the involvement of the Western powers, the differences overshadowed by political ideology of China and Africa will become increasingly prominent. African public opinion is changing. The so-called 'universal values' that had been considered as a by-product of Western 'colonialism' now are having a gradual effect on intellectuals and the 'middle class' in Africa.

The influence of public opinion is increasing and strengthening within the politics of Africa. If China does not change the top line timely, that only keeps friendly cooperation with the government in Africa and does not care about the fate of ordinary people, it risks moving away from the African people. But if China intervenes in African politics, it means giving up on their old diplomatic principles. There are signs that some African political leaders are in doubt about the Chinese traditional African foreign policy, and have further doubts of China's motives to strengthen its relations with Africa. There is the fundamental belief that only the pursuit of economic benefits from the view of mercantilism, or the idea of becoming involved in the African political and economic transformation process would be the reasons why China will remain as Africa's common ally in the future. This presents China with a huge dilemma.

5.4.2 African Energy in the Development of China's Economy

According to the 2010 statistics, the EU accounted for at least 33 % of the share of Africa's oil exports. America was aware of the rich oil resources in Africa and turned her attention to Africa, so 36 % of African oil exports were to the USA. Therefore, African oil exports to the USA and Europe equate to around 70 %, in comparison the exports of oil to China are less than 10 %. To give a further example, UK Shell entered Nigeria more than 30 years ago and their exploitations have polluted the local environment. Thus, in this current day and age, Nigeria's oil reserve is so low that they have to now import gasoline. Another example is Sudan. Their oilfield has been under the control of the USA. In contrast to common knowledge despite the fact that China exports oil from Sudan, they also invest in a series of relevant midstream and downstream industries to help Sudan refinery, develop chemical industry, and so on. Today, Sudan has become self-sufficient in the supplying of oil. Chinese oil development in Sudan created more than 10 million jobs, increased revenue of Sudan, and improved people's welfare and well-being.

China's African oil strategy is divided into oil imports and oil companies' investment. China began importing crude oil from Africa in 1992, at the time imports amounted to 500,000 tons, that is, 4.4 % of total imports. It rose to 2.13 million tons in the following year, accounting for 14 % of the total import volume (Cha Daojiong 2006). Since then, the sources of oil are changing but China's oil imports have increased despite volatilities. In 2000, China imported 16.95 million tons of oil from Africa, accounting for 24.1 % of China's total oil imports. In 2009, China imported 8.9 million tons, 41.7 million tons, and 12.2 million tons from North Africa, West Africa, and Southeast Africa, respectively, together accounting for 26 % of China's total oil imports (BP 2010 pp 8), wherein Angola, Sudan, Congo (Brazzaville), Equatorial Guinea, Gabon, Cameroon, Algeria, Libya, Nigeria, Chad, and Egypt were China's main oil suppliers. In 2009, China imported a total of 204 million tons of crude oil, of which China's oil imports from Africa have reached 30.39 % of China's total oil imports (Liang Ming 2011).

Since the Chinese government regarded energy security as the major issue which affects national development and stability, it seems necessary that it becomes a major player in international energy cooperation. This cooperation has been primarily conducted through national leaders' meeting and negotiation of international cooperation of energy during their exchange visits, and has consequently been embodied by the state-run oil companies. Such as Hu Jintao's visit to Kazakhstan in 2003, where he signed the 'Investment Demonstration Research agreement of Joint Development of Kazakhstan – China Oil Pipeline's Subsection Construction' and 'the Agreement of the Chinese National Petroleum Company to Further Expand Investment in Oil and Gas of Kazakh'. In February 2004 after a trip of Hu Jintao to Hu Algeria, Gabon, and Egypt, China began to purchase oil from Gabon, Egypt, Nigeria, and other countries and in the meanwhile, it also signed new oil agreements with Cameroon, Guinea, and other countries. At the end of April 2006, Hu Jintao visited Morocco, Algeria, and Kenya; in addition, he signed a $ 4 billion worth of oil development agreement with Algeria. The China National Offshore Oil Corporation also signed an agreement with Kenya, and got the exploration rights of six oilfields with over 115,000 square kilometres in northern and southern of Kenya.

In early 2006, the Chinese government published 'White Paper on China's African Policy'. It said in the sixth part of 'resources cooperation' that 'Strengthen the exchange of information and cooperation in resource fields of China-Africa. Chinese government encouraged and supported competent Chinese enterprises in accordance with the principle of mutual benefit and common development, to jointly develop and rational use of resources with African countries in various forms, and to help African countries turn the resource advantages into competitive advantages, to promote the sustainable development of African countries.'

5.4.3 Non-economic Factors in China's African Energy Diplomacy

Because of the inertia of thinking that the West's long-term control of African political, economic, and social spheres would minimise the Chinese influence, China made efforts to increase its global footprint. American scholars insist that China's African oil strategy jeopardised the USA's global hegemony (Giry 2004). United States-China Economic and Security Review Commission thought that China has been sought energy cooperation with the countries concerned by the USA. China's growing energy needs, coupled with its rapidly expanding economy, would bring the US concerns of economy and security. American scholar Daniel Volman believes that China seeking oil in Africa will encounter the USA. It has been a threat to US security interests (Klare and Volman 2006 pp 297–309). British scholar Ian Taylor also believes that the purpose of China's investment and development in Sudan oilfield is to control the source of the oil, and to interfere in international oil market by obtaining cheap oil, thereby manipulating the global oil market to change Western-dominated oil security system (Taylor 2009 pp 13–24). They criticised China Export–Import Bank for providing $ 2 billion in loans to Angola. In exchange, Angola supplied 40,000 barrels of oil per day and a many construction contracts to China. They think China's action precluded the International Monetary Fund's (IMF) sanctions against Angola (Tull 2006 pp 459–463). Western scholars that accuse China insisted on not imposing sanctions against Sudan to get oil and exporting weapons to Sudan (Taylor 2006 pp 937–959).

Western government officials and academics continue to criticise China for the implementation of the new policy of economic colonialism in Africa. When British Foreign Secretary Jack Straw visited Nigeria in February 2006, he said what China was doing in Africa today was most of what they did in Africa 150 years ago (The Telegraph, 23 August 2006). European and American scholars accuse China's deeds in Africa as a form of 'surgical colonialism', in order to grab Africa's natural resources with minimal problems. The China–Africa cooperation was just gentler than previous exploitations, when comparing the Portuguese and Spanish conquest in America in the sixteenth century and Britain, France, and Germany carving out Africa in the nineteenth century (Bergesen 2012). Some Western scholars believe that there is no fundamental difference between China's 'plundering of resources' in Africa and Western colonialism. What China is doing in Africa is 'neo-colonialism' or 'economic imperialism'. China–Africa economic exchanges not only 'hit' the same industry in Africa. What's more, they are unable to address local employment problem. There is a claim that China is s political control of African countries, with Sudan being a fundamental example (Giry 2004).

Western non-governmental organisations and the public media seem more willing to interpret the oil cooperation between China and Sudan from a political perspective. They took Darfur crisis as an opportunity to publish a large number of reports and comments with a strong propensity. Western governments' think tanks were good at doing more empirical research and comprehensive analysis based on the needs of national policy. In their view, the studies on relations of Sino-US, US–Africa, and Sino-Africa are to maintain the existing world energy orders. Oil cooperation between China and Africa is only a subordinate subject (Jaffe and Lewis 2002 pp 115–134).

The West took China's unconditional economic assistance to Africa as a barrier or destruction of West's promoting Western-style democracy in Africa. American scholar Stephanie Giry believes that China's presence in Africa undermined the US efforts to promote a democratic model there (Giry 2004). In July 2005, US Congressman Christopher Smith pointed out in the regular meeting of House International Relations Committee that 'China's activities in Africa offset the efforts of promotion of African nation and good governance in the past 15 years' (Klare and Volman

2006). This actually is not a new political state. Political games of China and the West in Africa did not begin today. Since the Maoist era, China has been taking Africa as a unique political force against the West to develop relations with; this process has merely continued to the modern age. China does not agree with the values of the West, or does not think it is right that the political reforms of the West are being implemented in Africa. There is no doubt that China will never abandon the development of political relations with Africa when China develops economic relations with Africa, including energy relations. On the contrary, the political relationship of China and Africa becomes closer because of the increasingly close economic relationship. The Chinese government does not mince words. China pursues a comprehensive relationship with Africa, and not only economic relations. China's foreign policy in Africa is not in order to control Africa, but an effort to obtain international political support in Africa. China truly takes Africa as a political friend and a brother to treat with equality. This was stressed by Hu Jintao, 'The Chinese people have always been and will always be equal, mutual trust and sincere friends of African people; mutual benefit, win-win cooperation partners; good brothers.' Chinese Foreign Minister Wang Yi said, 'In March 2013, Xi Jinping President's first visit after taking office that was destined for Africa. It reflected the fraternal bonds of friendship towards the African people' (Wang, *People's Daily*, 2013).

Because of the rapid development of China's economy, the sharp rise in demand for energy, coupled with energy being a common concern for semi-strategic materials in the world, has got the Western world's attention. Of course, driven by economic interests, some Western oil companies have been constantly denouncing Chinese oil development in Africa through various media. Erica S. Downs believes that Chinese loans to Angola are mostly for oil investment, because there are no significant relations between political reforms in Angola and China. Sudan's Darfur crisis is the legacy of nineteenth-century European powers' partition of Africa and colonial ruling, and is the struggle caused by the competition for resources between tribes in recent years. However, one thing is for certain, China does not abuse human rights for oil resources (Downs 2007 pp 42–68).

In fact, China's economic development lead to the explosive growth of demand for oil; the USA cannot avoid competition with China through the single deterrence strategy. The USA should work with China to promote China towards the direction the USA desired (Taylor 2006 pp 937–959). China's rapid development in Africa brought the USA both opportunities and challenges (Pham 2006, pp 241–248). The Center for Strategic and International Studies published 'China Balance Sheet', in which pointed it out that, firstly, Chinese investment in Africa brought Africa more external resources. Because of the competition from China, Europe, the USA, Japan, and India all increased their investment in Africa. Secondly, the diversity of economic investments changed the dominance of Western investment patterns that African political and economic autonomy strengthened. American scholar Deborah Brautigam pointed out that China was not an unpaid donor in Africa. China supplied loans, machinery and equipment, and building services to Africa, and the latter paid with oil and other resources to the former. It was a win–win cooperation (Brautigam 2009 pp 17–24). Edward Friedman, a scholar from the University of Wisconsin, believed that Chinese revolutionary forces made Africans shake off the shackles of poverty (Friedman 2009, pp 1–20).

Erica S. Downs argued that Chinese oil strategy in Africa threatened USA's energy security. He believed that commercial gain was the main motivation of Chinese state-owned oil companies to seek overseas oil and gas resources. Currently, with the high integration of global energy markets, especially oil markets, production of oil and gas of the Chinese state-owned oil companies in overseas, especially oil of those Western oil companies unable or unwilling to invest in exploring, actually increased the energy supplies of international markets. It was helpful to ease the pressure on oil prices (Downs, 'China's Quest for Overseas Oil' 2007 pp 54). What he said is a basic fact. The USA's ability to control the international oil market is far bigger than China. The USA has abundant oil reserves, also has a world-class oil extraction technology, and there is no problem for the USA to protect the domestic oil supply. The so-called American oil scarcity is a relative concept which is in comparison to the international market, rather than the absolute scarcity of oil. It is essentially different from China's oil supply and demand relations. With the rapid economic development, Chinese energy shortage is imminent.

The conventional coal-dominated energy model has been completely unable to meet the needs of social development. To meet the need of energy by the international market is necessary. If China's energy strategy in Africa impacted America's global energy strategy, it is because China's rapid growth in energy demand upset the existing world energy order of America and the world political order that the USA made efforts to build through its world oil order. In other words, the centre of the USA's oil security is not oil, but politics, international politics of American system. Some researchers from Middlesex University in the UK believed that African oil-producing countries were now sovereign states and these countries allowed foreign oil companies to develop their oil resources by bid. Western oil companies have already pre-empted the deep-sea oil in West Africa by virtue of technology. China missed it because of technical reasons. It is a fallacy that China is competing for African oil with the USA (Jedrzei 2007 pp 229–251). Overall, the Chinese oil development in Africa is in accordance with the international economic order model. Because stable and mature oil-producing countries have been divided up between Western powers, it is not easy for China to get a share. In 2000, when Petro China Company Limited (Petro China) under China National Petroleum Corporation (CNPC) got listed in New York, it was seriously obstructed by US human rights organisations. Petro China originally expected to raise $ 50–100 million, but only received a $ 3.1-million payment. It means that it is very difficult for Chinese state-owned companies to get into the Western market without being impacted by Western political philosophy. China can only take risks to invest where the Western powers cannot or do not want to invest in, including troubled countries of Iraq, Iran, and others.

The internationalisation of most African countries is far less than the Middle Eastern countries. Africa has not established stable economic relations with the international markets. It offers China an excellent chance to develop economic relations rapidly with Africa using existing friendly political relations.

Because of the ideas that Africa is lagging behind in the stage of social development and indigenous African political forces are alien to Western society, many Western powers do not want to see greater economic development in Africa at this stage. They believe that rapid economic development in Africa would be a threat to the Western-dominated world political order if African people have not accepted Western values. The principle of 'Common Development' of China implied in Africa clearly undermines the world political and economic order that the West constructed and maintained. Some scholars believe that China's behaviour in Africa is not like what mainstream Western media reported and the judgement should be based on the actual feelings of the African people. A series of social effects that were about brought by Chinese oil companies in Africa cannot be matched by Western oil companies (Brookes 2007 pp 17–24).

5.5 African Problems in the Development of China

Africa has brought great opportunities, but also a lot of political or economic problems to China. After the implementation of the comprehensive economic reform in China, the economic and trade relations between China and Africa are becoming more and more diversified. In addition to the government, more and more economic entities are becoming involved. These economic entities can be divided into state-owned enterprises, private enterprises, individual businesses, and so on. At the same time, considering the different interests of related departments of China, there are many unprecedented problems in the cooperation with Africa, such as the priority of the project, size, assessment of political risk and economic risk, and so on.

With the expansion of Sino-African cooperation in recent years, China has become Africa's largest trading partner and Africa has become China's second largest contract market, the second largest source of oil imports, and the fourth largest investment destination. The Chinese foreign ministry stated, 'every country must have multiple import channels of energy, and now there is no one country can meet the needs of China's oil demand alone'. The implementation of China's energy diplomacy is very comprehensive. It is almost all-embracing from national leadership to company, from the political cooperation to economic cooperation, from expanding military support to reliance on commodity trade.

Construct scientific, rational, and sustainable relations between politics and economy. At present, China and Africa pay far more attention to the implementation of economic and trade cooperation than the political cooperation. This is far different from the Sino-African relations before the twenty-first century when political relations were far more important than the economic and trade relations. China cannot maintain the old state in the last century where economic relations were subordinate to political relations, nor cause a new state where political relations subordinate economic relations. So there is a need to build a reasonable state of politics and economics. Therefore, serious thought should be given to transform the deep economic cooperation and the increasing volume of trade into the effective political and diplomatic power.

Construct the interactive system of the two sides. At present, the cooperation project between China and Africa is mostly in the charge of China unilaterally. This situation should change. China should mobilise the enthusiasm of Africa in cooperation and form a real cooperation mechanism by strengthening communication in politics and creating a better environment for investment and trade in economy to jointly control problems in the process of cooperation. In recent years, Sino-African relations have been criticised by Western public opinion. There are also some different voices for the China and Africa relationship from African native intellectuals, media, and institutions or organisations who echo the West. It is a normal phenomenon in the process of China's rapidly developing relations with Africa. But the voice supporting China is still the mainstream view in Africa. What China is looking for is cooperation without preconditions, not Western 'democratic transformation'. There still is a market for it in Africa. Although some Westerners think that China destroyed their efforts to implement 'democracy' in Africa, some African intellectuals influenced by Western thought also believe that intergovernmental cooperation of Sino-Africa is not conducive to the transformation of African societies. But the main problem is still development in Africa, which is a basic social consensus.

Africa so far has not risen to the main stage of competition for China and the West. China is fit for Africa's development phase and needs. In other words, the content and way of cooperation between China and Africa are suitable for the current Africa. In this regard, the West has no advantage at all. The Western high technology, high standards, high cost, and high investment are not suitable for a plethora of nations who are still in the basic stage of development. Since 2009, China has become the largest trading partner of Africa. China's trade with Africa in 2014 was four times that in 2006. In recent years, personnel exchanges between China and Africa have reached to about 3 million a year. There is no doubt that China and US-led Western powers are controversial, even oppositional in many aspects, due to the huge differences in political ideology. In Western groups, China is considered a heterogeneous state both politically and economically. It can be said that the Western Group led by the USA will not accept China as one of them, as long as China's political system remains unchanged, or the Chinese Communist Party is still in power. This is an indisputable fact. Due to the explosive development of China's economy, the rapid growth of economic aggregate, and the great purchasing power of society, Western countries have to take the attitude of approval or acquiescence to some of China's international behaviour, but their rejection of China will not change fundamentally. With China's economic growth, the Western powers will be more vigilant against China and anti-Chinese sentiments will be stronger. That is to say, the current seemingly close relationship between China and the West is a false impression, which is a complete relationship of interests or the relationship of economic complementarity. It is extremely unstable. With any changes, China's threat theory will become out of hand, such as the 'South China Sea dispute' today.

In contrast, the Sino-African relationship is different. As for the Chinese, there is no record of colonial plunder or slavery as the Europeans or no cultural discrimination of social values as Americans in Africa. There are just common historical experiences such as being bullied by the West and the common desire for the rapid development of society. The growing power of China is seen as a political representation of the Third World or developing countries by many African countries. This is a good foundation for China to establish friendly relations and political mutual trust between China and many African countries. International support of Black Africa is necessary for China to develop international leadership. Taking the UN reform as an example, China playing the Africa card effectively stopped Japan from becoming a permanent member of the Security Council.

Under powerful offensive of the Western public opinion, apparently, the Chinese government has been forced to accept the international order under the American system. Of course, this acceptance is under the condition that the traditional Chinese concept of state sovereignty remains unchanged. Yu Hongjun, Vice Minister of Foreign Liaison Department of the CPC Central Committee, said, 'Today, it has been widely recognized that the national rights cannot be violated in the theory and practice of international relations, but the emphasis on national responsibility is obviously inadequate. Therefore, it is necessary to apply the concept of "balance of power and responsibility" to the national relationship. If the idea that "states were born to bear international responsibility" can achieve the same status with the philosophy of "inviolability of sovereignty", the relationship between countries may be much more harmonious than it is now and the possibility of conflicts and war will further reduced' (Yu 2014, pp 65). The theory of 'states were born to bear international responsibility' is closely related to 'divine power'. The Chinese government has always been firmly opposed to it, because there is a great chance of it being abused without set criteria and standards set by an independent international organisation. If this 'God given power' is abused by some Western political power, it may cause threat to China's national security. Yu Hongjun not only admitted the strong power of 'states were born to bear international responsibility' in the current international political game but also proposed to parallel it with the 'inviolability of sovereignty' that China has consistently adhered to, as the two major current international behaviour standards; this is a huge change. 'Respect for national sovereignty' and 'non-interference in internal affairs' are two protective waistcoats of the Chinese to defend the regime security and system safety. Although, with China's national power growing, it is almost impossible for external powers to undermine China's regime by war, the Chinese government is still reluctant to easily give up the legal principle of political public opinion.

China is an active peacekeeper in Africa and has actively made efforts to help African countries achieve reconstruction after conflicts. So far, China has sent the largest number of peacekeeping personnel to Africa between the five permanent members of the UN Security Council and has been involved in the 16 UN peacekeeping operations in Africa. At present, there are more than 1800 Chinese peacekeeping personnel in Africa.

China continues to strengthen its participation in political efforts to solve the problem of African hot spots actively and has become an indispensable player in promoting crisis intervention and regional stability. China has completed the conversion from the 'spokesman' (stating the government's position) to 'the messenger' (responsible for passing negotiation messages between the West and Africa) to the 'mediator'. With China continuing to strengthen cooperation with Africa, it will continue to adhere to the traditional principle of non-interference in internal affairs. Despite the West and even some African countries calling on China to abandon the traditional political ideas, the principle of non-interference is in fact not only China's respect for Africa but also the protection of China's political security.

5.6 Development of Relations of China with Africa Recently

On December 4, 2015, the Chinese government published the second paper of 'China's African policy' in Johannesburg, which further enhanced China's relationship with Africa, in which China put forward the goal of establishing and developing a comprehensive strategic partnership of cooperation and to consolidate and reinforce a community of common visions of Sino-Africa. It stressed that China has always supported Africa's development sincerely by implementing a policy of non-interference in the internal affairs of the African countries, abstinence from imposing Chinese values against the will of Africans, and not attaching any political conditions with regard to their assistance to the Africans. China adhered to promote peace by development and to gain development through peace; China firmly supported Africa to develop independently and sustainably and to 'solve Africa's affairs in an African way' by which means all issues relating to Africa's durable peace and sustainable development should be 'proposed by Africans, agreed by Africans and dominated by Africans'. The chapter stressed to promote China–Africa cooperation in a multidimensional way, including political trust, the promotion of international affairs, pragmatic economic and trade agreements, development, humanities exchanges, consular and migration, judicial and police, and even cooperation in promoting peace and security in Africa and dealing with non-traditional security threats. Energy and resource cooperation that has been stressed and exaggerated repeatedly by the Western media is only one part of this cooperation. In addition, this chapter emphasised the spirit of 'build nest to attract phoenix' and 'teach a man to fish' to help Africa for development (*Xinhua net*, December 5, 2015).

Relative to the paper of 'China's African policy' in January 2006 that 'declared objectives and measures of China's policy towards Africa, planning cooperation in each field in a period of time in the future, keeping China-Africa relations in a long-term stable development, mutual benefit and cooperation and going to a new step' (Ibid.), we can clearly feel that the Chinese government has laid significant emphasis on Africa since the era of Deng Xiaoping. There's energy and resource demand, but more importantly political demands for China to realise its dream of becoming a world power. The Chinese government insists that the role of Africa in the stage of international political affairs is very important and irreplaceable. Since 2006, it was stressed that 'China is the biggest developing country in the world', then by 2015 it was stressed that 'China has become the world's second largest economy, and is an important participant, builder and contributor of the current international system.' Although the Chinese government has always taken Africa as an ally in international political affairs, China now seems to be working hard to make herself the protector of political interests of the African people. This change is worth noting. As China's status changes in the economic and political spectrum of the world, it obviously cannot fully reflect the relationship between China and Africa that simply takes the Chinese–African relationship as one of supply and demand of energy and resources; at least it cannot comprehensively reflect the strategic relationship for both.

In international politics, the conflicts and problems between China and its neighbouring countries continue to emerge and become more and more obvious. The Taiwan Strait issue has become more uncertain. The South China Sea and East China Sea issues have become more and more internationalised. These have led to China being in dire need of international supporters. The African countries have been giving China strong support in international political affairs and they occupy a quarter of the seats in the UN, so they are important for the Chinese government. Recently, the international game on the arbitration of South China Sea applied by the Philippines and judged by the UN maritime court was a very typical case. The traditional concept of 'national sovereignty' showing respect to each country's political system and development model or the policy of non-interference make it easier for both sides to form political alliances, although this type of political union may be very weak and often uncertain. The West attacks China for its authoritarian and even non-humanitarian regime when supporting Africa, but China reiterates the point that it is respecting the 'national sovereignty' and non-interference principles. In addition, as the USA is trying to build a political alliance to curb the development of China in East Asia, the support from the African nations is an invaluable asset when it comes to the decision-making process on the global front for China.

In terms of economic development, the future of China's economy is not clear and the whole national economy lacks the growth momentum. Africa is not only an important supplier of energy and resources but also an important market for China's economy to keep sustainable development. The size and low price of Chinese goods make it easier to meet the needs of the African market. Africa has become the second largest energy supplier to China, and China has become Africa's largest economy and trading partner. And there is a reason to believe that this trend will go on. Of course, these increasingly close economic relations, to a certain extent, are not disparate from China's ongoing financial support. Since Xi Jinping took office, China's capital investment in Africa, including aid, has reached unprecedented levels.

It is the same in the demand for non-traditional security. China's massive investment and huge economic interests in Africa meant that China could not sit idly and watch Africa sink into turmoil, especially as it concerned countries and regions closely related to China's interests. In the early stage of the investment, a serious lack of risk assessment resulted in mass investments in unsafe hubs and states. This coupled with the fact that millions of nationals immigrated to Africa for employment and economic purposes forced the Chinese government to pay greater attention to the national image and to strengthen national relationships with Africa, and in some degrees to intervene in the security affairs of relevant nations or regions. It is a typical example of China sending troops to Sudan. Of course, such intervention at least so far is still entirely defensive and is to safeguard interests of the Chinese state, enterprises, and citizens. There is no sign which shows that such behaviour violates the basic principle of 'non-interference in the internal affairs of other countries' that China has always adhered to. China has greatly changed its attitude towards the international peacekeeping system led by the UN, and has began to actively support and intervene both economically and personally. It can be said that the UN international peacekeeping system has become the main way for Chinese government to safeguard overseas rights and interests of state, enterprises, and citizens, in addition to 'escort' or 'evacuation' in special conditions. However, the Chinese overseas peacekeepers have recently been attacked by the local armed forces and there have been casualties. It has become a new diplomatic problem for China, and methods in which they could solve these problems or at least reduce casualties are not yet clear.

The economic relations between China and Africa have greatly developed, but the position of these relations in China's foreign trade and economic cooperation are still relatively low. China's main economic and trade objects are still the EU, the USA, as well as the neighbouring countries and regions. From this point of view, political factors seem more important than economic factors in the future relationships of China and Africa. Of course, foreign trade volume is not high for China, but it may be huge and irreplaceable for Africa. For example, China provided $6 billion in loans to Congo Republic in 2008, which is almost equivalent to this country's GDP and is far beyond the country's ability to repay. Such diplomatic and economic coordination is common in China's aid to Africa, which often causes the West to question the purpose of the extraordinary aid. In recent years, due to the rising cost at home, many of China's private enterprises have moved to Africa. It has become a trend. Some of the enterprises lacking a sense of social responsibility completely maximise purchases and profits. This brought many legal, environmental, labour, and other problems and has stained China's economic activities in Africa. How to solve these practices is also a future problem.

Over the years, the relationship between China and Africa has become closer and deeper. There has been a consensus on mutual reciprocity, mutual benefit, and mutual support. With the development of the relationship, the emergence of new problems and needs within the implementation of China's global influence, it seems important in both China and Africa's best interests to ensure Sino-Africa relations develop in a healthy and stable manner and that they overcome incumbent problems in an efficient yet pragmatic manner.

References

Bergesen, A. J. (2012). The new surgical colonialism China Africa and oil. http://www.allacademic.com/meta/p237190_index.html

BP (2010, June). *Statistical review of world energy.* pp 8.

Brautigam, D. (2009). *The Dragon's Gift: The real story of China in Africa* (pp. 17–24). Oxford, New York: Oxford University Press.

Brookes, P. (2007, February 9). *Into Africa: China's grab for influence and oil, Heritage lectures.* No.1006, (pp. 2–4).

Cha D. (2006). Zhongguo zai Feizhou de Shiyou Liyi: Guoji Zhengzhi keti (China's oil interests in Africa: An international political issue). *International Politics Quarterly.* Beijing (No. 4).

China's African policy. (2015, December 5). *Xinhua net.*

China's State Council Information Office. (2010). *Zhongguo yu Feizhou de Jingmao Hezuo (China-Africa Economic and Trade Cooperation).* Beijing: Demos Publishing Company.

DDRS. Farmington Hills, Mich: Gale 2011a No. CK3100127315.

DDRS. Farmington Hills, Mich: Gale 2011b No. CK3100276982.

DDRS. Farmington Hills, Mich: Gale 2011c No. CK3100295954.

DDRS. Farmington Hills, Mich: Gale 2011d No. CK3100572009.

DDRS. Farmington Hills, Mich: Gale 2011e No. CK3100015295.

Deng, X. (1993). *Selected Works of Deng Xiaoping* (Vol. 3). Beijing: Demos Publishing Company.

DeRoche, A. (2007, May). Non-alignment on the Racial Frontier: Zambia and the USA, 1964-1968. *Cold War History, 7*(2), 241.

Ding, M. (2010). Youyi zhi qiao lian wanly-Xinzhongguo yu Feizhou Guanxi Suxie (Bridge of friendship linking million miles – A sketch of new Sino-Africa relations) Materials from *CPC History* Taiyuan (No. 5).

Downs, E. S.. (2007, September). China's quest for overseas oil. *Far East Economic Review, 170*(7).

Downs, E. S.., & Erica S. (2007). The fact and fiction of Sino-African energy relations. *China Security, 3*(3) Summer.
Friedman, E. (2009). How economic superpower China could transform Africa. *Journal of Chinese Political Science, 14*(1).
FRUS. 1964a-1968. vol. 24, Africa U.S. Government Printing Office No. 463 http://history.state.gov/historicaldocuments/frus1964-68v24
FRUS. 1964b-1968. vol. 24 Africa, U.S. Government Printing Office No. 465 http://history.state.gov/historicaldocuments/frus1964-68v24
Giry, S. (2004, November 15). China's Africa strategy out of Beijing. *The New Republic.*
He, Y. (1993). Yuanjian Tanzan Tielu de Juece Guocheng (The decision process of aiding Tanzania Zambia railway) Literature of Chinese Communist Party Beijing No. 4. President Kaunda's Speech in 'Tunduma Completion Ceremony', *Sino-Turkey Company Archives,* 22 July 1973.
Jaffe, A. M., & Lewis, S. W. (2002). Beijing's oil diplomacy, survival. *Global Politics and Strategy, 44*(1).
Jiang, An. (2013). Mao Zedong Waijiao Sixiang de Lishi Luoji. *Chinese Social Sciences Weekly,* Beijing December 27.
Klare, M., & Daniel, V. (2006). America China and the scramble for African's oil. *Review of African Political Economy, 33*(108).
Liang, M. (2011). Feizhou Shiyou Maoyi (African Oil Trade: A Perspective of China). *Journal of International Economic Cooperation,* (4).
Mao, Z. (1952). He Zhongyangshe,Saodangbao,Xinminbao san Jizhe de Tanhua (The interview with three correspondents from the central news agency, The Sao Tang Pao and the Hsin Min Pao). In *Selected Works of Mao Tsetung* (Vol. 2). Beijing: Demos Publishing Company.
Mao, Z. (1960a). Biele Situleideng (Farewell, Leighton Stuart). In *Selected works of Mao Tsetung* (Vol. 4). Beijing: Demos Publishing Company.
Mao, Z. (1960b). Lun Renmin minzhu zhuanzheng (On the people's democratic dictatorship). In *Selected works of Mao Tsetung* (Vol. 4). Beijing: Demos Publishing Company.
Mao, Z. (1960c). Zai xin zhengzhi xieshang huiyi choubeihui shang de Jianghua (Address to the preparatory meeting of the new political consultative conference). In *Selected works of Mao Tsetung* (Vol. 4). Beijing: Demos Publishing Company.
Mao, Z. (1986). Lun shi da Guanxi (On the ten major relationships). In *Selected readings From the works of Mao Tsetung* (Vol. 2). Beijing: Demos Publishing Company.

Mao, Z. (1994a). Dabai Diguozhuyi de renhe Tiaozhan (Defeat any provocation from imperialism). In *Mao Zedong on diplomacy*. Beijing: Central Party Literature Press, World Knowledge Press.

Mao, Z. (1994b). Diguo Zhuyi shi bu kepa de (Imperialism is not terrible). In *Mao Zedong on diplomacy*. Beijing: Central Party Literature Press, World Knowledge Press.

Mao, Z. (1994c). Dijie Zhong Su Tiao Yue he Xieyi de Zhongda Yiyi (The significance of Sino-Soviet Treaties and agreements). In *Mao Zedong on diplomacy*. Beijing: Central Party Literature Press, World Knowledge Press.

Mao, Z. (1994d). Feizhou de Renwu shi fandui Diguozhuyi (Africa's mission is to oppose imperialism). In *Mao Zedong on diplomacy*. Beijing: Central Party Literature Press, World Knowledge Press.

Mao, Z. (1994e). Feizhou shi Douzheng de Qianxian (Africa is the front line of the struggle). In *Mao Zedong on diplomacy*. Beijing: Central Party Literature Press, World Knowledge Press.

Mao, Z. (1994f). Guanyu sange Shijie de huafen Wenti (About three worlds' division issue). In *Mao Zedong on diplomacy*. Beijing: Central Party Literature Press, World Knowledge Press.

Mao, Z. (1994g). Guojia bulun daxiao yinggai yilv pingdeng (Countries should be equal regardless of the size). In *Mao Zedong on diplomacy*. Beijing: Central Party Literature Press, World Knowledge Press.

Mao, Z. (1994h). Guo yu Guo zhijian zuyi yinqi Huaiyi, fang'ai Hezuo de Wenti dou yao Jiejue (Any problem may cause suspicion or impede cooperation between countries should be solved). In *Mao Zedong on diplomacy*. Beijing: Central Party Literature Press, World Knowledge Press.

Mao, Z. (1994i). Heluxiaofu de Rizi bu hao guo (Khrushchev's life is not easy). In *Mao Zedong on diplomacy*. Beijing: Central Party Literature Press, World Knowledge Press.

Mao, Z. (1994j). Heping Gongchu Wuxiang Yuanze shi yige changqi de Fangzhen (The five principle of peaceful coexistence is a long-term policy). In *Mao Zedong on diplomacy*. Beijing: Central Party Literature Press, World Knowledge Press.

Mao, Z. (1994k). Heping wei shang (Peace is above all). In *Mao Zedong on diplomacy*. Beijing: Central Party Literature Press, World Knowledge Press.

Mao, Z. (1994l). Shijie shang youren pa gui,ye youren bupa gui (There are some one afraid of ghost but some one not in the world). In *Mao Zedong on diplomacy*. Beijing: Central Party Literature Press, World Knowledge Press.

Mao, Z. (1994m). Shou yapo de Renmin ziji zong shi yao qilai de (The oppressed people always rise up). In *Mao Zedong on diplomacy*. Beijing: Central Party Literature Press, World Knowledge Press.

Mao, Z. (1994n). Tong Niboer Guowang Mahengdela he Wanghou de Tanhua (Talks with King Mahendra and Queen of Nepal). In *Mao Zedong on diplomacy*. Beijing: Central Party Literature Press, World Knowledge Press.

Mao, Z. (1994o). Tong xiongdi guojia tuanjie yizhi, tong yiqie guojia jianli youhao guanxi (Solidarity with fraternal Countries and establish friendly relations with all countries). In *Mao Zedong on diplomacy*. Beijing: Central Party Literature Press, World Knowledge Press.

Mao, Z. (1994p). Women hen xinshang Faguo zhezhong duli Zhengce (We appreciate the independent policy of France very much). In *Mao Zedong on diplomacy*. Beijing: Central Party Literature Press, World Knowledge Press.

Mao, Z. (1994q). Women tong suoyou Feizhou Guojia Renmin de Guanxi dou shi haode (Our relations with the People of all African countries are good). In *Mao Zedong on diplomacy*. Beijing: Central Party Literature Press, World Knowledge Press.

Mao, Z. (1994r). Women xiwang Alabo Guojia tuanjie qilai (We hope Arab countries to unite). In *Mao Zedong on diplomacy*. Beijing: Central Party Literature Press, World Knowledge Press.

Mao, Z. (1994t). Xiqu lishi jiaoxun, fandui daguo shawen zhuyi (The lessons of history, against chauvinism). In *Mao Zedong on diplomacy*. Beijing: Central Party Literature Press, World Knowledge Press.

Mao, Z. (1994u). Yibiandao dui budui? (Is that right to lean to one side?). In *Mao Zedong on diplomacy*. Beijing: Central Party Literature Press, World Knowledge Press.

Mao, Z. (1994v). Zhongjian Didai you liangge (There are two intermediate zones). In *Mao Zedong on diplomacy*. Beijing: Central Party Literature Press, World Knowledge Press.

Mao, Z. (1994x). Zhong Ri Guanxi yu Shijie Dazhan Wenti (The Sino-Japan relations and the problems of world war). In *Mao Zedong on diplomacy*. Beijing: Central Party Literature Press, World Knowledge Press.

Mao, Z. (1994y). Zhongguo he Bajisitan yinggai chengwei haopengyou (China and Pakistan should be good friends). In *Mao Zedong on diplomacy*. Beijing: Central Party Literature Press, World Knowledge Press.

Mao, Z. (1994aa). Zhongguo Renmin zhichi Aiji Renmin shouhui Suyishiyunhe (Chinese people support Egypt's recovery of the Suez Canal). In *Mao Zedong on diplomacy*. Beijing: Central Party Literature Press, World Knowledge Press.

Mao, Z. (1994ab). Zhong Yin Bianjie yao Yongyuan Heping Youhao (The border of China and Nepal would be always peaceful and friendly). In *Mao Zedong on diplomacy*. Beijing: Central Party Literature Press, World Knowledge Press.

Nadine, A. (1976). *Nasser* (Fan Yu, trans.) Shanghai People's Publishing House.

People's Daily. Beijing June 22, 1951.

Petterson, D. (2002). *Revolution in Zanzibar: An American's cold war tale*. Boulder, CO: Westview Press.

Pham, P. J. (2006). China's African strategy and its implications for US interests. *American Foreign Policy Interests, 28*, 239–253.

Tao, W. (Ed.). (2003). *Meiguo dui hua Zhengce Wenjianji [American China Policy Document]* (Vol. 1, 2nd ed.). Beijing: World Knowledge Press.

Taylor, I. (2006). China's oil diplomacy in Africa. *International Affairs, 82*(5).

Taylor, I. (2009). Unpacking China's resource diplomacy in Africa. *Centre on China's Transnational Relations Working Paper*, (No. 19).

The Telegraph. (2006, August 23). Chinese moves spawn a new order http://www.telegraph.co.uk/finance/2945957/Chinese-moves-spawn-a-new-order.html

Tull, D. M. (2006). China's engagement in Africa: Scope significance and consequences. *Journal of Modern African Studies, 44*(3), 459–479.

Wang, Y. (2013, September 10). Jianchi Zhengque Yiliguan, Jiji Fahui fu Zenren Daguo Zuoyong—Shenke Linghui Xi Jinping Tongzhi guanyu Waijiao Gongzuo de Zhongyao Jianghua jingshen' (Adhere to the correct views on righteousness and benefit concept, actively play the role of a big responsible country – deeply understand the spirit of the Xi Jinping's important speech on foreign affairs). *People's Daily*, Beijing (Section 7).

Wang, Y. (2014). Tansuo Zhongguo tese daguo Waijiao zhi lu (Exploring the road of major-country diplomacy with Chinese characteristics). In Information Office of the State Council (Ed.), *Interpretation of the new concept of China's diplomacy*. Beijing: China Intercontinental Press.

Ye, Z. (2014). Xi Jinping de jiu ge Waijiao Xinlinian (Xi Jinping's nine new diplomatic concepts). In Information Office of the State Council (Ed.), *Interpretation of the new concept of China's diplomacy*. Beijing: China Intercontinental Press.

Yu, H. (2014). Zhongguomeng yu Heping Fazhan Linian zhong de Zhongguo Waijiao (China's diplomacy of China's dream and the peaceful development concept). In Information Office of the State Council (Ed.), *Interpretation of the new concept of China's diplomacy*. Beijing: China Intercontinental Press.

Zhonggong Dangshi Ziliao. (1994). *The history of the Chinese Communist Party information*, (Vol. 42). The History of the CCP Press.
Zhonghua Renmin Gongheguo Jingji Dangan Ziliao Xuanbian. (1960). (1949–1952) Collection of Financial Records of the People's Republic of China (1949–1952), Foreign trade volume. Beijing: Economic and Management Press.
Zhong Mei Guanxi ZiliaoHuibian. (1960). *Compilation of Sino-US Relations* (Vol. 2 (1)). Beijing: World Knowledge Press.
Zhou, E. (1984a). Heping Gongchu Wuxiang Yuanze (Five principles of peaceful coexistence). In *Selected works of Zhou Enlai* (Vol. 2). Beijing: Demos Publishing Company.
Zhou, E. (1984b). Women de Waijiao Zhengce yu Fangzhen (Our foreign policy and guide line). In *Selected works of Zhou Enlai* (Vol. 2). Beijing: Demos Publishing Company.
Zhou, E. (1990a). Xinzhongguo Waijiao (On new China's diplomacy). In *Zhou Enlai on diplomacy*. Beijing: Central Party Literature Press.
Zhou, E. (1990b). Zai Ya Fei Huiyi quanqi Huiyi shang de Fayan (Speech in the plenary session of the Asia-African conference). In *Zhou Enlai on diplomacy*. Beijing: Central Party Literature Press.
Zhou, E. (1990c). Zhonghua Renmin Gongheguo de Waijiao Zhengce (Foreign policy of the people's republic of China). In *Zhou Enlai on diplomacy*. Beijing: Central Party Literature Press.

Part II

Chinese Companies in Africa

6

The China Challenge: Cameroonians Between Discontent and Popular Admiration

Ute Röschenthaler and Antoine Socpa

6.1 Introduction

Cameroon's relationship with China dates back to the 1970s. It intensified in the 1990s when Cameroon welcomed alternatives to the Structural Adjustment Programmes imposed by the World Bank. At that time also, China sought to open its markets and win allies in Africa. This coincidence opened up opportunities of cooperation for both countries who considered this collaboration beneficial for their political and economic interests. China was in search of political allies, new markets, and space for its large population. Cameroon needed political stability, development

U. Röschenthaler (✉)
Goethe University, Frankfurt, Germany
e-mail: roeschenthaler@em.uni-frankfurt.de

A. Socpa
University of Yaounde I, Yaounde, Cameroon
e-mail: asocpa@yahoo.com

Y. C. Kim (ed.), *China and Africa*, The Palgrave Macmillan Asian Business Series, DOI 10.1007/978-3-319-47030-6_6

without interference in its internal affairs, straightforward business relationship (Konings 2011: 18; see also Sautman 2006), and employment opportunities for its youth. China proposed brotherly relations, a win–win situation for both and project-related loans and investments, which represent an attractive alternative to the upsetting neoliberal economic and political reforms of the 1980s and 1990s. This collaboration now keeps going for two decades, but what can be said about its results?

Most studies on Asians in Africa have focused in a general way on state-funded cooperation and produced a homogenised image of China's influence on the continent and either praise or criticise its engagement. Others draw a more differentiated picture considering national specificities, local peculiarities, and the different national policies towards China.[1] Studies on the relationship of China with Cameroon are still few but their number has increased in the past years. They include studies by African Forum and Network on Debt and Development AFRODAD (2011), Julius Amin (2015), Charles Ateba Eyene (2010, 2012), Assemblée Nationale du Cameroun (1975), Piet Konings (2011, chapter 8: 177–203), Gweth (2011), Reinhold Plate (2005), Hilaire de Prince Pokam (2015), David Sinou (1985), and Joachim Tedié (2014).

These authors look at the topic from different perspectives; some are more, others less, critical about the impact of China's activities in Cameroon. The most straightforward embracement of China's presence comes from pro-government circles (see e.g. Ateba Eyene 2012; Etian 2011). Others rather note that a great number of cheap consumer goods are of minor quality, do often not meet safety standards, and their arrival also weakens local industries, entrepreneurs, and traders (AFRODAD 2011; Konings 2011: 1, 18; Pokam 2015). But how do these observations relate to the narrative that China's aid is based on equality, mutual benefit, and respect for the sovereignty of the host? Most of the loans are theoretically unconditional and interest-free, with an emphasis on mutual benefit and noninterference (Bräutigam 2008; Rotberg 2008: 7), but how far does the equality reach and who wins more in this venture?

[1] See, for example, Ikhouoria (2010), Kamau (2010), Khan Mohammad (2014); see also the special issues 43, 1 and 44, 1 of the *Journal of Current Chinese Affairs*, edited by Karsten Giese, and several studies listed by Konings (2011: 179).

Is the Chinese presence able to solve the challenges of unemployment for Cameroons' youth who roughly at the same time began to migrate to Asia (Alpes 2011; Deli 2011; Fleischer 2012; Konings 2011; Pelican 2014; Röschenthaler forthcoming)?

This chapter follows these issues and emphasises the importance of looking at the cooperation not from a monolithic perspective. It is necessary to differentiate between the similar but also different interests that are at stake within the Cameroonian society and also between China's development policy and the activities of Chinese migrants in the country. The chapter is concerned with the different Cameroonian actors and the predicaments that they feel the Chinese presence entails. Most people appreciate the variety and availability of affordable consumer goods, but also complain of competition and loss of trade opportunities. Few studies mention that Cameroonians regularly travel to Asian countries such as UAE (Dubai) and China to import trade goods (Etian 2011; Pelican 2014).

The concerns of these commercial actors and the related norms and activities will be the focus of this contribution. Therefore, their voices and experiences will be given room as they are muted in most studies on the role of China in Africa. They reflect the inherent contradictions in the Chinese presence in their country and bring out the unequal treatment of Cameroonians and Chinese by their governments in this reflection that actually challenges the narrative of equal and brotherly partnership between China and African countries. This becomes visible on two levels: first, when the situation of Cameroonian and Chinese entrepreneurs is compared in Cameroon, and second, when the situation of Chinese migrants in Cameroon is compared with that of the Cameroonian migrants in China. Our research provides first insights, although more research has to be carried out on the topic.

The chapter is based on research by the two authors, together with several Cameroonian assistants, particularly between 2013 and 2015. Altogether 33 long interviews were carried out with Cameroonian traders in Douala, Yaounde, and Bamenda, in addition to observation and short interviews with Chinese and Cameroonians in shops, different markets, and commercial streets. We have also talked to Cameroonian traders and entrepreneurs who regularly travel to China. The chapter also draws on research by one of the authors in China during the same time frame.[2] For the larger political context, we above all rely on local newspapers, official documents, and the available scholarly literature.

This chapter examines the Chinese engagement in Cameroon and its impact on the local economy from the point of view of different economic stakeholders and their interests. We have structured our discussion into seven sections. The first three provide a brief overview of the history of Cameroon's relationship with Asia and some of China's investments and development projects in the country and their evaluation. The fourth and fifth sections discuss private Chinese migration and their commercial activities in Cameroon. We then turn to the perspective of the Cameroonian economic actors and their experiences and perceptions on Chinese traders; and in the final section, we look at the role of diasporas for their home countries and compare this role for Chinese and Cameroonian economic actors. With these elaborations, we want to show that Chinese activities in Cameroon are not either beneficial or detrimental but that the situation is more complex; it brings development for both countries, but the extent to which it does this is entirely unequal.

6.2 The Evolution of Sino-Cameroonian Cooperation

In order to understand the circumstances in which the complexities of the Sino-Cameroonian cooperation developed, it is necessary to briefly look at Cameroon's post-colonial history and its relationship with Asia.[3]

Cameroon's independence from France in 1960 went along with agreements that Ahmadou Ahidjo, Cameroon's first president (1960–1982), signed and which guaranteed its former colonial power close political, social, military, and economic privileges, including the safety of French investments in Cameroon (for details, see Takougang and Krieger 1998: 38). At the same

[2] The research was carried out in the framework of the project "Africa's Asian Options" (AFRASO), which is supported by the Goethe University Frankfurt and the German Ministry of Foreign Affairs. We are also grateful to Diderot Nguepjouo for his comments.

[3] The People's Republic of China already played a role in Cameroon's struggle for independence from France, when it supported the Marxist inspired revolutionary movement Union des Populations du Cameroun (UPC).

time, Cameroon—as did other African countries as well—looked for further international partners and began to cooperate with Taiwan (Sinou 1985), Pakistan, and Indonesia (see Geschiere and Konings 1993).[4] Taiwan provided generous development aid, irrespective of ideology, whereas China, at that time, supported countries with a socialist government. Cameroon's relations with Taiwan lasted from 1960 to 1971 when Cameroon redirected its interest to China, which was looking for allies among African countries who would vote it into a seat in the UN Security Council. In 1971, indeed 26 of 50 African states voted for China (that replaced Taiwan). In the same year, on 26 March 1971, Cameroon established diplomatic ties with the People's Republic of China (AFRODAD 2011: 17; Konings 2011: 190; Tedié 2014), which resulted in the signing of a number of agreements, the first of which was a general trade agreement in 1972.

During the Cold War, China cooperated with the West, focused on its economic modernisation and reduced its interest in Africa. During that time, Cameroon refused to take sides and supported neither the USA nor the Soviets. It decided for a self-reliant form of planned or communal liberalism for its national development (Konings 2011: 14), in which the state became the sole operator in the import-substituting industrial sector through the Société National d'Investissement. Although this development format was characterised by authoritarianism and patrimonialism, Cameroon became one of the successful states in Africa between the late 1970s and 1985. Cameroon's success was interrupted by the 1986 world market crisis and the subsequent Structural Adjustment Programmes that the World Bank implemented to liberate economies, remove price subsidies within internal markets, commit to privatisation, encourage foreign investment, reduce governmental payroll, and so on. When this did not lead to good results, the World Bank introduced the concept of good governance that ought to conform African states with neoliberal doctrines. These measures greatly overlooked African realities; they did not change much to the better but rather increased ethnic identity politics and rent-seeking behaviour with a contraproductive impact on development.[5]

[4] Much more than Taiwan, Pakistan and Indonesia were involved in the trade of consumer goods since 1982. They were competing in this field with Bamileke traders.

[5] AFRODAD (2011: 19); Konings (2011: 2–3, 14–15); Nyamnjoh and Geschiere (2000); see Konings for an analysis of why the Structural Adjustment Programmes did not work in Cameroon

On the backdrop of these evolutions and the upsetting experience of the Structural Adjustment programmes, it is understandable that Cameroon welcomed China's offer to act as a friend and supporter who promised development without intervention. In 1997, when Premier Li Peng visited the country, Cameroon and China signed further agreements for the reciprocal protection and promotion of investments. Cameroon participated in China's first Forum on China–Africa Cooperation (FOCAC) in 2000 and supported China to become a member in the World Trade Organization in 2001 (AFRODAD 2011: 18). In 2002, the two countries signed another agreement for economic and commercial cooperation. Cameroon also assisted in the third FOCAC summit in Beijing in 2006, and further agreements were signed in 2010.[6]

Chinese Development Assistance is aligned with Cameroon's priorities and includes long-term public loans with low interest rates, grants, and private loans through the Chinese Exim Bank. This assistance was boosted by China's general new intervention strategy in Africa and proclaims to serve mutual interests and gains (see for China's more general policies in Africa, Alden 2007; Broadman 2007; Medeiros 2009). During that time, Cameroon formulated its millennium goals, which entail a number of medium-term objectives to be reached until 2035, including poverty alleviation, becoming a middle-income and a newly industrialised country, consolidating democracy and national unity while respecting the country's diversity (AFRODAD 2011: 20, 35). Facing the millennium goals, President Paul Biya, Cameroon's second president since 1982, encouraged in public speeches in 2006 and 2007 Chinese investment in all economic sectors (*Cameroon Tribune*, 2 February, 2007, quoted in Konings 2011: 192).

due to ignorance of the heterogeneity of social interest groups and the specific role of elites, the youths, and civil society organisations in the country.

[6] For a list of agreements, see AFRODAD (2011: 17). Regular visits of Chinese officials to African countries and African officials to China intensified from 1996 onwards; for a list of the state visits, see Chinese foreign ministry (2006) and Medeiros (2009: 157).

6.3 Chinese Investment in Cameroon

Chinese investment began in the 1970s. It was revitalised in the 1990s and has grown substantially since then. The list of Chinese investments is impressive, hence we briefly summarise the more important ones (for further details, see AFRODAD 2011: 21–24; Ateba Eyene 2012; Chinese foreign ministry 2006; Konings 2011: 177–203; Pokam 2015).

The projects of the 1970s include mainly medical and infrastructure measures. From 1975 onwards, China regularly sent medical teams to Cameroon. In 1977, a grant agreement was signed for the construction of the National Congress Hall in Yaounde, which was followed by the construction of the Lagdo Dam in the North Region of Cameroon from 1978 to 1984. In 1989, a microlab was set up at Yaounde University. As Konings notes, few traditional donors would have financed such prestige projects (2011: 198–200).

Since the mid-1990s, cooperation with China augmented. Cameroon (along with many other African countries) intensified its export of cotton to China, a world-leading exporter of clothes which imports its cotton mainly from the USA (Konings 2011: 182; Rotberg 2008: 6). China also began to provide quotas of scholarships per year for Cameroonians to study in China.[7] In 1997, China's Zhejiang Normal University created a Mandarin language-teaching centre in Yaounde and provided training for more than 300 professionals. In 2007, this centre was transformed into a Confucius Institute, with branches in Douala, Maroua, and Buea.

From 2000 onwards, Chinese companies were contracted to begin with iron ore exploration at Mbalam. Later, also the Chinese Sinosteel subsidiary, SinosteelCam S.A., explored iron at the Lobe concession near Kribi. In 2002, the China Geological Engineering Group and the China Hydropower Foreign Project Company began with oil exploration, drilling, and road-building. In 2005, the Chinese ZTE society cooperated with Cameroon Postal Services (Campost) to establish electronic letters. Following the 2006 FOCAC summit, more projects were agreed upon. About ten Chinese

[7] For different figures of scholarships, see Amin (2015), Chinese Foreign Ministry (2006), AFRODAD (2011: 21), Konings (2011: 199). The Cameroonian government grants fellowships for doctoral studies in China as well.

companies are active in the construction of infrastructure, and among them are the Shaanxi group and China Road and Bridge company which constructed 12.8-km road extensions in Douala in September 2006.

In January 2007, the Ministry of Agriculture implemented huge agricultural projects in the Cameroon's Centre and West Regions. The Chinese company Shaanxi State Farms—a big enterprise that produces, transforms, and trades agricultural products—established a 5000 (some say 10,000 or even 15,000)-hectare plantation. A related project of US$ 62 million is carried out by a Sino-Cameroonian joint venture, Sino-Iko Agricultural Development Company, and exploits 200 hectares in Nanga Eboko (173 km north of Yaounde, in the Upper Sanaga Division, Centre Region) for the production of rice, cassava, and maize as well as fruits, vegetables, and poultry. The farm serves as an agricultural demonstration centre that is used for technical training, experimental research, and sustainable development studies and ought to reduce Cameroon's dependence from abroad. The firms have employed 10,000 Cameroonians, but the majority of the workers are Chinese. The population and various civil society organisations protested against the state's large-scale sale (or lease for 99 years) of local people's land to China and the poor conditions at which local workers have been employed (Konings 2011).

In April 2009, the Chinese oil company Yan Chang signed a renewable contract with Cameroon's National Hydrocarbon Company (SNH) to start four-year exploration activities on two onshore blocks in Zina and Makari in the Extreme North Region, at a cost of US$ 18 million. Yan Chang receives 75 per cent of the share on the blocks and SNH 25 per cent. More recently, Addax Petroleum, which belongs to Sinopec, obtained the exclusive right for explorations at the Rio del Rey (project Iroko).

Further projects include the partnership of Huawei with Camtel, the national telephone company, in the frame of which Huawei offers its service to Camtel as a mobile phone and internet provider and also constructs a network of optic cable of 3200 km through the entire country, which it offers to private operators.[8] China also constructed the Palais des Sports in Yaounde and stadiums in Limbe and Bafoussam, but most workers for these projects were imported from China.

[8] For the realization of the optic fibre network the Chinese contracted a Vietnamese company that was working on it in 2014 (conversation with Vietnamese workers in Yaounde, June 2014).

Chinese companies also constructed numerous hospitals in the country, including a 200-bed hospital in Yaounde, hospitals in Bafoussam, Guider, and Mbalmayo, and a centre to combat malaria. They constructed a drinking water production facility in Ayato at the outskirts of Douala with a 150,000 m^3 additional water capacity. The ministry of Urban Development and Housing commissioned the Chinese company Shenyang to build 10,000 homes and develop 50,000 plots of land.

China's timber imports from African forests (Cameroon, Congo, Equatorial Guinea, Gabon, and Liberia) have tripled since 1993, of which many come from unlicenced or dubious loggers. China is the largest importer of Cameroonian wood products. The Hong Kong-based Sino-French joint venture Vicwood with a total of 532,537 hectares is one of the 23 logging concessions exploited by nine companies in Cameroon. National companies are financially supported by their Chinese trade partners and work according to the requirements of the latter, that is, different from Cameroon's timber exports to the EU and the USA; they have no consideration for forestry exploitation standards, log sizes, and species. Additionally, there are independent Chinese timber traders operating in Douala, and numerous unlicenced and illegal loggers (AFRODAD 2011: 24; Konings 2011: 182).

China also provides military assistance and exports arms, and Cameroon regularly sends military staff to China for training, and visits of military delegations between the two countries are frequent (for a list, see Chinese foreign ministry 2006).

Presently, Chinese construct a deep water port in Kribi and dams in Memvele and Mekin in the South Region of Cameroon (*Cameroon Tribune*, 11 March 2013, p.3). The construction of the Memvele dam is one of the largest projects, financed through the Exim Bank, which began in 2010 and is supposed produce electricity from 2017 onwards. Plans for future projects include amusement parks in Douala and the development of tourism facilities to attract Chinese tourists to Cameroon.

In addition to Cameroonian and Chinese enterprises, other international investors carry out projects or explore project opportunities in Cameroon. South Koreans were involved in road construction in the 1980s and Japan was constructing primary schools. Further countries with investment interests include companies from Brazil, France, India, Nigeria, Morocco, Singapore, Spain, Thailand, Tunisia, and Turkey.[9]

6.4 Cameroonian Perspectives on Chinese Investment

As the brief overview illustrates, the Chinese are present not only in strategic key sectors such as oil, infrastructure, development, forestry, and agriculture but in almost all economic sectors. After the two governments have signed general agreements on concessional loans for project packages with open clauses, Cameroon is free to choose projects for which the corresponding financial resources are allocated through the Chinese Exim (import and export) bank. Then companies are invited to hand in project proposals proposals. The most promising of them is awarded the contract.

Compared to traditional donors, the advantage for Cameroon is that it can set its own priorities without further interference as far as democracy, human rights, safety, and environmental standards are concerned. The overall amount of Chinese loans is considerable but compared to those of traditional donors remains relatively small, and there have also been several debt cancellations (AFRODAD 2011: 21, and several tables; Konings 2011: 18, 185, 198). Not even all projects seem to be a financial gain for China, hence scholars suggest that apart from searching natural resources and expanding its markets, China is interested more in restoring its image, gaining its international prestige, and legitimising its regime in relation to the West, more precisely US hegemony. Africa is a large market, but the USA is an even more rewarding market for China (Konings 2011: 185; Pokam 2015: 62; see also Kernen 2007).

Generally, the popular response to China's investments is ambivalent. Some scholars argue that China's help is long-term and motivated by real friendship and that Cameroon needs China as it would be unable

[9] MINMAP (2015); US Department of State (2013); the government-near newspaper *Cameroon Tribune* regularly reports about foreign investments, for example in 2013, on Brazil (26 February, p. 7; 4 March, p.3), China (22 February p.12; 11 March, p. 3, 13), Japan (11 March, p. 32; 30 May, p.10; 5 June, p. 3), Morocco (26 February, p. 3), Turkey (1 April, p.8–9; 5 June, p. 29; 11 November, p. 5).

to build up such infrastructure on its own, more so that it might help decolonising African minds (Ateba Eyene 2012). However, obviously there are different understandings of how development is achieved. The former ambassador of China in Cameroon, Xue Jinwei, emphasised that Cameroon was not at all losing due to the Chinese presence and that China would do its best to respond to the most urgent needs of the Cameroonian people and augment its capacities of self-development. Therefore, Cameroon would give priority to the sectors of public health, education, agriculture, telecommunication, and infrastructure (according to an interview with *Cameroon Tribune*, 16 November 2010, cited in Pokam 2015). Pokam does not question this, but insists that what Cameroonians need is to profit more from employment and technology transfer; Chinese should not only sell them manufactured products but teach them how to produce these goods themselves in order to become economically independent: "Cameroon needs its own enterprises to become an emerging economy on the horizon of 2035 as this is the wish of its president" (Pokam 2015: 20, our translation).

Our informants stated and Konings also confirms that Cameroonians normally do not get enough jobs, as Chinese companies import their own labourers even for small jobs, not to talk about management positions in Chinese projects (Konings 2011: 196). Plate (2005) and Tedié (2014) emphasise the benefits of the cooperation but also the necessity of adjustments. Chinese companies ought to be committed to employ far more local workers and intensify the transfer of technological knowledge. Cameroonian markets needed protection, and Cameroonian society was left to cope with the high number of Chinese migrants. Tedié (2014: 173) also suspects that neither the East nor the West was serious friends of Cameroon as each of them pursues their own interests when negotiating contracts. Hilaire de Prince Pokam (2015: 90–91), too, acknowledges that the Chinese contribute much to the country's development and provide access to affordable products, but he rightly worries that the Chinese products also weaken the Cameroonian economy.

On a political level, Chinese loans might be unconditioned, but China does not deliver these loans to domestic banks but only via the Chinese Exim bank. Therefore, this money is not actually free, more so as it does not work for the African economy but for China. Additionally, the realisation of development projects also entails the transformation of the environment with consequences for the well-being of coming generations; the expulsion of people from their land and the question of adequate compensation for the loss of their homes, land, and sacred forests which form part of their cultural identity. The exploitation of natural resources such as minerals and timber is measured in terms of the money they bring, whereas the costs of environmental and climate damage for future generations and the personal losses for individuals on whose land the projects are carried out are ignored but might create long-term complications.

Koning also notes that labour unions and civil society groups complain about poor environmental and labour standards in Chinese ventures and the breakdown of local industries (2011: 18). The fresh flower industry is a good example. Fresh flower plantations succumb to Chinese plastic flower imitations and sellers in Yaounde told us in 2014 that they can sell far less flowers than before. Customers also often prefer plastic flowers that do not perish, and only for festivities, people afford the more expensive fresh flowers.

In short, we see that there is agreement on the general beneficiality of Chinese projects for the development of Cameroon, but there are also different ideas of what kind of development is needed and of how this can be achieved, that is, whether the supply of infrastructure projects and service enterprises is sufficient or whether Cameroonians need to not only be receivers but encouraged to manage their own companies. Additionally, it is important to understand that different interest groups inside the Cameroonian society might have different ideas on this. For example, there are long-lasting political fears that certain ambitious and successful ethnic groups might become economically too powerful and need therefore stronger political guidance, whereas others vote for a liberal economy which, however, must remain in the hands of Cameroonians.

Cameroonians who are not employed by the state face a double challenge: state projects engage Chinese companies who largely employ Chinese workers and do not provide the dearly needed employment for young Cameroonians and the increasing number of private Chinese economic actors who rather than serve as a resource create complicated scenarios of competition for Cameroonian traders and entrepreneurs.

6.5 Chinese Migration to Cameroon

Chinese migration to Africa more generally began from the eighteenth century onwards when living conditions became difficult in some of the Chinese coastal areas and European powers needed indentured labourers to assist them with their colonial projects, particularly in Southern Africa; a second wave of Chinese followed in the 1960s and 1970s; and a third and still ongoing wave came in the 1990s after the opening up of the markets after the Cold War (Li 2012, 2013).

In Cameroon, as we outlined earlier, Chinese arrived since the 1970s in the framework of the Sino-Cameroonian development projects, which brought medical teams and temporary Chinese workers. Between 1971 and 1995, the number of Chinese in Cameroon remained low; only from the 1990s onwards, a growing number of individual small- and large-scale traders looking for opportunities began to settle in the country (Konings 2011: 191; Pokam 2015: 13).

The background of massive Chinese migration is that due to the reforms of the late 1970s, thousands of Chinese lost employment as civil servants and had no other choice than to leave the country. China even encouraged them to found enterprises abroad and committed them morally (and legally) to maintain relations with their home country. In 1995, Jiang Zemin urged unemployed Chinese to move abroad and become global actors. Since 1998, the Chinese government supports every infrastructural enterprise in Africa, negotiates tax suppression, and Chinese banks provide credit without, or with very low, interest. The foundation of the China–Africa Development Fund is one of the measures to facilitate the implantation of Chinese enterprises in Africa. In 2008, the Chinese government encouraged Chinese companies to purchase farmland overseas for the production of crops (especially soybeans) for export that helps guarantee China's food security (Pokam 2015: 50; Rotberg 2008: 4).

China's emigration is basically a migration of poor people, unemployed workers, and expropriated farmers. As part of the agreements of 2007, China also negotiated with the Cameroonian government the facilitation of migrants' settlement in Cameroon. Due to this agreement, Chinese are the only foreigners in Cameroon who obtain visas of one and a half years, even without a work contract.

The actual number of Chinese in Cameroon is difficult to ascertain. According to the Chinese embassy in Yaounde, there were 1500 Chinese in Douala and 2000–3000 in Yaounde in 2009 who came mainly from Fujian and Zhejiang provinces (Konings 2011: 191). In 2013, another source mentions 4000 Chinese in Cameroon (*Mutations*, 27 March 2013, cited in Pokam 2015: 14). Others estimate their number between 20,000 and 30,000 or even much higher (Konings 2011: 191).

Chinese migrants become a quickly growing diaspora that is supported and fostered by politics. This migration follows the well-known model according to which migration begins with employment in development projects, and these workers, in turn, facilitate the arrival of family members and friends. These in turn begin to work as traders, offer services to Chinese workers, sell food in restaurants, open drinking spots, and so on. Chinese migrants continue to strongly rely on family and clan solidarity (Pokam 2015: 13, 51) and create transnational relationships that connect home country and the diaspora.

To secure their interests as a diaspora group, Chinese businesspeople have created an association, the Chinese General Association of Industry and Commerce in Cameroon, in whose board the more important Chinese entrepreneurs are represented. This association coordinates Chinese economic activities in the country. It was founded when Chinese shop owners felt they were harassed by Cameroonian fiscal and customs officers and the entire Chinese communities went on strike for several days in 2006. At state visits, the association reports to representatives of the Chinese government about harassments and other problems, and Chinese officials then negotiate better conditions and security for their diaspora (see also Anon 2007; Pokam 2015: 52).

6.6 Private Chinese Commercial Activities

Many Chinese migrants followed their government's suggestion to leave their country and make a living abroad. In Cameroon, they invested in various economic sectors. The Chinese government even encouraged its diaspora in Cameroon to create joint ventures with African counterparts (Konings 2011: 184), but not many positive examples are known.

Among the early arrivals of Chinese businesspeople are fishermen who practise industrial fishing with trawlers along the Atlantic coast. Cameroonian consumers appreciate the large fish; however, these entrepreneurs make easy profit with their unsustainable fishing methods and outdo local fishermen who with their modest equipment can no longer make a living (according to *The Post*, 22 October 2007, cited by AFRODAD 2011: 24; Konings 2011: 192–196).

Another field that is highly profitable for Chinese businesspeople is Chinese traditional medicine (CTM). Many Cameroonians consider CTM effective and affordable, so that meanwhile CTM has become such a success that medicaments are sold everywhere and towns have at least one private Chinese clinic (Konings 2011: 197; see also Candelise 2011; Monteillet 2010; Wassouni 2010). Soon also the issue of fake medicaments and problematic practices came up and the Cameroonian ministry made attempts to regulate certain practices such as acupuncture, which are only allowed in two of the largest Chinese hospitals (Pokam 2015:40–41). Among the companies that sell medicaments are Tianshi, Tasli, Somai, and Meilun (Pokam 2015: 26, 39). They hire Cammeronians who trade their products in various places or act as middlemen and resell them to other mobile drug sellers.

Chinese have also opened shops with cheap household products all over the country. The first Chinese shops opened in the 1990s. In the 2000s, more and more shops opened not only in the city centres but also in poor neighbourhoods. In some of Douala's and Yaounde's neighbourhoods, entire Chinatowns have emerged. They consist of a series of family-owned shops and small-scale enterprises. In Akwa in 2008, there were about 70 Chinese shops and at the Marché Congo 30, plus many Chinese restaurants (Konings 2011: 197; Pokam 2015: 14–16; see also Ma Mung 2000; Bruneau 2010).

In Yaounde, in 2013, we noted that entire streets around the Marché Central were completely in Chinese hands. Most of these shops sell a mixture of household goods, textiles, electric products, furniture, beauty products, health products, clothing, decoration, artificial flowers, and small machines. We noted in several shops at least 50 different types of health teas for all kinds of problems. These shops usually have a controller who sits above level so that he or she can easily supervise the entire shop. In some of them, the personnel are Chinese only; others employ additionally Cameroonians, both young men and women. They help selling, respond to the Cameroonian customers, translate their orders to the Chinese, and help transport goods from the warehouse to the shop. Many also work as security persons for the Chinese. Some of them stated that they enjoyed their work, but after talking a while, they forwarded that the work culture was very different and that each of the parties would seek ways to draw their own advantages from the situation. Many also complained about the low salaries, but accepted to work with the Chinese as it was at least a job.

Cameroonians benefit from the employment opportunities in private Chinese enterprises, especially in shops, restaurants, and clinics. These jobs, however, do not require specific skills, are often without employment contract, poorly paid and only short-term. Shop assistants are easily dismissed as soon as the owners have learned to communicate in the local language. Chinese employees, too, complained to us about the Cameroonians and noted disagreements about cultural norms. However, in spite of many complications, friendly relationships have also emerged among Cameroonians and Chinese.

In 2013 and 2014, the Chinese whom we observed in Yaounde were mainly selling from their shops; our Cameroonian informants, however, often complained that as more Chinese had arrived from 2000 onwards, they began to apply aggressive sales' strategies and carry out not only wholesale but also retail and even street selling. Cameroonian traders told us how surprised they were to see "white street vendors" in the cities of Cameroon. These young Asian women and men move in the streets and popular areas to offer products ranging from watches and mobile phones to textiles and food. Their strategies to attract customers are not very different from those of Cameroonian street vendors. They shout at people and even harass them in public places and also in private homes. Observers and potential clients react with surprise, curiosity, and even mistrust. They ask themselves, as one interview partner stated, "How can one explain that a white man sells in the street like a common Cameroonian? How can someone move far away from Asia and pay an air ticket to come to Africa simply to be a street vendor?" The Chinese street vendors (some are still very young) don't differ from

Malians, Nigerians, or Senegalese who also leave their countries to come to Cameroon to carry out petty jobs. People understand that Africans are doing this. But, as one informant observed, the Chinese "have bloody eyes," meaning they know no shame. People wonder how Chinese men and women coming from so far can do the same type of job as Africans.

For many Cameroonians, this is difficult to understand. More so, it appears to them as a paradox that China is known as a world power and provides Cameroon with financial resources for development projects and that the same country sends unskilled Chinese manpower to labour in these projects that could be easily recruited locally. Furthermore, Chinese citizens whose government assists Cameroon in its development process lower themselves to open small shops in the neighbourhood as would do any common African, and as if this was not enough, they are not ashamed to hawk or sell doughnuts in the street. Cameroonians often see the reason for their irritation in the policies of their own political leaders: "Biya has sold Cameroon to Chinese … he has opened all the doors … we are invaded by the Chinese." Similar statements are widespread among people from various sections of society.

People do not only wonder about this behaviour but feel that the activities of Chinese individuals contradict established trading norms. The example of a Chinese trader illustrates what Cameroonian businesspeople regard as unfair competition. A Chinese woman of 21 years arrived in Cameroon in 2011 at the invitation of her uncle, who runs a shop selling flowers and gadgets for decoration in the city of Douala. She observed that the phone business flourished in the Cameroonian market and asked her father in China to send her a stock of 10,000 mobile phones of all brands. When the order was delivered, she showcased samples in their supermarket with the indication "large consignment of mobile phones … wholesale." The wholesale price for a Sony phone T8000i was 12,000 FCFA (about 18 Euros). Cameroonian petty traders rushed in to buy some of them, which they intended to resell for 15,000–20,000 FCFA (about 23 and 30 Euros). The Chinese woman, however, turned into a street vendor as well and walked in the city streets and into the administrative offices to sell the same phones sometimes even at a much lower price than the wholesale price (i.e. for 8000 or 10,000 FCFA). When the Cameroonian street vendors offer their price to a customer after the passage of the Chinese trader, they are treated as a crook and customers say to them: "You Cameroonians, you want too much profit. … I'll buy directly from Chinese source." This looks like unfair competition, which is actually clearly spelled out in the law (Republic of Cameroon, laws no. 90 and 98 of 1990 and 1998) and needs to be applied more strictly in the case of Chinese traders.

As noted earlier, the Asian traders have difficulties to understand the Cameroonian consumer preferences, as one of them remarked: "We alone can know the taste of the people of our country. So what do Chinese do? When we come up with the goods, a Chinese finds a way to photograph them and then faxes the picture to his partner company in China. His business partner over there reproduces similar products and sends them to him in Cameron. Sixty days after, he receives it and 'destroys' the business."[10] This example also shows that Chinese traders are quick to observe what local traders are selling; then they order the same product in large quantities from China and sell it, even in rural villages, for a price that is lower than that of Cameroonian traders. Many of our informants mentioned that they never knew what the Chinese in the country were planning to do next. They were also irritated that Chinese did not exchange ideas with local people but decided everything among themselves. Cameroonians therefore felt insecure and challenged to constantly develop new strategies to remain on the market. Several traders told us that the Chinese presence encouraged their creativity whereas the Chinese would not create but only imitate what they see with them.

Traders also told us that the Chinese would sell not only imported Chinese goods but also "traditional" Cameroonian products. One Chinese became well known as a Makossa singer and sold his music on CDs (see also Pokam 2015: 21). Our informants complained that Chinese traders also began to sell doughnuts, an occupation of Cameroonian women who produce them in the morning and sell them for breakfast (see also Mbori 2005). Others have opened street kitchens to sell *fufu* and *eru* (pounded yam with a liana vegetable), the favourite food in the Southwest Region. Chinese prostitutes have been observed in Douala working for half the

[10] It has been noticed that Asian traders use Cameroonian networks that are composed of their employees to have relevant information on Cameroonian traders' stocks and order lists of products.

price than Cameroonian prostitutes (Ndjio 2009, 2014; see also Pokam 2015: 20; Konings 2011: 191). Chinese traders also sell cheap wax prints with the popular designs of the Cameroonian textile company Cottonière industrielle du Cameroun (CICAM).

Our informants concluded that Chinese were only thinking about money and would assume that Africans simply like cheap commodities. Often, the cheap Chinese products are dubious in quality in contrast to those that Cameroonian entrepreneurs import and which the Cameroonian middle classes prefer. Obviously, the bad quality does not prevent people from buying. However, Cameroonians generally prefer good quality products even though they have to economise. Hence, a range of different qualities has emerged on the Cameroonian market and one product is often available in several qualities. Most traders talked of three qualities: first, the cheapest and lowest are usually imitated products; the second are medium quality for a medium price, often also imitated but from better materials; and the third are best quality and original brand names of good material and manufacture, which are often imported by Cameroonian traders themselves.

Scholarly literature on Chinese in Cameroon—and this is true for other African countries as well—does only rarely consider that African traders have quite successfully travelled to China to import goods for the local market, despite many obstacles and even before the majority of the Chinese migrants arrived. In the beginning, the importation and marketing of Asian products in Cameroon were made exclusively by a young generation of Cameroonian businesspeople who regularly travelled to Asian countries several times a year for this purpose. Cameroonian traders first went to Dubai (Pelican 2014), and when China opened its markets, many of them continued to China and travelled to Guanghzhou and later also to Yiwu. Some buy products in China and also other better-quality products in Dubai.

Those who travel to China are established entrepreneurs with capital to travel and buy substantial quantities of goods, often several containers a month. Those with less capital and warehouse space join with other traders to share a container. Other Cameroonians travel to China and establish themselves there as brokers and entrepreneurs, due to the lack of employment opportunities in their country (see Alpes 2011). They mediate between African traders and Chinese companies and factories. All these Cameroonians are not poor migrants but come from middle-class families. Most of them have advanced education and arrive with capital.

They struggle on two levels. First, they feel they do not get enough support from their government to carry out their business and have to pay higher taxes than Chinese traders; second they face the challenge to obtain a visa, which is granted for a very short time of two to four weeks only, during which they have to order products, visit trade fairs to update their knowledge of novelties, supervise the shipping, and undergo substantial paperwork for the export of the Chinese products and the import to Cameroon.

Despite the many challenges, obstacles, and the Chinese competition, many of these traders are successfully selling clothing, shoes, fashion, and other items because, as they say, Cameroonians know the local consumer preferences better than foreigners. But, our informants also observed that fewer Cameroonians travel to China as before because for many the journey is no longer very rewarding. The situation has rather reversed. Asian traders now come themselves to sell the products from Asian factories in the country. They tend to force Cameroonian economic entrepreneurs out of business, which upsets local merchants who are excluded from areas over which they previously held a monopoly. The Chinese traders not only import products from their countries of origin, but now also increasingly push into the local distribution networks to reach consumers and do wholesale, semi-wholesale, and even retail and street vending.

The situation is most complicated for those traders and entrepreneurs who survive from the production or sale of similar products than those that the Chinese have come to sell as they feel the Chinese intrude in their business and prevent them from making a living (see also examples in Ampiah and Naidu 2008; Bredeloup and Bertoncello 2006 for Senegal and Cap Verde; Rotberg 2008: 25). To this adds that Cameroonian traders are in competition also among themselves, and they have not created associations to defend their interests.

6.7 How Cameroonian Businesspeople Experience Chinese Competition

The opinion of Cameroonian traders about their Chinese colleagues depends on which type of trade they carry out. Those Cameroonian retailers who do not travel to Asia themselves but obtain their trade goods from Chinese shops tend to see the arrival of Chinese as more or less beneficial for their business opportunities, as the Chinese bring new products and the low prices help consumers with limited financial means to buy these goods from them. One trader in Yaounde explained: "Their arrival was appreciated because they have helped us a lot. Yes, I have to admit this. Their arrival has made life easy for all because the prices are affordable compared to the time when these products were not yet here. That's why we say that the white man is powerful, the white man works." A good example of how Cameroonians have successfully appropriated a Chinese product that has changed the lives of many are the motorbikes that serve as intra-city and inter-village taxis. Since the mid-2000s, even in small towns and villages, for example in Mamfe, motorbike taxis have largely replaced the car or bush taxis. As the motorbikes are affordable, many young people make a living as motorbike taxi drivers (for a study on the motorbike taxis in Douala, called *bendskin*, see Konings 2006).

Another trader from Douala gave a similar estimation: "The arrival of Asians in the market is a good thing; it bothers me individually; but it's good for the nation because if you're all alone you cannot do anything, you know even with 500 FCFA (about 0.75 Euros) you can have a good pair of shoes. That's fine. [...] If the Chinese were not there, how would people live? Life would have been too expensive. So we need these Chinese." Sometimes even the Chinese traders depend on Cameroonian entrepreneurs, as a phone seller in Douala observed: "I would say in the phone domain, when they [the Chinese] come here, they cannot do without us, they do not have a real shop [for phones] here. We are the ones supplying the market. When they arrive, they come to us to propose their products. And it is up to us to see at what price we sell in order to make some profit."

Other Cameroonian traders are much more critical and worried. They evaluate the presence of Asians in the Cameroonian market as a "loss of earnings." These entrepreneurs believe that Asians are masters in the art of unfair competition. Many of them assume that the breakthrough of Asian traders is facilitated by customs and tax reduction that the government offers to the newcomers.[11] An informant in Yaounde explained this: "If a Chinese sees me

[11] Such a behaviour of the political authorities is not new. Indeed, in the mid-1980s, Cameroonian businessmen accused the regime of Paul Biya of having "introduced the Indo-Pakistani wolf in sheepsted of the Cameroonian economy" (Geschiere and Konings 1993: 338, our translation).

with a shoe like this one that I bought at 12,000 FCFA, he will copy it and sell the fake version at 4,500 FCFA. You see, that it is already influencing the price level. And also, the Cameroonian government does not allow young Cameroonians to express themselves normally. This system allows Chinese to retail … [however] they ought to be limited to wholesale. When they leave the retail trade to young Cameroonians, they could still make it in business; they could buy products, sell and make a living."

Of still other traders, people say they "eat behind the Chinese," which means, they hide behind them to do business or behind whom Chinese hide and invest. There are indeed Cameroonian traders who have local Chinese partners or partners in Asia. These Cameroonian businesspeople exploit customs facilities enjoyed by Asian traders to make their own business. However, the majority of Cameroonian traders agree on the fact that they cannot imagine to work with Asian businesspeople because of their reluctance. Indeed, Cameroonian traders accuse their Asian colleagues of not being open and carrying out underground practices. Also, most Chinese refrain from cooperating and sharing their experience with Cameroonian traders who would be willing to work with them. A trader in Yaounde explains: "I cannot say that I have relationships with Chinese traders who buy from China and sell in Cameroon because they are people who do not really allow you to discover their business strategies because they are afraid you're going to copy them. So they don't give you any opportunity. […] Some will say they represent […] a Chinese company in Cameroon; so they work for the company and are not self-employed. So understanding them is complicated. When you ask them: 'When you go to China for New Year celebrations, where do you go then?' They tell you they leave for their village to rest. So, a Chinese does not easily disclose his secret. Especially, when he knows that you have the power and the capacity to rival him, he does not allow you to be able to discover his secret."

In short, Cameroonian and Chinese businesspeople find it difficult to collaborate. Cameroonians have created strategies to cope with the presence of Chinese traders. Their first strategy consists in avoiding selling the same items as the Asians because these generally have a substantial commercial capital, business networks, and the advantage to get the better prices at home in Asia, which gives them the freedom to sell at unbeatable prices. Hence, a businessman in Douala argued: "We are neither in collaboration because you cannot even approach them nor in conflict. We're trying to get along with what we have. There is a difference between what they sell and what we sell. The products that we offer to customers are different from theirs."

The second strategy is selling the same items as the Chinese at the same price as these, although it does not benefit the Cameroonian traders. However, it has the advantage of continuing with one's trading activities, as a trader in Yaounde explains: "With this competition, I avoid doing the same things as Chinese do. Since Chinese deal in substandard products, I try to deal in quality stuffs, no matter the cost. When I return from China, I take the time to retail with a very low profit margin given that the purchasing power of Cameroon has declined. I apply a margin that will allow me sell everything within three months. If unfortunately a Chinese charges lower than me for the same product, I lower mine to match his just to get rid of the product. [...] As soon as he comes with a big consignment, you are forced to sell at his prize, otherwise once customers are used to his prize, there is no way to make them buy at a higher prize. You know, the goods that are for sale, when you keep them for a long time they become perishable."

A third strategy is to praise the quality of one's own products, even if they are of the same quality than those of the Chinese, and insist that the latter are only imitations. Traders will also plead for the solidarity of their country people to buy with them and not with strangers and argue that they ought to develop Cameroon and that buying from Chinese or Asian shops is developing someone else's country. To this end, we found that some Cameroonian traders recruit youth or "tacklers" (called "appacheurs" in popular parlance) whose daily task is to guide or orientate customers to their shops against a percentage of the purchased product or a daily fixed amount of money.[12]

Traders were also worried about the increasing difficulties of obtaining visas for business travels to China. One of them, a Douala-based informant, even suspected that their Chinese counterparts used their relations at the Chinese embassy to prevent them from obtaining a visa to travel freely to China. He complained: "I think that since last year or the year before last, getting a visa for China has become difficult because it seems Chinese traders had complained to their embassy arguing that

[12] Obviously, Chinese traders carefully observe this game to develop their own strategy. Further studies need to be carried out on the "appacheurs" of both groups.

Cameroonians had a very important purchasing power and that they were selling the same things as the latter and so they were not making any profit; it may be a policy to monopolise the Chinese market sectors."

Many Cameroonian businesspeople who travel to Asia have observed that it becomes less profitable to make the journey, as they feel that the Chinese do not respect the established Cameroonian market order and additionally, profit from having direct contacts to factories in China where they get better prices. A trader in Douala complained: "A Chinese who has all the advantages [of getting cheap goods in China] will wholesale a shoe at five thousand and retail the same shoe at five thousand as well, whereas a Cameroonian retailer has to buy the shoe at five thousand and resells it a higher price to earn something." This situation diminishes traders' interest for business with Asia and especially with China.

Hence, another trader in Yaounde explained: "It will lead to a situation whereby petty businessmen with small turnovers will no longer be able to survive. The proof is that usually you start the year with ten but by the end of the year, only five or less are still in business. The majority buys from Chinese and from a few traders who are located in Douala Central Market. In the Douala Central Market, there are not yet many Chinese; there are mostly Cameroonians. But Akwa is full of Chinese. They are the new masters of Akwa. They have no rival there." The great majority of Cameroonian businesspeople are worried by the growing Asian presence in the commercial sector and their business practices. They also feel that they are left alone by their government. They argue that other earlier foreign diasporas such as the Lebanese and Greek did not create such a competition but followed the unwritten local trade regulations.

Consequently, businesspeople proposed a number of recommendations: first, Asian traders should only be allowed to do wholesale which would allow retailers to continue to make a living from trade. Second, the obtention of visas should be facilitated and the costs reduced, but for this, the trade agreements would need to be revised and Cameroonians should be allowed to obtain residence permits in China. At least they should be able to have the same rights in China as Chinese have in Cameroon. Third, there should be equal treatment in terms of customs duty, or better, nationals should have advantageous treatment, as is the case for Chinese in China. Fourth, a functioning quality control is needed that guarantees the good quality of those products that Asians sell to African consumers. Five, there should be technology and knowledge transfer and training for Cameroonians. Six, foreigners, especially Asians, should not be treated more favourably than Cameroonians in order not to weaken the incipient national economic power of its citizens. Seven, there should be firm controls to eliminate abuses of power at customs and tax collections.

Altogether, however, many Cameroonian businesspeople readily acknowledged the beneficial aspects of the Sino-Cameroonian relations and that the availability of their products had improved the living conditions of many people. One trader in Yaounde observed that "today, it is practically difficult to see a child who goes to school barefoot. This alone is already something." Some businesspeople even suggested that rather the importation of European and American products should be limited, which would allow Cameroon to open exclusively to Asia because Asia's products were affordable for everybody. They emphasised that the Chinese brought development and democratised consumption of goods. And nowadays, some brand new Chinese vehicles are of almost the same price or even cheaper than old imported vehicles from Europe.

Nevertheless, a number of Cameroonian businesspeople also developed new strategies and opened up alternative opportunities to the import of commodities from other African countries such as South Africa, West African countries or the Maghreb, or they redirect their trade to Europe and North America. There they look for high-quality and second-hand goods such as shoes, textiles, indoor and outdoor clothing, cosmetics, food and health products. Middle-class consumers highlight the quality of these products and often mock themselves about those who buy from Asians. Hence, the Cameroonian commercial landscape is highly dynamic and the Chinese presence also inspires Cameroonians to excel in inventiveness.

6.8 The Role of Migrant Diasporas for Their Home Societies

The Chinese presence is not only beneficial and challenging for Cameroonians but also more beneficial for China and its migrants' home communities. Diasporas of the past have often been perceived as lost for their societies of origin, whereas scholars increasingly note that many contemporary diasporas are veritable resources for their home societies. Migrants keep contact and contribute to development by sending remittances, transferring knowledge, creating investment, and enabling relatives to move on (Akyeampong 2000; Kernen 2007; Mercer et al. 2008; Peil 1995; Rapoport 2005). This is also true for the Chinese diaspora in Cameroon.

The larger part of the gains that the Chinese diaspora generates in Cameroon with their enterprises does not become productive for Cameroon but is almost immediately transferred to Chinese banks or via money transfer institutions to China. The Chinese (and the Indian) diasporas are among the largest diasporas, and China is one of the countries that receives the largest amounts of remittances worldwide. Indeed, Jérôme Elie, Marylène Lieber, and Christine Lutringer (2011) argue that the reason why India and China are no longer considered to be developing countries is to a large part due to their numerous diasporas and the huge amounts of remittances they regularly send back home. As far as African diasporas are concerned, scholars tend to observe that the amounts of remittances are considerable as well but have not yet created development to the same extent than in China or India.

Chinese private activities do not only solve China's problem of unemployment to a certain extent, but, as Pokam (2015: 47–68) notes, the Chinese diaspora is highly instrumentalised as a resource by its government. Additionally, the diaspora profits from bilateral agreements of China and the favourable conditions that the Chinese government negotiates with the host societies for opening up new territories and creating enterprises. The Chinese government keeps a strong grip on its growing global diasporic population that is increasingly well organised and allows it to gradually gain soft power influence. More generally, the global presence of the Chinese diaspora allows China to gain access to all continents. According to Pokam, between 1978 and 2000, the Chinese government made 360 laws that concern the overseas Chinese and their duties to contribute to the development of their home country. It even encourages its diaspora to adopt the nationality of the host society to integrate itself to be better able to found enterprises and act successfully (Pokam 2015: 51, 53). Pokam (2015: 62) argues moreover that the presence of the Chinese diaspora with its numerous ventures not only is popular and entrepreneurial but also represents a political strategy.

Migrants also tend to appropriate the new space in the host country by creating structures in the style of their home country. When Chinese construct new buildings, they include elements of Chinese architectural style; they introduce new types of food, decorate their places with red lampions, place Chinese letters at their company buildings and shops, and carry out festivities in public. They create entire commercial zones that transform the image of a place to be recognisable as Chinese. These urban enclaves have a strong concentration of the Chinese population and assemble living quarters, shops, restaurants, and clinics for CTM. Those markers of territorial appropriation help them diminish the risk of dissolving their identity and be assimilated into the host country. The appropriation of space into zones such as China towns inscribes itself into a collective project that ties the Chinese together in clan and family solidarity. More generally, Chinese rely in their endeavour upon strong bonds of mutual financial help from local compatriots and the global diaspora (see Bruneau 2010; E. Esoh 2005; Ma Mung 2000; Michel and Beuret 2008; Plate 2005).

The consolidation of the Chinese diaspora in different host countries and the contribution of their activities to the development of their home country have been described as globalisation from below in a positive way as a form of empowerment. But how does the same issue present itself in the case of Africans in China? When African activities are described as globalisation from below, they are rather associated with a shadow economy, illegal activities, and informality (Mathews et al. 2012). In recent years, as our research shows, Cameroonians have experienced increasing complications when they want to obtain visas for China and if they are successful, the duration of their visas is only two to four weeks. Yet, more often more time is needed for placing orders and purchase commodities in China. Cameroonians feel disadvantaged in comparison to Chinese traders who can stay in the country for more than a year without complications.

To a much greater extent than Chinese in Cameroon, Cameroonians who wish to do business in China have to follow specific regulations and it is usually difficult to obtain residence permits, even if they are married to a local partner in China. Africans are a considerable clientele for Chinese commodities in China itself. They are addressed in trade fairs with advertisements and commodities specifically produced for African markets. Entire halls of fairs have names to attract foreign customers. Already in China, Africans help China a lot to sell their products as brokers and find a market for Chinese goods. As African migrants cannot return home empty-handed, they often have no choice but to stay on without valid documents and try to survive with brokering jobs.

In Cameroon, Chinese are encouraged to open businesses, whereas for Cameroonians it is very difficult to do this in China; they cannot open businesses except they have substantial amounts of capital or do this under the name of a local business partner. Others have invested in China through marriage relationships but face insecurity due to their residence and property status.[13] The observation that China makes it more and more complicated for Africans to obtain visas and engage in successful trade in China creates the impression that China does not wish to see the African diaspora as a resource for their country's development; it is less interested to have Africans coming to China for business but only for study and visits as consumers (see Röschenthaler 2016 for a similar study on Cameroonians in Malaysia).

In contrast, the successful settlement of Chinese migrants in Africa is encouraged by the backing of Chinese government that has negotiated favourable conditions for its diaspora in the host country. Such helpful negotiations are lacking in the case of Cameroonians in China. Cameroonians are not treated in the same encouraging way as Chinese in Cameroon, due to different governmental policies, which do not provide the two diaspora groups with the same opportunities. This provides a picture of a quite unequal relationship.

Different from China that sees Africans as consumers, in Cameroon there are no signs that attract Chinese to African shops. Cameroonians complained that the Chinese would not come to buy anything from them; that the Chinese would stick together, speak their own language, rely strongly on family networks, rent shops in the same building, support only each other and refuse to mix with Cameroonians, except for

[13] There is a growing number of scholarly studies on the situation of Africans in China, especially in Guangzhou and in Yiwu; for an overview on this literature, see Cissé (2015), Marfaing and Thiel (2015), and other articles in the special issues of *The Journal of Pan African Studies* 7, 10, 2015, edited by Adams Bodomo.

business (Pokam noticed the same, 2015: 76). Cameroonians complained that Chinese would even grow and produce their own food for daily consumption themselves so that the local people could earn nothing from these guests; instead, they would try to outdo them and deprive them of their long-established businesses.

The beneficial aspects of the Chinese presence in Cameroon and the positive rhetoric of brotherly cooperation that underline China's long-term endeavour in the country (Pokam 2015: 62–69) are countervailed by an increasing economic inequality. China and Cameroon have the same objective when they wish to develop their countries and economies, but the question is whether the same recipe will be efficacious for realising the objectives of both countries. China's presence makes the Cameroonian economy dependent on Chinese ventures (as earlier on Western development aid) as it does not create enough employment and weakens local industries. Instead, Cameroon-owned enterprises ought to be strengthened. Seen from this perspective, Chinese activities are more beneficial for China than for Cameroon as China is above all in a situation of geopolitical competition between Washington and Brussels and needs the support of African countries; hence, China's activities in Africa form part of an attempt to enlarge its global influence sphere more generally both from above and from below.

6.9 Conclusions

China's engagement in Cameroon has achieved substantial development in infrastructure, health, and cultural institutions with much less money than traditional development aid. Compared to traditional donors, the conditions under which these projects have been carried out are favourable for African countries and also ensure that China's own economy is profiting. Loans are provided without much interest but do not flow freely and have to be managed by the Chinese Exim bank. As such, they are very efficient and cannot be misused. Probably, Rotberg (2008: 1) is right in noting that "China hardly wants to colonise, but it has immense mercantilist ambitions." China needs Africa's raw materials to feed its industries and ultimately also America's substantial demand for consumer goods. China does not need to conquer Africa with military means, but if the number of Chinese migrants continues to grow and their economic authority increases then it will be of no surprise that local economic actors become alarmed. They have the impression that the presence of Chinese migrants might represent a form of economic colonisation despite the positive developments and affordable consumer goods that arrived with the Chinese presence.

One challenge is that there are a lot more promises that need to be kept and there is a blind spot in the calculation of the trade balance when environmental damages that future generations will have to face are not added to the costs of exploitation. Another complication is that governments and their people do not necessarily have the same opinion, as opinions and interests are heterogeneous in a society. Governments need to redistribute their gains from bilateral cooperation with their populations in a beneficial and sustainable manner. It is not enough that infrastructures are developed, a few jobs created, and cheap consumer goods made available when most Chinese enterprises are actually very reluctant to employ Cameroonians, when several domestic economic sectors are weakened by Chinese competition, which is supported by negotiations with the host government. Governments might have different interests than civil society organisations and other interest groups that rather ought to join efforts to develop the country. Chinese in Cameroon and Cameroonians in China should be treated on an equal basis and at least enjoy similar governmental encouragement.

Cooperation with China has different outcomes in different countries, due to diverse histories and colonial legacies but also due to the way governments negotiate favourable policies. Some negotiate with China for a balanced participation and secure their own economy, others, such as Cameroon, neglect this part because they fear the empowerment of their local entrepreneurial classes and rather support foreign enterprise, investment, and banks. The ongoing "Chinarisation" of Cameroon's sociocultural and local economy, through huge capital investment in so-called developmental big ambitious projects and the insidious imposition of Chinese culture (teaching of Chinese language in schools and research institutes), seems to be a considerable risk for the future of the country. In the long run, the neglect of the domestic economy, of local entrepreneurship and trade, might create a dangerous potential for conflict and revolts, so that it is highly recommendable that governments enforce their legal system in favour of their citizens and develop measures of care for local economic needs that contribute to support local enterprise and eventually an independent domestic economy.

References

AFRODAD. (2011). *Mapping Chinese development assistance in Africa: An analysis of the experiences of Cameroon*. Causeway/Harare: African Forum and Network on Debt and Development.

Akyeampong, E. (2000). Africans in the diaspora: The diaspora in Africa. *African Affairs, 99*, 183–215.

Alden, C. (2007). *China in Africa*. London: Zed Books.

Alpes, M. (2011). Bushfalling: How young Cameroonians dare to migrate. PhD Dissertation, Amsterdam University. http://dare.uva.nl/document/342146

Amin, J. (2015). Sino-Cameroon relations: A foreign policy of pragmatism. *African Studies Review, 58*(3), 171–198.

Ampiah, K., & Naidu, S. (Eds.). (2008). *Crouching tiger, hidden drangon*. Scotsville: University of KwaZulu-Natal Press.

Anon. (2007, July 12). Douala: Les commerçants chinois font grève. *Mutations*. Online edition. http://www.cameroun-info.net/stories/0,19777. Accessed 10 Dec 2015.

Assemblée Nationale du Cameroun. (1975). Protocole d'accord entre le gouvernement de la République Unie du Cameroun et de la République Populaire de Chine relatif à l'envoi par la Chine d'une équipe médicale au Cameroun, Yaounde.

Ateba Eyene, Charles. 2010. La pénétration de la Chine et les espoirs de la rupture du pacte colonial avec l'occident. Yaounde: Staint-Paul.

Ateba Eyene, C. (2012). *Émergence du Cameroun a l'horizon 2035: L'apport de la Chine. La cooperation de développement, ses succès et ses craintes*. Yaounde: Editions Saint-Paul.

Bredeloup, S., & Bertoncello, B. (2006). La migration chinoise en Afrique: Accélérateur du développement ou "sanglot de l'homme noir". *Afrique Contemporaine, 2*(218), 199–224.

Brautigam, D. (2008). China's foreign aid in Africa: What do we know? In R. Rotberg (Ed.), *China into Africa: Aid trade and influence* (pp. 197–216). Washington, DC: Brookings Institution Press.

Broadman, H. (2007). *Africa's silk road: China's and India's new economies frontier*. Washington, DC: World Bank.

Bruneau, M. (2010). Diasporas, transnational spaces and communities. In R. Bauböck & T. Faist (Eds.), *Diaspora and transnationalism: concepts, theories and methods* (pp. 35–49). Amsterdam: Amsterdam University Press.

Candelise, L. (2011). La medicine chinoise au delà des frontiers chinoises. La confrontation de ses pratiques avec la médecine conventionnelle en France et en Italie. *In Perspectives Chinoises, 3*, 44–52.

Chinese Foreign Ministry. (2006). Cameroon. http://www.china.org.cn/english/features/focac/183577.htm. Accessed 16 Dec 2015.

Cissé, D. (2015). African traders in Yiwu: Their trade networks and their role in the distribution of 'Made in China' products in Africa. *The Journal of Pan African Studies, 7*(10), 44–64.

Deli, T. T. (2011). Les migrants et les commerçants camerounais à Doubaï : une contribution à l'anthropologie de la migration. PhD Thesis, Université de Yaoundé I.

Elie, J., Lieber, M., & Lutringer, C. (2011). Migration et développement: les politiques de la Chine et de l'Inde à l'égard de leurs communautés d'outremer. *Revue international de politique de développement, 2*, 215–230.

Esoh, E. (2005). 'L'immigration en Afrique noire dans le contexte de la mondialisation. www.lestamp.com/.../publication.esoh.htm. Accessed 20 Dec 2015.

Etian, E.-É. (2011). *Vingt ans d'expérience en Chine Un Africain raconte*. Paris: l'Harmattan.

Fleischer, A. (2012). *Migration, marriage and the law: Making families among Cameroonian "Bush Fallers" in Germany*. Berlin: Regiospectra Verlag.

Geschiere, P., & Konings, P. (1993). *Itinéraires d'accumulation au Cameroon*. Paris: Karthala.

Geschiere, Peter and Francis Nyamnjoh. 2000. Capitalism and Autochthony: The seasaw of Mobility and Belonging. *Public Culture 12*, 2: 423-452.

Gweth, G. (2011, January 24). La stratégie de puissance chinoise en Afrique vue du Cameroun. *Geostrategies*. http://archives-lepost.huffingtonpost.fr/article/2011/01/24/2381921_la-strategie-de-puissance-chinoise-en-afrique-vue-du-cameroun.html

Ikhuoria, E. (2010). The impact of Chinese imports on Nigerian traders. In A. Harneit-Sievers, S. Marks, & S. Naidu (Eds.), *Chinese and African perspectives on China in Africa* (pp. 128–138). Kampala: Pambazuka Press.

Kamau, P. (2010). China's impact on Kenya's clothing industry. In A. Harneit-Sievers, S. Marks, & S. Naidu (Eds.), *Chinese and African perspectives on China in Africa* (pp. 108–127). Kampala: Pambazuka Press.

Kernen, A. (2007). Les strategies Chinoises en Afrique: Du pétrole aux bassines en plastique. *Politique Africaine, 105*, 163–180.

Khan Mohammad, G. (2014). The Chinese presence in Burkina Faso: A Sino-African cooperation from below. *Journal of Current Chinese Affairs, 1*, 71–101.

Konings, P. (2006). Bendskin drivers in Douala's new bell neighbourhood: Masters of the road and the city. In P. Konings & D. Foeken (Eds.), *Crisis and creativity: Exploring the wealth of the African neighbourhood* (pp. 46–65). Leiden: Brill.

Konings, P. (2011). *The politics of neoliberal reforms in Africa: State and civil society in Cameroon*. Bamenda: Langaa.

Li, A. (2012). *A history of overseas Chinese in Africa to 1911*. New York: Diasporic Africa Press.

Li, A. (2013). China's Africa policy and the Chinese immigrants in Africa. In C. Tan (Ed.), *Routledge handbook of the Chinese diaspora* (pp. 59–70). London: Routledge.

Ma Mung, E. (2000). *La diaspora chinoise: Géographie d'une migration*. Paris: Ophtys.

Marfaing, L., & Thiel, A. (2015). Networks, spheres of influence and the mediation of opportunity: The case of West African trade agents in China. *The Journal of Pan African Studies, 7*(10), 65–84.

Mathews, G., Ribeiro, G. L., & Vega, C. A. (2012). *Globalization from below: The Worlds other economy*. London: Routledge.

Mbori, L. (2005). 'Chinese doughnuts producers perturb Bamileke traders'. *The Cameroon Post* 25 July. http://allafrica.com/stories/200507260036.html. Accessed 20 Dec 2015.

Medeiros, E. (2009). China's foreign policy actions. In *China's International behavior: Activism, opportunism, and diversification*. Santa Monica: Rand Cooperation.

Mercer, C., Page, B., & Evans, M. (2008). *Development and the African Diaspora: Place and the politics of home*. London/New York: Zed Books.

Michel, S., & Beuret, M. (2008). *La Chinafrique: Pékin à la conquête du continent noir*. Paris: Grasset.

MINMAP (Ministère des Marchés Publics). (2015). 'Résultats de l'avis général d'appel à manifestation d'intérêt en vue de la réalisation du Plan d'urgence triennal', *Cameroon Tribune* 3 June.

Monteillet, N. (2010). L'africanisation de la médecine chinoise à Yaoundé. In L. Ludovic (Ed.), *Le pluralisme médical en Afrique* (pp. 223–237). Yaounde: PUCAC.

Ndjio, B. (2009). Shanghai beauties and African desires: Migration, trade and Chinese prostitution in Cameroon. *European Journal of Development Research, 21*(4), 606–621.

Ndjio, B. (2014). "Magic body" and "cursed sex": Chinese sex workers as bitch-witches in Cameroon. *African Affairs, 113*(452), 370–386.

Peil, M. (1995). Ghanaians abroad. *African Affairs, 94*, 345–367.
Pelican, M. (2014). Urban lifeworlds of Cameroonian migrants in Dubai. *Urban Anthropology, 23*(1–3), 255–309.
Plate, R. (2005). *Coopération economique et commerciale Chine-Cameroun: état des lieux* Yaoundé: Friedrich Ebert Stiftung. http://library.fes.de/pdf-files/bueros/kamerun/05225.pdf
Pokam, H. d. P. (2015). *Migration chinoise et développement au Cameroun*. Paris: l'Harmattan.
Rapoport, H. (2005). 'The economics of migrants' remittances', *Institute for the Study of Labour* Bonn.
Republic of Cameroon. (1990). Law no. 90/031 of 10 August 1990, regulating commercial activity in Cameroon, Yaounde: Présidence de la République.
Republic of Cameroun. (1998). Law no. 98/013 of 14 July 1998, relating to competition Yaounde: Présidence de la République.
Röschenthaler, U. (2016). *Asian-African Encounters*. In constant search for money to survive: African youths in Malaysia. In Arndt Graf and Azirah Hashim (Ed.), Amsterdam: Amsterdam University Press.
Rotberg, R. (2008). China's quest for resources, opportunities and influence in Africa. In R. Rotberg (Ed.), *China into Africa: Aid trade and influence* (pp. 1–20). Washington, DC: Brookings Institution Press.
Sautman, B. (2006). Friends and interests: China's distinctive links with Africa (Working paper 12). Hong Kong: Center on China's Transnational Relation. http://www.cctr.ust.hk/materials/working_papers/WorkingPaper12.pdf
Sinou, D. (1985). *Les relations economiques sino-camerounaises (1960–1984)*. Yaounde: IRIC.
Takougang, J., & Krieger, M. (1998). *African state and society in the 1990s: Cameroon's political crossroads*. Boulder: Westview Press.
Tedié, J. (2014). *Coopération Chine-Afrique. Inpact sur les infrastructures du Cameroun*. Paris: l'Harmattan.
US Department of State 2013. (2013). Investment climate statement, report of April 2013. http://www.state.gov/e/eb/rls/othr/ics/2013/204615.htm. Accessed 20 Dec 2015.
Wassouni, F. (2010). La médicine chinoise au Cameroun: Essai d'analyse historique (1975–2009). In L. Lado (Ed.), *Le pluralisme médical en Afrique* (pp. 223–237). Yaounde: PUCAC.

7

The Economic Determinants of Chinese Foreign Direct Investment in Egypt

Hany Elshamy

7.1 Introduction

Foreign direct investment (FDI) is investment by a multinational corporation (MNC), based in a 'source' country, in a subsidiary or affiliate located in a foreign 'host' country. FDI, as a key element of globalisation and of the world economy, is a driver of employment, technological progress, and productivity growth. It plays an important role of filling the development, foreign exchange, investment, and tax revenue gaps in developing countries (Anyanwu 2012).

By the end of the twentieth century, FDI had effectively replaced trade as a driver of economic growth in less developed and emerging economies. In 2002, there were an estimated 65,000 MNCs with about 850,000 worldwide affiliates employing about 54 million employees, a rise of 141 per cent over the 1990 employment figure for MNCs (UNCTAD 2002).

H. Elshamy (✉)
Tanta University, Cairo, Egypt
e-mail: ElShamyhany@hotmail.com

Y. C. Kim (ed.), *China and Africa*, The Palgrave Macmillan Asian Business Series, DOI 10.1007/978-3-319-47030-6_7

Over the same period, the stock of outward FDI increased from 1 trillion dollars to 6.6 trillion dollars, and MNCs accounted for about 10 per cent of the world's GDP and about 33 per cent of the world's exports (Bhaumik and Gelb 2005).

The proportion of the capital formation for developing countries which were financed by FDI rose from 4.7 per cent in 1970 to 13.8 per cent in 2006 (Foryth et al. 2009). The net inflows of FDI in Egypt had increased by 95 per cent from 440.1 to 858.2 million dollars during the second quarter of the fiscal year 2011/2012 compared to the same period the previous year, according to the monthly report by the Central Bank of Egypt.

The European Union (EU) investments are still on top of the FDI list, hitting 656 million dollars, up by 30 per cent during the second quarter of the current fiscal year, in accordance with the report. Britain comes first among the EU states with 335.4-million-dollar investments being pumped into the Egyptian market. Belgium, France, and Greece come next in terms of investment inflows. Arab investment inflow rose by 23.3 per cent from 314.6 million dollars to 362.1 million dollars.

The Chinese FDI in Egypt is not as much as the other counties, despite the fact that it has increased from 6922.457 million dollars (constant prices 2000 = 100) in 1985 to 95,877.79 million dollars (constant prices 2000 = 100) in 2012 (GAFI 2012). The organisation of this chapter is as follows: Sect. 7.2 presents some literature on FDI theories. The methodology is explained in Sect. 7.3. The results are presented in Sects. 7.4, and 7.5 concludes.

7.2 Literature Review

This section presents a brief review of a set of representative studies based on competing theories of FDI.

7.2.1 The Classic Theory of FDI

Drawing an analogy with the pure theory of trade, the classic theory of international capital flow argues that if the rate of return on capital under autarchy varies across countries, the opening up of trade in capital will lead to a flow of capital from countries with lower returns to those with higher returns (Shamsuddin 1994). Thus, FDI is a function of international differences in the rates of return on capital. The existing empirical work does not provide any conclusive evidence for this hypothesis. Analysing manufacturing FDI from the UK and Canada into the USA during 1950–1971, Blais (1975) found empirical support for the differential-rate-of-return hypothesis. Contrary to the finding of Blais (1975) and Weintraubus (1967), Walia (1976) observed no significant relationship between the US capital flow and the relative rates of return.

7.2.2 Portfolio Theory

The classic theory of FDI cannot explain why we observe simultaneous inflows and outflows of FDI in many countries. Furthermore, it focuses only on the rate of return, ignoring the risk factor associated with the investment project. The later factor has been captured by the portfolio theory (Shamsuddin 1994). Grubel (1968) is the first to apply this theory in the context of international capital movement. This theory suggests that if the rates of return on various investment projects across countries have a less than perfect correlation, a firm can reduce its overall risk exposure by diversifying its investment internationally.

This theory, however, has been criticised for the fact that in a perfect capital market, firms need not diversify their portfolio internationally to reduce risk for their shareholders because individual investors can do so by directly diversifying their individual portfolios. Thus, under the assumption of perfect competition, the portfolio approach cannot explain international capital flow.

7.2.3 Market Size Hypothesis

This hypothesis postulates that FDI is a positive function of the market size of the host country. The market size is usually measured by the GDP of the host country. Most empirical studies support the market size hypothesis. Reuber et al. (1973) observed that flows of per capita FDI into the less developed countries (LDCs) were positively correlated with their GDP. Edwards (1991) investigated the distribution of the Organisation for Economic Co-operation and Development (OECD) FDI across 58 LDCs for the period 1971–1981.

They found that the higher the real GDP of a country, the larger was its share in the total OECD FDI in the LDCs. It is worth noting that the size of the market in the host country is likely to influence the FDI undertaken to produce importables rather than exportables. Recent work points to the rise of offensive market-seeking motives driving Chinese multinational enterprises (Buckley et al. 2007) and posits that this activity may increasingly be directed towards large markets.

7.2.4 Other Determinants of FDI

Other determinants of FDI include location-specific advantages, economic and political stability, and the debt experience of the host country. The supply of cheap labour in developing countries has been recognised in the literature as an important determinant of FDI. Riedel (1975) observed that relatively lower wage costs have been one of the major determinants of the export-oriented FDI in Taiwan. Furthermore, the location aspect of the mainstream or general theory, as encapsulated in Dunning's eclectic paradigm, suggests three primary motivations (Dunning 1977, 1993):

A. foreign-market-seeking FDI;
B. efficiency (cost reduction)-seeking FDI;
C. resource-seeking FDI (including a subset that is known as strategic-asset-seeking FDI)

it is very rare to find a study which investigated the determinants of the Chinese FDI in Egypt. However, Buckley et al. (2007) investigated the determinants of the Chinese outward direct investment (ODI). They found the Chinese ODI to be associated with higher levels of political risk in the host country. Moreover, Chinese ODI had fundamental motives to be associated with the host country's market size and the host's natural resource endowments.

7.3 Methodology

In this part, I will test some hypotheses which have been presented in Sect. 7.2. I can summarise theses hypotheses as follows:

A. Hypothesis l: Is Chinese FDI in Egypt associated positively with the Egyptian market size?
B. Hypothesis 2: Is Chinese FDI in Egypt associated positively with the Egyptian endowments of natural resources?
C. Hypothesis 3: Is Chinese FDI in Egypt associated positively with the Egyptian endowments of ownership advantages?
D. Hypothesis 4: Is Chinese FDI in Egypt associated negatively with the Egyptian inflation rates?
E. Hypothesis 5: Is Chinese FDI in Egypt associated negatively with rising levels of political and economic risk in Egypt?
F. Hypothesis 6: Is Chinese FDI in Egypt associated positively with the Liberalisation of the Chinese FDI policy in 1992?

To test these hypotheses, I formulated an econometrics model. The model used in this study is adapted from Buckley et al. (2007) model. This model suggests the following log-linear model:

$$\text{LFDI} = \alpha + \beta_1\text{LGDP} + \beta_2\text{LORE} + \beta_3\text{LPATENT} + \beta_4\text{LINF} + \beta_5\text{LPOL} + \beta_6\text{D92} + \varepsilon_t \quad (1)$$

This chapter depends on annual data collected from the World Bank and the General Authority for Investment and Free Zones Information (GAFI) and Decision Support Division for the period 1985–2011.

The data has been transformed into natural logarithms as we expect non-linear ties in the relationships on the basis of theory and previous empirical work. Table 7.1 explains these variables.

Table 7.1 The determinants of Chinese FDI in Egypt

Variable	Description	Expected sign	Type of determinants
LGDP	GDP per capita in Egypt	+	Market seeking
LORE	The ratio of ore and metal exports to merchandise exports of Egypt	+	Resource seeking
LPATENT	Total (resident plus non-resident) annual patent registrations in Egypt	+	Strategic asset seeking
LINF	Annual Inflation Rate in Egypt	–	Cost seeking
LPOL	Egypt's political risk rating (higher values indicate greater stability)	+	Stability and safety seeking
D92	Influence of Deng's South China tour (1992). It is a dummy variable which takes value 1 since year 1992 and 0 before year 1992	+	Policy liberalisation in China

7.4 Empirical Results

First, I conducted the co-integration analysis. I use this technique as it is very suitable to the data as the original values of the variables are not stationary, so I made unit root tests, and I found that some variables are stationary at the first difference, so I considered it to be suitable to use the co-integration analysis. Table 7.2 shows the results of the Augmented Dickey–Fuller (ADF) test on the first difference based upon the Mackinnon *P* values at various lag lengths. The preferred lag length based upon the Akaike information criterion indicates that co-integration is generally accepted.

Table 7.2 shows the estimation results using co-integration analysis. I find that Egyptian market characteristics (measured by the size of economy, LGDP), natural resource endowments (LORE), asset-seeking FDI (LPATENT), inflation rates in Egypt (INF), political risk (LPOL), and policy liberalisation (D92) are all significant and correctly signed. These findings support all the hypotheses. I find that Egyptian market size (LGDP) has a positive influence on Chinese FDI in Egypt, with a 1 per cent rise in the variable increasing Chinese FDI by 0.26 per cent. This indicates that market seeking was a key motive for Chinese FDI in the period under study (Hypothesis l). This result is supported by Buckley et al. (2007).

Table 7.2 Co-integration analysis

Dependent variable (LFDI)	Coefficients	Significant
Independent variables		
Constant	−42.12	*
LGDP	0.257	***
LORE	0.162	**
LPATENT	0.092	*
LINF	−0.231	***
LPOL	2.123	**
D92	0.532	***
CDRW	1.35	
ADF tests	Favoured lag length = 2	Favoured lag length = 2
ADF(0)	0.005	0.004
ADF(1)	0.063	0.024
ADF(2)	0.065	0.007
ADF(3)	0.072	0.005

ADF figures show the Mackinnon approx *P*-value
*** = significant at 1 %; ** = significant at 5 %; * = significant at 10 %

The policy liberalisation variable (D92) is also positive and significant. This supports the argument that the qualitative changes in Chinese policy that took place in 1992, the year of Deng Xiaoping's visit to the southern provinces, did mark a significant step towards liberalisation in a number of FDI-related areas, and positively influenced the value of approved Chinese FDI for that year (Hypothesis 6). This results confirmed by Buckley et al. (2007) as he argues that policy changes freed Chinese firms to invest abroad for reasons other than the promotion of exports; that is, they were able to service foreign markets directly.

Table 7.3 shows the ECM. This technique is a short-run analysis, so I use it to be sure that the co-integration analysis (long run analysis) results are constant with these short-run analysis results. The results are in synthesis with the co-integration results. Most importantly of course, the lagged error is negative and significant. This confirms the acceptance of the long-run relationship, which is further validated given there are no problems with any of the diagnostic tests presented (the AR(1) test for first order residual autocorrelation, the ARCH(1) test for autoregressive conditional heteroscedasticity and the Jarque-Beta test for normality).

Table 7.3 Error correction mechanism (ECM)

Dependent variable (LFDI)	Coefficients	Significant
Independent variables		
Constant	−38.11	*
LGDP	0.221	**
LORE	0.154	**
LPATENT	0.072	***
LINF	−0.211	**
LPOL	1.85	**
D92	0.421	***
Lagged error	−0.452	***
No. of observation	27	
F-statistics	8.33	***
Adjusted R^2	0.76	
DW	2.15	
AR(1)	1.42	
ARCH(1)	1.82	
Normality	2.12	

*** = significant at 1 %; ** = significant at 5 %; * = significant at 10 %

7.5 Conclusions

This chapter empirically analyses the determinants of the Chinese FDI in Egypt by estimating a single model equation which employs long-run co-integration analysis and short-run analysis (ECM). These analyses use annual data from 1985 to 2011. I find a conventional result for market size. I infer from the significant role played by the Egyptian natural resource endowments that the institutional environment has strongly shaped Chinese FDI, leading to significant natural resources-seeking FDI. I also find that policy liberalisation in China has had a positive influence in stimulating Chinese FDI in Egypt.

There are implications of this research for our understanding of the Chinese FDI strategies of firms from other emerging markets, such as Egypt. Firstly, state direction over firms (whether formal or informal) is likely to generate a signature in the locational pattern of outward investment that would not be predicted by the general theory of FDI, which assumes that firms are profit maximisers. Secondly, liberalisation is a very powerful instrument for emerging economies. According to the results of this chapter, improving the availability of sufficiently qualified labour, focusing on the establishment of sound institutions, and opening up to international trade will make Egypt's locational characteristics more favourable to potential investors.

With respect to further work, an issue requiring investigation, possibly of a qualitative nature, is whether or not and how Chinese investors are influenced (as are industrialised country firms) by concerns of due diligence, risk evaluation, and ethical considerations in Egypt. Similarly, how patterns of FDI are affected by formal and informal political links between China and Egypt.

References

Anyanwu, J. (2012). Why does foreign direct investment go where it goes?: New evidence from African Countries. *Analyze of Economics and Finance, 13-2*, 425–462.

Bhaumik and Gelb (2005) Bhaumik, S.K., and S. Gelb. 2005. "Determinants of Entry Mode Choice of MNCs in Emerging Markets: Evidence from South Africa and Egypt." Emerging Markets Finance and Trade 41, no. 2 (March–April): 5–24.

Blais (1975) Blais, Jeffrey P. (1975) A Theoretical and Empirical Investigation of Canadian and British Direct Foreign Investment in Manufacturing in the United States. Ph.D. Thesis, University of Pittsburgh.

Buckley, P., et al. (2007). The determinants of Chinese outward foreign direct investment. *Journal of International Business Studies, 38*(4), 499–518.

Dunning, 1977 Dunning, J.H. (1977) 'Trade, Location of Economic Activity and the MNE: A Search for an Eclectic Approach', in B. Ohlin, P.O. Hesselborna nd P.M. Wijkmon(eds.) TheI nternational Location of Economic Activity, Macmillan: London, pp: 395–418.

Dunning, J. (1993). *Multinational enterprises and the global economy.* Wokingham: Addison-Wesley.

Edwards, S. (1991). Capital flows, foreign direct investment, and debt- equity swaps in developing countries. In H. Siebert (Ed.), *Capital flows in the World Economy: Symposium. Tubingen: Institute fur Weltwirtschaft an der Universitat Kiel.*

Forsyth, D. et al. (2009). *Development economics.* McGraw-Hill.

Grubel, H. (1968). Internationally diversified portfolios. welfare gains and capital flows. *The American Economic Review, 58*, 1299–1314. London

Reuber, G., et al. (1973). *Private foreign investment in development*. Oxford: Development Centre of the OECD.

Riedel (1975) Riedel, James (1975) The Nature and Determinants of Export-oriented Direct Foreign Investment in a Developing Country: A Case Study of Taiwan. Weltwirtschaftliches Archiv 3: 505–528.

Shamsuddinr, A. (1994). Economic determinants of foreign direct investment in less developed countries. *The Pakistan Development Review, 33*(1), 41–51.

Walia (1976) Walia, Tirlochan S. (1976) An Empirical Evaluation of Selected Theories of Foreign Direct Investment by U.S. Based Multinational Corporations. Ph.D. Diss., New York University. Graduate School of Business Administration.

Weintraubus (1967) Weintraub, Robert (1967) Studio empirico sulle relazioni di lungo andare tra movi- menti di capitali e rendimenti differenziali. Rivista Intemazionale di Scienze Economiche e Commerciali. 14: 401–415.

8

Learning to Collaborate: The Case Study of a Chinese–Kenyan CSR Effort

Irene Yuan Sun and Wang Yuan

8.1 Introduction

The economic ties between China and Sub-Saharan Africa (SSA) have expanded tremendously over the past decade. Trade between China and SSA has grown by 26 percent per year since 1995, reaching a total value of US$170 billion in 2013. Yet this increase has not been not symmetric—in 2013, when the share of Chinese trade to SSA was 24 percent of the total, SSA's share in Chinese trade reached just 3 percent of its total (Pigato and Tang 2015). Moreover, in 2013, China became SSA's most important export partner. China now accounts for 27 percent of

The name of the SOE was not to be revealed in this chapter per the request of the SOE.

I.Y. Sun (✉)
McKinsey & Co, Washington, DC, USA
e-mail: irene.y.sun@gmail.com

W. Yuan
UN, Beijing, China

Y. C. Kim (ed.), *China and Africa*, The Palgrave Macmillan Asian Business Series, DOI 10.1007/978-3-319-47030-6_8

SSA's exports, compared with 23 percent for the European Union and 21 percent for the United States (Pigato and Tang 2015).

Chinese outward foreign direct investment (FDI) to Africa also experienced significant expansion in the past decade. The 2014 data from the Chinese Ministry of Commerce (MOFCOM 2014) indicates that Chinese FDI flows to SSA reached US$3.1 billion in 2013, representing 7 percent of global investment in the region, approaching that of the United States at 7.3 percent. Chinese FDI stock in SSA in 2013 is recorded at US$24 billion, about 5 percent of SSA's total FDI stock (Pigato and Tang 2015).

Lying in the eastern end of the African continent, Kenya is a lower middle-income country with total GDP of US$60.94 billion in 2014.[1] In recent years, Chinese–Kenyan ties have deepened considerably, including in trade, infrastructure, immigration, and investment. China's exports to Kenya grew rapidly from 2005, and in 2013, its value reached US$3.2 billion, seven times the 2005 value. In turn, Chinese imports from Kenya reached US$53 million in 2014, three times the value of that in 2005 (Fig. 8.1). In the

[1] World Bank Data: http://data.worldbank.org/country/kenya

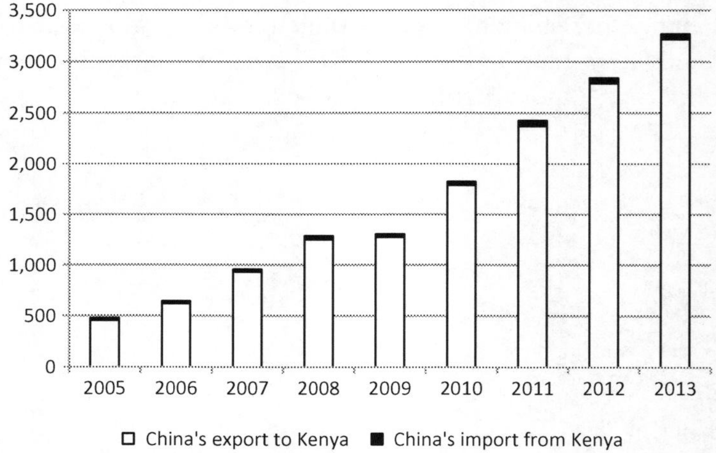

Fig. 8.1 China–Kenya trade, 2005–2013 (US$, million) (Source: National Bureau of Statistics, P.R. China)

infrastructure realm, since China's first construction project in Kenya, the Moi International Sports Center in the 1980s, China has completed various road, airport construction, hospital, and water treatment projects, earning a reputation for high quality and quick execution. Currently, Kenya hosts more than 40,000 Chinese people and around 400 Chinese state-owned and privately owned enterprises (SOEs and POEs), and Chinese businesses in Kenya are spread across every sector in a significant way, especially in the construction business (Wang and Luo 2015).

However, there exists considerable concern about the social, environmental, workplace, and economic responsibilities of Chinese businesses. Chinese presence in Africa is viewed with suspicion, especially from the Western press, in which Chinese businesses' human rights record, labor practices, and environmental impact are often questioned. Within Africa, according to a recent report on Africans' perceptions of the business practices of Chinese nationals by the Ethics Institute of South Africa, only 11.1 percent African interviewees think that Chinese companies care about environmental protection. And when asked about whether Chinese companies take social, economic, or environmental responsibilities seriously, 70 percent of African interviewees think that social responsibilities are not taken into consideration when Chinese companies invest in African countries (Ethics Institute 2014). In Kenya, it is not uncommon to see Chinese-run projects facing corruption charges and environmental and social concerns published in the local press. The Mombasa–Nairobi Standard Gauge Railway project by China Road and Bridge Corporation, for example, attracted controversy around the lack of a proper bidding process, conflict related to land acquisition, and alleged corruption (Tuko 2015; Wafla 2014).

At the same time, the international community has proposed new expectations for inclusive, green, and sustainable business (UNDP 2015). The United Nations Sustainable Development Goals published in September 2015 encourages companies to take advantage of their financial, technological, and network resources to support the global development agenda, thus contributing to improvement in the global economic, environmental, and social spheres (UNDP 2015). The G20 Inclusive Business Framework also calls on the private sector to promote strong, sustainable, balanced, and inclusive growth and to boost economic resilience.

At least, some members of the business community have been responsive. Some prominent examples include Coca-Cola, which initiated the 5by20 program to enable the economic empowerment of 5 million female entrepreneurs across the company's value chain by 2020. Through collaboration with nongovernmental organizations, governments, and businesses, 5by20 provides access to business skills training, financial services, assets, and support networks of peers and mentors (Coca-Cola 2005). Non-consumer facing businesses have also gotten involved; one example is German chemical giant BASF, which joined hands with GIZ to strengthen inclusive ecosystems for food fortification in Tanzania.

Increasingly, the concepts of corporate social responsibility (CSR) and sustainable development have been recognized by Chinese companies operating both domestically and overseas. Since 2000, when the 'going global' policy became a national strategy, the Chinese government has published a series of guidelines and policies to promote the sustainable development of Chinese companies overseas (UNDP 2015). The *Green Credit Policy*[2] issued by the China Banking Regulatory Commission in 2012 requires banks to promote green credit operations by strengthening supervision responsibility and information disclosure. These guidelines emphasize management of both environmental and social risks (Greenovation Hub 2014). The *Measures for Supervision and Management of Overseas Centrally State-owned Enterprises*[3] by the State-owned Assets Supervision and Administration Commission (SASAC) in 2011 requires that SOEs owned by the central government obey policies for economic and social development in host countries where they operate (Greenovation Hub 2014). This shows the determination by the Chinese government to steer Chinese overseas enterprises toward more positive impacts on local economy and community. The *Guidance on Environmental Protection in Foreign Investment and Cooperation*[4] issued in 2013 by MOFCOM and the Ministry of Environmental Protection

---

[2] 《绿色信贷指引》, full text available in China from http://www.cbrc.gov.cn/EngdocView.do?docID=3CE646AB629B46B9B533B1D8D9FF8C4A

[3] 《中央企业境外国有资产监督管理暂行办法》, full text available in Chinese at http://www.sasac.gov.cn/n1180/n1566/n11183/n11229/13624671.html

[4] 《对外投资合作环境保护指南》 Full text in Chinese available at http://www.zhb.gov.cn/gkml/hbb/gwy/201302/t20130228_248632.htm

requires that Chinese companies engaged in outward investment raise their level of awareness of and take steps related to environment protection. Specifically, this guideline asks companies to conduct environmental impact assessments (EIAs), abide by environmental laws and regulations of host countries, respect local religions and customs protect laborers' rights, and fulfill CSR projects (Greenovation Hub 2014). On paper at least, these three guidelines are fairly comprehensive policies articulating the social and environmental responsibility of Chinese overseas investment.

Compared to international policies and guidelines, however, these Chinese policies do have some gaps. For example, they rarely touch upon human rights and consumer issues. And a majority of the policies adopts a suggestive tone, while only the *Administrative Rules for Overseas Contracting* issued in 2008 by the State Council prescribes fines and punishing measures for Chinese companies engaged in unsafe operations, corrupt activities, or illegal sub-contracting activities overseas. This is also the only policy that prescribes specific fines to illegal operations. Moreover, many policies issued by SASAC focus on central government-owned SOEs; for instance, in 2012, SASAC required all 121 SOEs that it supervises to issue annual CSR reports (Chinanews 2011), but given SASAC's jurisdiction, this policy does not cover the large number of SOEs owned by provincial and local governments, nor POEs.

In addition, a disconnect exists between policy and practice. There are two reasons for this. First, for many of the guidelines and policies issued by the Chinese government, compliance is not mandatory. Instead, they are non-binding recommendations, guidelines, and voluntary agreements. Only a few take the form of regulatory requirements, compulsory standards, and concrete requirements for foreign operations (Bosshard 2008; Mol 2011; Compagnon and Alejandro 2013). Thus, in practice, some Chinese developers operating overseas do not conduct EIAs, for example, because the need to comply with the 2013 Guidance on Environmental Protection is not compulsory (Greenovation Hub 2014).

A second reason that Chinese businesses sometimes fail to meet the social and environmental responsibility standards set out in Chinese government guidelines is that there is often a gap between headquarters and country teams within Chinese companies. That is, the guidelines and principles are adopted by the headquarters of Chinese transnational corporations and banks, often located in China, but often lack full comprehension, supervision, and transparency at the level of project implementation in Africa. Added to this is the context of lack of stringent enforcement by the mother company (or state agency in the case of state-owned companies), Chinese credit institutions, and local African enforcing agencies (Global Environmental Institute 2011). Given the challenge of doing business environments that are often new and unfamiliar to country-level managers, it is easy to understand why for country teams, implementing suggested Chinese government guidelines would sometimes fall to the end of a day's to do list.

That said, there are signs that at least some Chinese companies operating in Africa are beginning to implement major CSR programs. One example is Chinese Information & Communications Technology (ICT) giant Huawei, the largest telecoms equipment company in the world, which established Huawei Training Centers in its major overseas markets (Gradl 2012). The company set up six training centers across Africa and provided training programs to Huawei employees as well as the general public (Huawei 2012).

8.2 Project Background and Objectives

The project described in this chapter was an initiative of the Sino-Africa Centre of Excellence Foundation (SACE Foundation). Established in 2013, the SACE Foundation is an applied research think tank that focuses on building knowledge and driving constructive action on Sino-Africa issues in commerce, education, culture, and politics. Based in Kenya and with a representative office in China, the SACE Foundation has received official acknowledgment and support from the Chinese Embassy in Kenya, the China–Africa Development Fund, and several research institutes based in China. The authors of this chapter are former employees of the SACE Foundation in Kenya.

In 2014, the SACE Foundation conducted a firm-level descriptive survey of 75 Chinese companies in Kenya of various sizes, sectors, and shareholding nature. The survey found that Chinese companies frequently cite corruption, theft, and disorder as major barriers to doing business in Kenya. According to respondents, skilled labor is often difficult to find, and regulatory regimes are sometimes difficult to understand and navigate. This was a major finding: as much as Africans have concerns about Chinese businesses operating in their home countries, Chinese businesses experience equally acute challenges. Hence, the SACE Foundation team felt that concerns on both sides would need to be addressed in order for the Chinese–Kenyan relationship to become truly mutually beneficial.

The case of employment generation was particularly intriguing. Despite the common local perception among Africans that Chinese businesses are reluctant to hire employees locally, the SACE Foundation survey found that 93 percent of Chinese companies hire local employees. In addition, 78 percent of full-time employees among all surveyed companies are locals, and 95 percent of part-time employees are locals (Wang and Luo 2015). At the same time, however, inadequately skilled workforce is perceived to be a major obstacle for doing business in Kenya. Chinese companies that engage in labor-intensive businesses, such as construction and manufacturing, are major contributors to local employment; yet during interviews, they frequently complained that it has been hard for them to find qualified and adequately skilled Kenyan workers (Wang and Luo 2015).

The negative perception of Chinese companies by Kenyans and the perceived challenges of doing business in Kenya by Chinese companies are interlinked problems. Only by solving one can the other be solved to make Chinese investment in Kenya mutually beneficial and sustainable for the long term. In this conception, CSR becomes one promising avenue toward improving the sustainability of Chinese investments in Kenya. Despite altruistic efforts of individual companies, however, Chinese companies in Kenya have typically not engaged in CSR with intentionality nor at scale. Hence, the SACE Foundation initiated this pioneering project to create a proof-of-concept CSR project for a large Chinese SOE operating in Kenya. The belief was that a well-designed CSR program by a Chinese company would signal to Kenyan stakeholders about the potential for mutually beneficial partnership and prove to other Chinese companies that CSR projects in Kenya would be a worthwhile investment. Hence, the SACE Foundation initiated this project in 2014 with four aims:

1. Create local social and economic impact on Kenya;
2. Improve the sustainability of Chinese business in Kenya;
3. Devise a concrete model for Chinese–Kenyan and cross-sectoral collaboration; and
4. Draw lessons that other countries and companies can learn from.

8.3 Project Design

From the beginning, the project was conceived of as a collaborative effort between Chinese and African stakeholders across the private, public, and non-profit sectors. Hence, the overall project design was configured to provide ample time for identification of a core project objective that would fulfill the needs of various constituencies and allow space for complementary collaboration. A full first phase was devoted to this challenge identification, followed by a more detailed phase of project design, and finally institutionalization of the program (Table 8.1). Although the SACE Foundation team already hypothesized that workforce skills

Table 8.1 Summary of project phases and timeline

Phase	Description	Timing
1. Challenge identification	Needs assessment of Chinese companies as well as Kenyan stakeholders to determine potential areas of overlap. Through multiple stakeholder discussions, improving construction-related technical skills training in Kenya was identified as the target intervention field	3 months
2. Project design	Detailed program design and more detailed stakeholder identification and recruitment, involving Chinese and Kenyan government, UNDP, a Chinese SOE, SACE Foundation, and Kenya Technical Teacher's College (KTTC)	3 months
3. Institutionalization	Consultation services to the Chinese SOE and KTTC at the practical level, and the design and establishment of a high-level institutional support structure	3 months

building might be a productive focus for a CSR project, we also wanted to make sure all parties were in agreement and willing to invest time, energy, and resources into this area. Hence, the project phases were designed with the logic of using the process of challenge identification to build internal support among the various organizations to work together on a single project, then to collaboratively design the project as a first pilot experience of co-governing and co-implementing an important initiative. The rest of this section describes each of these phases in greater detail.

1. *Challenge Identification*: The primary aim of this first phase was to identify a single galvanizing issue that could bring together diverse constituencies across the Chinese and Kenyan, public and private sector constituencies needed for sustainable positive change (please see Fig. 8.5 for a visual conception of this idea that was used in various stakeholder meetings). The project team believed that the single best way to build effective coalitions was to work on something meaningful together. Hence, the project design built in ample time to listen to various constituencies about Kenya's business and social challenges and to seek advice on what area of work to focus on.

One of the critical choices was the choice of who to consult in this initial phase. Without knowing what the ultimate project focus would be, we chose to include a broad cross-section of Kenyan leaders and institutions, including a Kenyan elected official, technocrats, businesspeople, the Chinese embassy, and a non-profit leader. In total, eight leaders across the public, private, and social sectors in Kenya who also spanned the Chinese and Kenyan communities were consulted repeatedly in this phase.

In consulting these stakeholders, we began by probing their concerns about social development in Kenya. In this effort, we were aided by the related work of the SACE Foundation in the survey described above on the perceptions of Chinese businesses on doing business in Kenya. In stakeholder consultations, we first asked participants for their unbiased views on the major issues Kenya faces, but then also followed up by asking the participant's views on the other areas identified in the survey. We also asked stakeholders which obstacles seemed most addressable. Hence, even though obstacles such as corruption and personal safety ranked higher in importance for many stakeholders in the survey, skilled workforce availability was viewed as most addressable in conversation with stakeholders (Fig. 8.6). For the Chinese stakeholders, we also spent time understanding the typical design of their standard CSR projects in Kenya and what challenges they have encountered in the past (Fig. 8.7).

The result of these stakeholder consultations was a clear consensus around vocational education as the key area to tackle. For Chinese business, this was an area of significant potential cost savings, as recent wage trends in China had been on a steep upward trajectory, making the need to find quality local talent sources an increasingly pressing economic imperative. Our project team visited construction sites and interviewed construction foremen. According to these sources, bringing a Chinese technical worker to Kenya was already five to six times the cost of hiring a local worker at the same skill level, due to higher prevailing salaries in China and the market norm of paying for flight tickets, longer vacation times, medical insurance, accommodation, and transportation for Chinese workers in Africa. Moreover, since the summer of 2013, Kenya has narrowed its immigration policy, making it more expensive to bring in foreign workers. It now costs about KES 400,000 (US$ 4597) for a foreign employee to obtain a working permit for two years (let alone the tips paid to the immigration officer). There were also positive reasons to hire more locally: many Chinese companies expressed their desire to hire more locals to be sales managers and accountants due to their familiarity with the local context. Among the Kenyan government officials and civil society representatives we consulted, skills development was also a major priority area. For them, this issue was a way of addressing the high youth unemployment rates in the country, which reached 17 percent in recent years, according to the World Bank.[5] In addition to this high overall rate, there is also concern about the fact that 84 percent of employed youth are in vulnerable informal economy jobs (Munga and Onsomu 2014). Finally, for Chinese government, this was a potential reputational boost for the overall China 'brand' in Kenya (Figs. 8.2, 8.3, and 8.4).

[5] World Bank, "Unemployment, youth total," http://data.worldbank.org/indicator/SL.UEM.1524.ZS (accessed 6 December 2015).

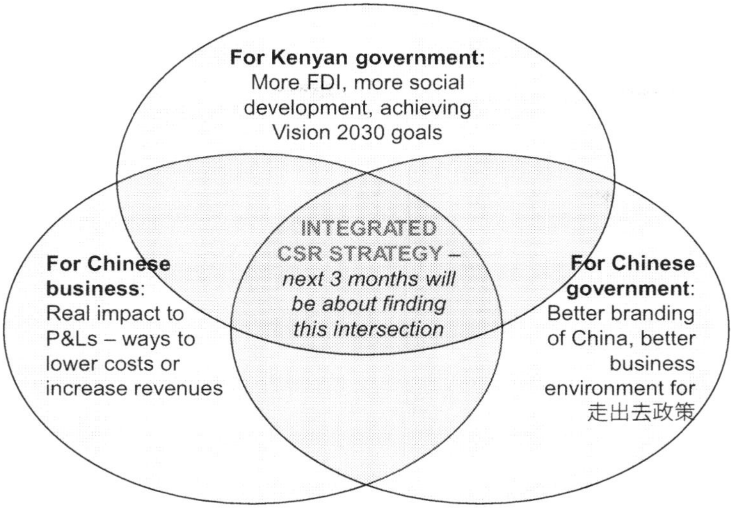

Fig. 8.2 Conception of stakeholder alignment used in project meetings

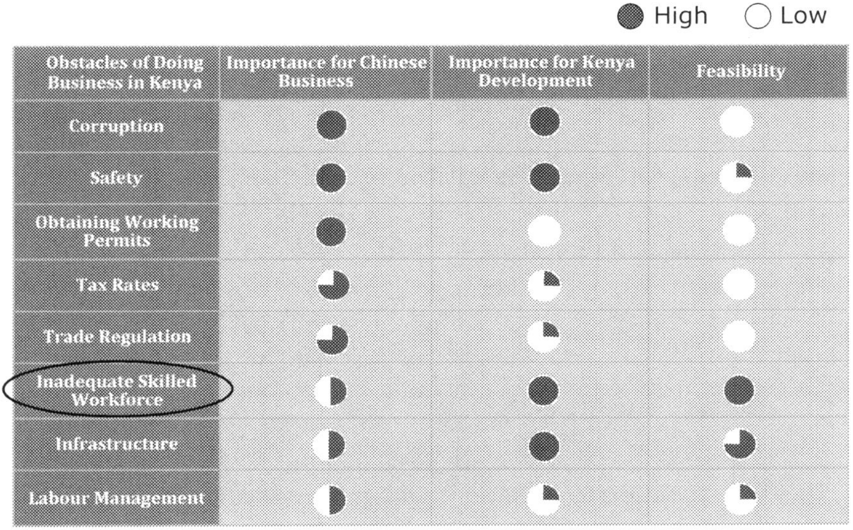
High
Low
Obstacles of Doing Business in Kenya
Importance for Chinese Business
Importance for Kenya Development
Feasibility
Corruption
Safety
Obtaining Working Permits
Tax Rates
Trade Regulation
Inadequate Skilled Workforce
Infrastructure
Labour Management

Fig. 8.3 Summary of stakeholder consultations about challenges of doing business in Kenya and addressability of these issues, 2014

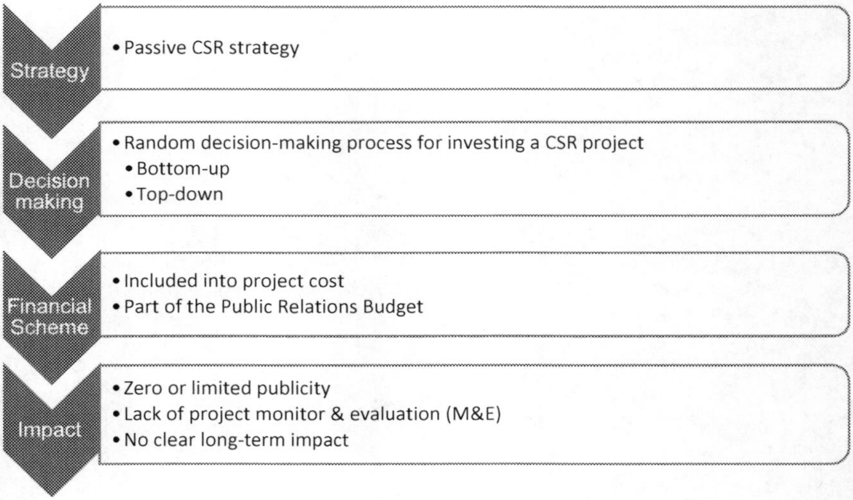

Fig. 8.4 Traditional Chinese companies' CSR project design & challenges, summarized from stakeholder consultations

2. *Project Design*: This phase involved working closely with technical staff within the Chinese SOE and the Kenyan Ministry of Higher Education to understand the existing problems in the current system and to design a program to address these barriers. As part of this phase, the core team conducted further interviews, including of multiple construction sites to understand current talent availability and needs, as well as workers' perspectives. We also conducted site visits and interviews at existing vocational schools to understand principal perspectives and to observe classes and exams in progress. Based on this work, five major barriers were identified: (1) teacher training and recruitment; (2) curriculum that emphasizes theory rather than practical skills; (3) ad hoc, informal recruiting methods; (4) cultural and language differences on the work-site; and (5) fragmented institutional reform efforts.

Through multiple consultations and joint problem-solving sessions, the stakeholders determined that the first three issues are both most immediate and most addressable through a partnership between the

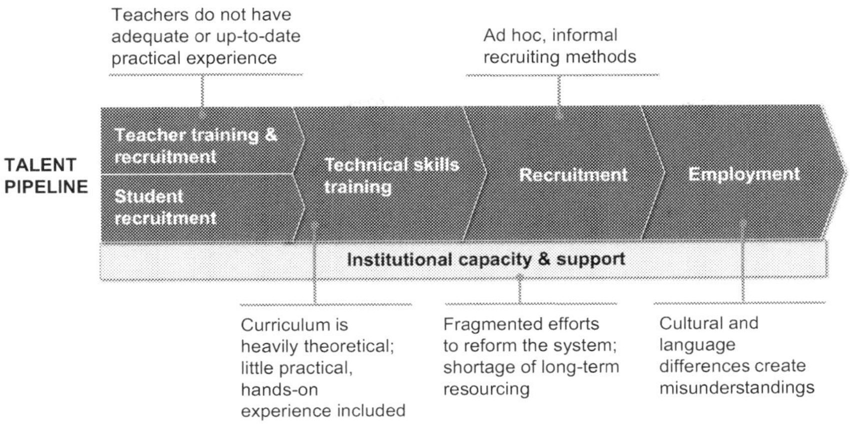

Fig. 8.5 Summary of Issues in Construction Industry Talent Pipeline

Chinese SOE and Kenyan vocational training institutions. Together, the stakeholders designed a training center called the Sino-Africa Industrial Skills Upgrading Centre (SAISUC). This training center would simultaneously produce ready-to-hire students with up-to-date skills and a corps of instructors familiar with modern-day industry standards and technology. This would be done through a train-the-trainers approach that heavily relies on pairing master trainers provided by and funded by the Chinese SOE with teacher trainees for three cycles of co-teaching. The proportion of theory versus practical work would also be turned on its head; with 80 percent of the time to be spent on real construction sites, the Chinese SOE was operating (Figs. 8.5 and 8.6).

3. *Institutionalization*: The institutionalization phase centered on assembling the right coalition of partners to fund and create the SAISUC (the Sino-Africa Industrial Skills Upgrading Center), training center, as well as putting in place the right governance structure to sustain and grow the project well into the future. On the project level, there were detailed discussions by cost category: who would provide each type of needed resource (e.g., land, building, machinery, operational funds, curriculum, practical projects for the students to work on). The governance of the overall initiative also entailed a different set of

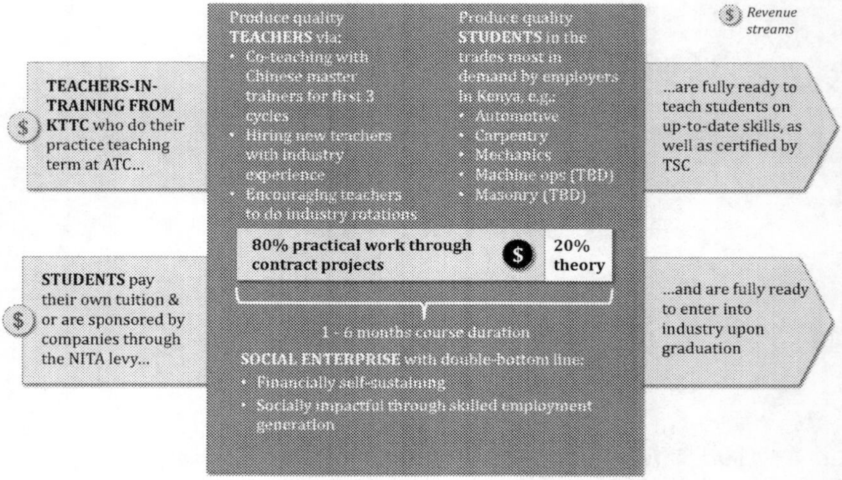

Fig. 8.6 Training Center Design

conversations and a more expansive partnership structure. Because the stakeholders envisioned that the project would grow over time to multiple sites across Kenya and possibly also encompass other issues related to skills training and employment in the future, the governance group was designed to incorporate broad representation across government, business, and civil society, on both the Chinese and Kenyan sides. The partners were designated either as principals—the primary institutions to oversee and 'own' the project for years to come—or as industry leads or technical partners to reflect more specialized roles (Fig. 8.7).

8.4 Project Progress

In February 2015, the Kenyan Technical Training Colleges (KTTC), the Chinese SOE, and the Kenyan Ministry of Higher Education signed a memorandum of understanding (MOU) under the facilitation of SACE Foundation. The Chinese government was a key partner notably missing

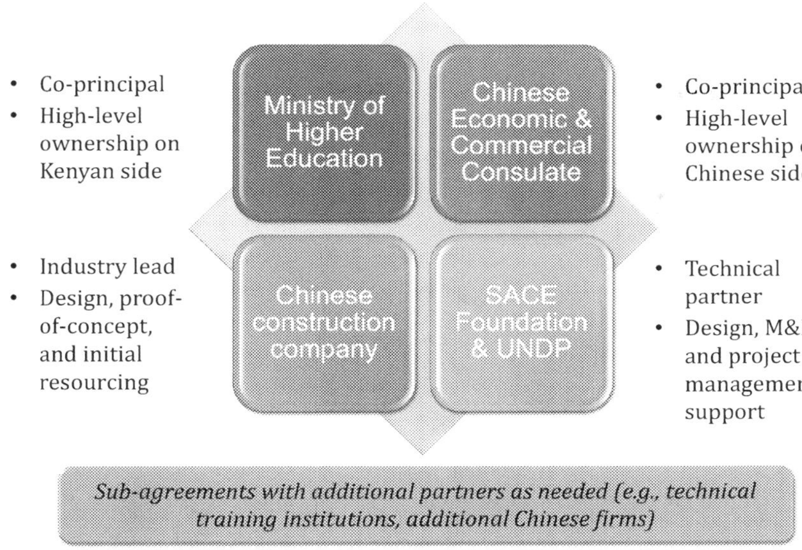

Fig. 8.7 Partnership Structure for Overall Governance

from the signatories: even though the economic councilor spoke highly of this effort on multiple occasions, the Chinese government's willingness to sign an MOU with a Ministry of Kenya and a Chinese SOE was low, likely due to bureaucratic inertia and lack of precedent. However, the model described here was introduced by the economic councilor to the China Communications Construction Company, another large SOE operating in Kenya, as a model to follow in developing a training program for their construction projects.

After the MOU, the project also ran into barriers on the administrative side. Seldom do Chinese companies incorporate CSR into their budgeting process. Within the construction industry, this problem is compounded by the fact that companies compete for projects based in largely part on price, creating pressures to slash any CSR budgets. The project design phase of this project benefitted from an unusually enthusiastic project manager within the Chinese SOE. Soon after the MOU was signed, however, he departed from the company for unrelated reasons. Although it is difficult to tell precisely what impact this had on the execution of this project, since that time, it has been an ongoing challenge to find adequate financial resources for this project. However, the company has continued to publicly express its support for the training center.

8.5 Lessons Learned

To our knowledge, this case was one of the first CSR projects involving a Chinese company in Africa that achieved such high levels of collaboration with local actors. As such, it generated lessons both about conducting CSR in any developing country situation, as well as specifically in the Chinese company and Kenyan local contexts.

There were three lessons from this experience that would apply to any CSR project in a developing country context. First, the effort required to facilitate collaboration across the public, private, and non-profit sectors was well worth the while. Our experience was that each sector brought unique comparative advantages: the private sector can move very quickly, especially on funding; the government can bring needed actors to the table; and non-profits can serve as independent and technically competent bridges between other organizations with sometimes divergent interests. Indeed, the issues that are most worthwhile to solve in our world today—whether the employment of youth or the health of mothers or the pollution in our environment—will require many more such coalitions of diverse actors.

Second, a sensible project design, a coalition of the willing, and resourcing is not enough to get a project off the ground, as bureaucracy is alive and well in developing country contexts. As one example, after we had designed the SAISUC (the Sino-Africa Industrial Skills Upgrading Center) and secured funding, teachers, a vocational school who had strong leadership and was excited to host the SAISUC, we celebrated, believing that our job was basically complete. It turned out, however, that a quasi-autonomous government agency controls teacher placement in Kenya, and that the vocational school in our program would have no claim on keeping the teachers trained by the program. Our design started unraveling: without assurance that they could quickly build a locus of competent training to send trainees to, the Chinese SOE balked at paying for the program. We learned an important lesson: the government is not a monolith, and although we were working closely with the Ministry of Education, there are other government actors that control important parts of educational policy. Care needs to be taken to understand in detail these overlapping jurisdictions and to design programs that fit within the requirements of all the various government bodies that a project will inevitably touch.

Third, we learned a lesson about sustainability in CSR projects. One of the major concerns of the Chinese SOE we worked with was that many previous Chinese CSR projects in Africa were small-scale and did not run on their own after many years. Hence, we made the decision from the beginning to design a model that would be economically viable on its own within three to four years. This would ensure lasting benefit to all stakeholders and to broader society, and ensure a fiscal discipline and sustainability-oriented mindset from the beginning.

In addition, we also learned important lessons about the CSR approach of Chinese companies in particular. African and Western media reports often paint Chinese companies operating in Africa as extractive, rarely if ever giving back to the societies in which they operate. Hence, we were surprised to learn from speaking to Chinese company representatives that all major companies are involved in local charitable work. In fact, they all donate money every year, usually through the Chinese embassy in Kenya as a channel. Through this experience, many Chinese company country-level managers felt that the funding would achieve more impact if there was more effort toward directing and designing specific programs for using these resources. Hence, although not present in all companies at equal levels, there undoubtedly exists pockets of enthusiasm within Chinese companies for trying to go from 'CSR 1.0' of simply donating money to good causes such as local schools to a 'CSR 2.0' that entails a more sophisticated approach of engaging more company resources in project design and execution. Against this backdrop, our project can be seen as an early experiment in pushing for 'CSR 3.0,' in which private sector companies seek their enlightened self-interest by investing in social goods; in this case, a Chinese construction company solves its rising skilled labor costs by investing in vocational education to reduce youth unemployment. In many ways, this trajectory mirrors the development of CSR as a concept among Western multi-national companies, such as when Walmart seized upon eliminating excess packaging as a way to save supply chain costs or when Unilever targeted environmental sustainability as a way of ensuring the steady supply of key agricultural inputs such as palm oil. Our experience through this Kenya work is that despite media reports to the contrary, Chinese companies do not represent exceptions to this broader trajectory. The fact that Chinese companies have largely yet to move in practice from CSR 1.0 to CSR 2.0 or 3.0 may therefore be more related to the relatively short history of Chinese firms going global, or to the difficulties in operationalizing these impulses into reality.

On a related note, we would be remiss not to recognize the unique challenges of bringing together the relatively insular and unique culture of Chinese firms and the diverse stakeholders in the developing countries in which they do business. Everything from language to food to meeting norms to the level of formality in interpersonal interactions has the potential for awkwardness at best and severe misunderstanding at worst. In this, we were fortunate to be a team of bilingual Chinese who have spent significant time both inside and outside of China. As such, we literally and figuratively translated among different stakeholders, sometimes serving as interpreters and at other times playing behind-the-scenes roles to explain other stakeholders' rationales and behaviors to concerned parties. If Chinese companies are to collaborate more with local stakeholders to help solve the pressing issues of today, more of such cross-culturally fluent and independent interlocutors will be needed.

8.6 Conclusion

In many ways, this was not a straightforward project. This work entailed countless rounds of stakeholder consultation, and many hours of debate. More than once, we thought the project would fail, and even today, despite the progress so far, the SAISUC (the Sino-Africa Industrial Skills Upgrading Center), training center remains underfunded and its future is far from assured. Nevertheless, we still see reason for optimism. As one of the first, if not the very first, CSR projects by a Chinese state-owned company to deeply engage multiple local stakeholders, it has already achieved its higher-order implicit aim of building trust and accumulating practical experience working together on a meaningful goal among diverse Chinese and Kenyan actors that normally see little of each other, much less work together in team-based, long-term ways. This accomplishment was brought home to us one day when we were out at a Kenyan vocational college, debating and tweaking the project design with the dynamic and experienced school principal. There were three Chinese and two Kenyans at the table. Among these five, there were two private sector representatives, a government representative, and two non-profit representatives. We all were focused on the same diagram, and one man even literally had his sleeves rolled up. Of course, we all hope that the training program we designed together will be realized, but even if this specific project does not ultimately materialize, the trust forged at that table is an asset to future Chinese–Kenyan relations and a reason onto itself to feel hopeful.

References

Bosshard, P. (2008, 29 May). *China's environmental footprint in Africa*. Retrieved Dec 10, 2014, from Pambazuka: http://www.pambazuka.net/en/category/comment/48442

Chinanews. (2011). 国资委:所有中央企业明年发布社会责任报告. Accessed on 5 Dec 2015 from http://www.chinanews.com/cj/2011/06-20/3121276.shtml

Coca-Cola. (2005). *5by20 by the Numbers*. Accessed on 6 Dec 2015 from: http://www.coca-colacompany.com/stories/5by20/infographic-5by20-by-the-numbers/

Compagnon, D., & Alejandro, A. (2013). RESEARCH ARTICLE: China's external environmental policy: Understanding China's environmental impact in Africa and how it is addressed. *Environmental Practice, 15*(3), 220–227.

Ethics Institute. (2014). *African's perception of Chinese Businesses in Africa, a survey*. Accessed on 5 Dec 2015 from http://www.ethicsa.org/phocadownloadpap/Research_Reports/AfricanPerceptionSurveyChineseBusinessWEBSITEVERSION.pdf

Global Environmental Institute. (2011). *Environmental policies on China's investment overseas*. Chinese Environment Science Press, State of Delaware, US.

Gradl, C. (2012). *Building a Strategic Alliance for the Fortification of Oil and Other Staple Foods (SAFO)*. CSR Initiative, Harvard Kennedy School.

Available at http://www.hks.harvard.edu/m-rcbg/CSRI/research/report_49_SAFO.pdf

Greenovation Hub. (2014). *China's Mining Industry at home and overseas: Development, impacts and regulation*. The Climate and Finance Policy Centre, Greenovation Hub. Available at: www.ghub.org/cfc_en/mining2014 (english), www.ghub.org/cfc/mining2014 (Chinese).

Huawei. (2012). *Bridging spaces, with you*. http://www.huawei.com/ucmf/groups/public/documents/attachments/hw_193077.pdf

MOFCOM. (2014). *Report on development of China's outward investment and economic cooperation 2014*. MOFCOM.

Mol, A. P. (2011). China's ascent and Africa's environment. *Global Environmental Change, 21*(3), 785–794.

Munga, O. & Onsomu, E. (2014). *State of Youth Unemployment in Kenya*. Brookings Institute. Accessed on 6 Dec 2015, from http://www.brookings.edu/blogs/africa-in-focus/posts/2014/08/21-state-of-youth-unemployment-kenya-munga

Pigato, M. & Tang, W. (2015). *China and Africa: Expanding economic ties in an evolving global context*. World Bank. Accessed on 5 Dec 2015 from http://www.worldbank.org/content/dam/Worldbank/Event/Africa/Investing%20in%20Africa%20Forum/2015/investing-in-africa-forum-china-and-africa-expanding-economic-ties-in-an-evolving-global-context.pdf

Tuko. (2015). Why standard gauge railway is a grand corruption scheme. *Tuko News*. Accessed on 5 Dec 2015 from http://tuko.co.ke/71666-standard-gauge-railway-kenya-cost-jubilee-government.html

Wafla, P. (2014). Corruption claims mar Jubilee's Standard Gauge Railway project. *Standard Digital News*. Accessed on 5 Dec 2015 from http://www.standardmedia.co.ke/article/2000108972/corruption-claims-mar-jubilee-s-standard-gauge-railway-project

Wang, Y., & Luo, Y. (2015). *China Business Perception Index: Survey on Chinese Companies' Perception of Doing Business in Kenya*. Globalethics.net. ISBN 978-2-88931-061-6 – China Ethics No. 3.

9

China and Namibia: An All-Weather Friendship Investigated

Henning Melber

9.1 Introduction

The rapid expansion of Chinese diplomatic links to African countries and the corresponding growing presence of Chinese companies and traders since the turn of the century have also been very visible in Namibia. While the bilateral relations between the two governments are making a reference to an "all-weather friendship", the Chinese engagement is perceived less enthusiastic among the local population and often viewed with reservations if not with outright suspicion and rejection, at times bordering to xenophobic behaviour and actions. Sino–Namibian relations can, subject to the eyes of the beholder, be classified as a matter of solidarity or xenophobia (Dobler 2008a). This dichotomy is reinforced by a political culture which tends to discourage "public debate on sensitive matters",

H. Melber (✉)
The Nordic Africa Institute, Uppsala, Sweden
e-mail: henning.melber@nai.uu.se

Y. C. Kim (ed.), *China and Africa*, The Palgrave Macmillan Asian Business Series, DOI 10.1007/978-3-319-47030-6_9

which "extends to the different perceptions about China's presence in Namibia from various sectors in society" (Amadhila 2013: 74).[1] The Namibian case and the divergent views at different levels of society is however no singular discrepancy but only one among several examples indicative of contrasting perceptions between government and citizens within the same country as regard to the role of China.

The difference to opposite views are also reflected in the general analyses of China in Africa (for summaries see i.a. Lee et al. 2007; Melber 2010, 2013a, b). There are concerned and critical voices within the general debate that are more reluctant than others to argue for a welcoming embrace to a new global player, which after all might not change the rules of the game but simply join the hegemonic club. Their fear is that China in the end merely offers more of the same. In particular, those representing a labour movement perspective argue that the employment conditions in Chinese companies tend to be even worse (see Jauch and Sakaria 2009; Jauch 2009). Others argue that Chinese and other companies representing emerging economies are contributing to a wider range of opportunities and should not be dismissed or ridiculed (Bräutigam 2010; Cheru and Obi 2010; Harneit-Sievers et al. 2010; Shinn and Eisenman 2012). They also maintain that malpractices by Chinese investors—put into perspective—would not exceed those by other external agencies. However, even highest-ranking Chinese officials are willing to admit that there is room for improvement. According to the Chinese news agency Xinhua (2013), the country's Vice Foreign Minister Zhai Jun at a forum on Chinese businesses in Africa stated on 18 March 2013, in Beijing: "Making quick money and leaving is a myopic action, and 'catching fish by draining the pond' is unethical".

This chapter offers a closer examination of the Chinese–Namibian relations and the differing perspectives. It summarises the political-diplomatic as well as the economic aspects and the responses by the stakeholders in Namibia based on the hitherto available studies and numerous reports in the local print media. It thereby seeks to add to other case studies investigating the political and economic realities in countries on the continent, where the Chinese presence has created new social facts and thereby also provoked a lively debate over the effects.

[1] For a shorter summary version of this instructive MA Thesis see Amadhila (2012).

9.2 A History of Chinese–Namibian Relations

It is most likely no exaggeration to assume that prior to the implementation of the transitional period under the United Nations (UN) supervision starting a year before Namibian Independence, on 21 March 1990, no citizens of the People's Republic of China had set foot on the territory occupied first by the Germans (1884–1915) and then by South Africa. But since the Bandung Conference in 1955, China emerged as a non-aligned global player in firm support of the anti-colonial struggles for national sovereignty. This also contributed to early good relations with the emerging nationalist movements fighting for the self-determination of the Namibian people.

The main support was originally during the 1960s offered to the South West African National Union (SWANU), established as the first national liberation movement in May 1959, followed in April 1960 by the South West African People's Organisation (SWAPO). SWANU initially had a similar status to SWAPO and was considered ideologically closer to the socialist bloc than SWAPO. It "was to build close ties with the East, and especially with China" already prior to the Sino–Soviet split (Gibson 1972: 123). While SWAPO as from the mid-1960s emerged as the dominant movement and SWANU lost terrain not least due to the prior's decision to resort to armed resistance, Chinese support to SWANU lasted throughout the decade, not least because SWAPO openly pursued a pro-Soviet stance. According to Gibson (1972: 141), the first SWAPO statement recorded, which was "warmly hailing' the Chinese people 'in their struggle against imperialism'", dated 15 September 1970. As he commented further, "one robin does not make a Red Spring". However, already during the late 1960s, SWAPO combatants had been sent for military training to China, underlining that the decision to resort to armed struggle was a decisive turning point in international support offered now to SWAPO, which reportedly also already at its 1969 congress in Tanga/Tanzania thanked China together with other countries "for the moral and material support it had given the movement" (Sherbourne 2007: 161).

The full Chinese support shifting from SWANU to SWAPO took place soon thereafter, when SWANU got lost in internal squabbles while SWAPO became increasingly recognized. Subsequently, "SWAPO was able to enjoy undivided support from both Communist powers, though its links with Moscow and the Socialist bloc were always of more importance, both on political and material level" (Taylor 1997: 111). With China's admission to the UN in 1971 and its status as permanent member of the Security Council, it assumed a more influential role on the international stage, which also benefitted SWAPO. United Nations General Assembly Resolution 3111 of 12 December 1973 recognized SWAPO as "the authentic representative of the Namibian people". This was amended by United Nations General Assembly Resolution 31/146 of 20 December 1976 to "sole and authentic". By then, increasingly friendly relations with China had unfolded. The fraternal relations between SWAPO and the Angolan UNITA (União Nacional pela Independência Total de Angola) under the leadership of Jonas Savimbi, dating back to the mid-1960s and prevailing until Angola's Independence in 1975, were certainly an additional factor, since the fiercely anti-Soviet UNITA received massive Chinese support. The close relations between the two organisations were, despite SWAPO's pro-Soviet tendencies, a rather natural bond: "rather than being based on political, social and economic aspects of a fundamental ideology, it rested on common regional and ethnic affinity, culture and history" (Hamutenya 2014: 87). With Angolan Independence, SWAPO's collaboration guided by pragmatism shifted towards friendly relations with the governing MPLA (Movimento Popular de Libertação de Angola). This reinforced the close links to the Soviet bloc and its Cuban ally, with material (including direct military) support far more important than that of China. SWAPO nevertheless maintained good relations with the Chinese. But, as Du Pisani (2014: 115) observes, the organisation did not open a diplomatic mission like in other countries to which SWAPO had friendly relations, despite President Nujoma visiting the People's Republic seven times during the 1970s and 1980s.

With the ease of the Sino–Soviet tensions as from the mid-1980s onward, new avenues for Chinese support to SWAPO opened up and reinforced the friendly relations. This was underlined when SWAPO's President Sam Nujoma was among the few African leaders who openly declared his support to China's violent oppression of the democracy movement after the June 1989 Tiananmen Square massacre. At a time when the transition to Independence under a UN-supervised interim period was implemented, Nujoma expressed in a message to the Chinese ambassador in Luanda "his understanding of [the] resolute action taken by the Chinese Government and the People's Army to put down the counter-revolutionary rebellion" and congratulated the Communist Party "on their victory in quelling the counter-revolutionary rebellion" (quoted in Taylor 1997: 115). A few months later, SWAPO took over political power and ever since then consolidated its dominance into a hegemonic de facto one-party state, while the Soviet Union as its so far closest ally and strongest support collapsed. This opened a new chapter for the relations between the Chinese and Namibian states.

China opened an embassy directly after Namibia's Independence in 1990. In 1991, an Agreement on Economic and Technical Cooperation defined the framework for trade and investment between the two countries. In 1995, Namibia opened its embassy in China and as Head of State Sam Nujoma added five more official visits to the People's Republic during his three terms in office in 1992, 1996, 1999, 2000 and 2004 (Du Pisani 2014: 116). On 20 July 2004, the increasingly closer exchange relations also in economic terms manifested in signing an Agreement on the Establishment of the Joint Commission of Bilateral Economy and Trade. But also in the areas of defence and security, a closer cooperation emerged with the procurement of military equipment from China as well as training of senior officers of the Namibian Defence Force at a military academy in Shanghai (Du Pisani 2014: 125). In the following sub-chapters, some of the more noteworthy interactions during the last decade are summarised. They offer an indication and evidence of the growing intensity of exchange patterns.

9.3 Diplomatic Activities Since 2006[2]

Namibia's Minister of Works announced during the parliamentary debate over the annual state budget on 21 June 2006 that the Chinese government had offered a generous grant to cover expenses for the new presidential

---

[2] This summary is based partly on information compiled in the Namibia chapters by the author in the volumes of the *Africa Yearbook. Politics, Economy and Society South of the Sahara*, published

residence under construction at the state house complex. From 16 to 18 November 2006, a 47-member Chinese delegation of government officials and business people visited Namibia. The head of delegation welcomed Namibia's support to the Chinese position on Taiwan and on human rights. He qualified the bilateral relations as a "natural alliance". A loan of N$ 189 million for the purchase of trains and an agreement on investment promotion and protection were signed. President Pohamba accepted the invitation for a state visit, which he undertook from 16 to 21 December 2006. He declared it served the purpose to strengthen economic ties with an old friend, who had helped Namibia to attain Independence through its material, diplomatic and political support to SWAPO during the liberation struggle. In this spirit, the cabinet established on 6 December 2006 an economic commission in support of closer Chinese–Namibian cooperation.

President Hu Jintao visited Namibia on 5 February 2007 as part of his tour to several African countries. Namibia expressed its support for the One-China policy and opposed the establishment of a Taiwan–Africa forum. The special ties were again underlined in late September 2007 at a farewell function for the departing Chinese ambassador. The two countries had signed some 20 agreements over the past four years and trade volume had tripled between 2003 and 2006. Chinese grants led to the construction of several public buildings by Chinese companies. But relations were temporarily strained in 2009 as a result of a series of financial scandals, in which Chinese companies were involved, and by Namibia's decision not to take up a preferential loan offer, which in its view was not really a bargain. Two Chinese news websites, which had reported on the involvement of the Chinese president's son in one of the scandals, were temporarily offline on 21 July 2009 and had the news removed. At the end of July, after the Chinese involvement in the Namibian fraud case became international news, the Chinese authorities deleted from search engines all references to "Namibia" and the names of the Chinese individuals and companies involved, thus preventing them from being accessed on the Internet and de facto eliminating Namibia from the Chinese map of the world.

---

since 2005 (Melber 2016). For a detailed list of high-level official visits and bilateral agreements signed between Namibia and China from 1990 to 2011 see the Appendices 2 and 3 in Amadhila (2013: 130–135).

In March 2010, the chairman of the Chinese People's Political Consultative Conference and the Vice-Minister of Foreign Affairs were for diplomatic consultations in Namibia, while former President Sam Nujoma and Trade Minister Hage Geingob attended the Shanghai World Expo on different occasions. Wikileaks caused some irritation by disclosing in December 2010 the claim by foreign diplomats that Namibia had allowed the resettlement of 5000 Chinese families in the country in compensation for a loan on which it had defaulted. Prime Minister Nahas Angula dismissed this allegation in a statement on 15 December 2010 as "unsubstantiated and mere fabrications", but it fuelled already existing suspicions that the Chinese received preferential treatment over and above anyone else.

China's Foreign Minister, Yang Jiechi, underlined these friendly relations through a visit on 5/6 January 2012. He signed with Foreign Minister Uutoni Nujoma another technical cooperation agreement for N$ 26 million (20 million Yuan). Jiechi qualified Namibia as an "all-weather friend", but advised to have an omnidirectional policy—or relations with East, West, and any other regional configuration, while reiterating that China was there to stay. The Namibian Deputy Minister for Trade and Industry declared at a business forum with a Chinese delegation on 6 March 2012 that China is an alternative market, more than double the size of the so-called lucrative European market, which created, through its Economic Partnership Agreement (EPA), humiliating agreements with unacceptable conditions. Suggesting that Namibia's agricultural products could be exported to China instead of the EU market, he added that, "this government does not sit idle in the face of humiliation". On 26 March 2012, Theo Ben Gurirab, former Foreign Minister and Prime Minister and the then Speaker of the National Assembly, addressed a Chinese delegation of around 25 Members of Parliament headed by the Vice Chairperson of the Standing Committee of the National People's Congress, Hua Jiamin. He strongly criticised the Western military and economic hegemony and warned that, "military intervention and regime change have replaced dialogue and peaceful co-existence". During a three-day visit, the Chinese Deputy Prime Minister Hui Lianghui signed on 2 April 2012, five cooperation agreements. While on a state visit to China, Prime Minister Hage Geingob (then designated next Head of State) met President Xi Jinping on

8 April 2014. He confirmed the will to create a favourable environment for closer collaboration with Chinese investors. Chinese business interests in Namibia remained high and the number of Chinese local residents remained a constant matter of speculation and provoked strong feelings among ordinary people.

In December 2014, a local newspaper claimed to have information that China had negotiated with the government to use the deep seaport of Walvis Bay as a naval base. The government vehemently dismissed this as unfounded speculations. On 30 March 2015, a top-ranking Chinese military delegation led by State Councillor and Defence Minister Chang Wanquan met Namibia's new President Geingob in Windhoek, thereby reinforcing the earlier suspicions. Questioned at a press conference the next day, Geingob declared that rumours might kill a country. Confronted with the same speculation during the BBC's "Hard Talk" on 1 December 2015, Geingob neither confirmed nor denied Chinese interest in the naval base. The US Embassy in Windhoek on 10 December 2015 categorically dismissed that the USA had approached the government with a view to obtaining a naval base in Walvis Bay, contrary to what Geingob had indicated during the "Hard Talk" interview.

Attending the Forum on China–Africa Cooperation (FOCAC) Summit in Johannesburg on 4/5 December 2015, Geingob met again with Chinese President Xi Jinping, whom he had visited as Prime Minister in 2014. In his speech, he emphasised that the partnership with China "is one built on long lasting and historic solidarity, as well as mutual respect. It is therefore offensive when we are lectured by certain nations and warned about the so-called Chinese colonisation of Africa" (Republic of Namibia/Office of the President 2015b: 3). He applauded a number of key Chinese investments in Namibia and praised, as invaluable, the two countries' deepening cooperation, especially with regard to infrastructure. On 5 February 2016, the Chinese Minister for Foreign Affairs, Wang Yi, paid a courtesy call to State House in Windhoek as a follow-up to the FOCAC Summit. He praised the Namibian Head of State for refuting the allegations against China, thereby testifying to the true friendship between the two countries. Geingob reiterated that now is the opportunity to establish with those who have been loyal supporters of the country's struggle for Independence, a win–win situation. When meeting

Netumbo Nandi-Ndaitwah, Namibia's Deputy Prime Minister and also Foreign Minister the same day, she applauded China for being "a true, trusted and reliable friend". At a media briefing, Minister Yi promised that Namibia shall receive a generous share of the 200,000 experts to be dispatched to Africa to assist local development. In late February 2016, the Chinese ambassador inaugurated a Chinese language classroom at the fourth school in the capital district.

9.4 Chinese Economic Engagement[3]

Chinese economic activities started off most visibly in the retail sector and major construction works. During the first decade after Independence, a countrywide net of Chinese trading shops started to mushroom. These reminded one of the "native shops" of earlier times, when (white) traders offered simple consumer goods to the African population even in remote areas (Namibia's population of now some 2.3 million people occupy some 825,000 square kilometres of mainly semi-arid and arid land). A database of the Ministry of Trade and Industry listed in 2009 more than 500 registered Chinese shops (Jauch and Iipumbu 2009: 262). Chinese shop-owners and shopkeepers, operating on a more modest scale elsewhere, are coming mainly from Fujian. They seem well connected and organised but often have no proper permits to run their business and depend on bribing officials to not be deported (Cissé 2016).

With the open border to the Northern neighbour Angola and the unfolding oil boom creating considerable purchasing power there, a flourishing hub fuelled by larger-scale Chinese (but also other expatriate) investments in wholesale and retail enterprises took off as from the turn of the century in the hitherto largely informal border town of Oshikango (since then upgraded and renamed into Helao Nafidi Town in 2006). Declared as an Export Processing Zone (EPZ), Oshikango boomed for years (cf. Dobler 2008b, 2009a, b), until the decline of the oil price directly affected the purchasing power from Angolan customers with devastating consequences for some of the Chinese trading businesses. Combined

[3] Based partly on summaries in Melber (2016) and other local media reports.

with the collapse of the exchange rate of the Angolan currency, the export from Oshikango to Angola declined between the second quarter of 2014 and the last quarter of 2015 by 85 %, resulting in a "crisis of epic proportions" (Iikela 2016). The closure of Chinese shops resulted in more than 700 local people being unemployed again. Asked for a comment, the Chinese ambassador Xin Shunkang stated: "We sincerely hope that local business survives the hard times with the help of the government" (New Era 2016)—obviously meaning the Namibian government.

Chinese companies also secured considerable stakes in the Namibian public works sector and established control over large parts of the construction industry, dominating competition for state tenders for office buildings, roads, railways, harbour and airport upgrades. Continued high unemployment and the gross disparities in income distribution among Namibians soon contributed to the build-up of anti-Chinese sentiments among ordinary people. The massive presence of Chinese, not least in the construction sector with large-scale projects under state tenders, resulted for the first time in public criticism by the National Union of Namibian Workers (NUNW), which is affiliated with SWAPO and largely loyal to government policies. In a press conference on 22 November 2007, its Secretary General expressed concern over the importation of cheap labour from China for public construction work.

The local construction industry laments the negative effects of awarding the most attractive public works tenders to foreign (mainly Chinese and North Korean) construction companies, which left the local industry ailing and resulted in retrenchments of Namibian workers. They bemoan the fact that Chinese bids (often subsidised by the Chinese government) undercut local offers at the expense of investment in Namibian capacity and work places, while on numerous occasions also violating Namibian labour legislation. A study of the trade union affiliated local Labour Resource and Research Institute (LaRRI) bemoaned already in 2009 that the business practices of Chinese companies often border to the dubious and that state tenders are awarded in deviation from the prescribed procedures (Jauch and Sakaria 2009). The low cost bidding strategy by Chinese contractors is based on lower salaries (often also for imported labour) and a much lower calculated profit margin, reportedly often limited to 10 %, while local and South African companies are said to apply up to 50 % profit margins (Niikondo and Coetzee 2009: 36; see also Dobler 2007: 101). The dominance of Chinese companies in the Namibian public works sector is illustrated by the fact that a tender for a highway expansion of 28-km road between Windhoek and Okahandja (the next town on the main road North of the capital) advertised in mid-2015, attracted 22 bidders, of which 16 were Chinese.

Mining operations with direct Chinese involvement considerably increased in recent years. Eastern China Non-Ferrous Metals Investment Holdings, the investment arm of the East China Mineral Exploration and Development Bureau, announced in early December 2011 the discovery of two billion tonnes of iron ore in the Kunene region and plans to open an iron mine and steel plant with an annual production of five million tonnes. Chinese investments were also announced towards the end of 2012 in the Omitiomire copper mine deposit, 120 km north east of Windhoek. In early December 2011, the wheeling and dealing around the ownership of Swakop Uranium, which controlled one of the largest known uranium deposits of the world at Husab, paved the way for further Chinese ownership through a takeover of Kalahari Minerals by China Guangdong Nuclear Power Corp in a £ 632 million (US$ 990 million) deal. Kalahari owned 43 % in Extract Resources, whose wholly owned subsidiary, Swakop Uranium, received a mining license to develop Husab as one of the biggest uranium mines in the world. Operations by a joint venture between local and Chinese partners announced the start of constructions for the N$ 12 billion project near Swakopmund towards the end of 2012. Husab as the third largest known uranium deposit in the world has a production potential of 15 million pounds uranium oxide per year. Once operational, it will rank Namibia as the second biggest producer on the world market. Construction at the Husab mine continued largely according to plan, but with complaints about the shortage of qualified workers and no secure long-term solution for water and energy supplies. During November 2015, dissatisfaction among locally employed workers over employment of large numbers of foreigners (mainly from Ghana and the Philippines) in jobs, which allegedly could be filled by qualified Namibians, erupted into a series of strikes and violent acts against infrastructure. Becoming operational during 2016, it is expected that the production (mainly for Chinese energy consumption and hence not dependent upon world market prices) will to a large extent compensate for the effects caused by a sluggish global economy and offset negative impacts on the mining industry. But securing reliable water and power supply without lasting damages to the natural habitat or at the expense of the ordinary users living in the wider area will continue to pose major obstacles.

Another major project by Chinese investors was announced by the Namibian cement importer Cheetah Cement, which is planning to set up within the next two years, for US$ 30 million, a cement plant aiming at a production output of 1.5 million tonnes annually under the locally based Whale Rock Cement. This will elevate Namibia's total cement production to 2.2 million tonnes per year with an average local consumption of about 600,000 tonnes per year and thereby enhance competition in the sub-regional markets (Oshili 2016).

While the Chinese presence in the mining sector and extractive industries continually expanded, trade relations took a temporary dip, with a decline in exports from N$ 1.8 billion in 2009 (mainly uranium, copper, lead and other natural resources) to N$ 1.2 billion in 2010. Imports shrank from N$ 2.9 billion in 2009 (mainly cars, telecommunication, furniture, machinery and other manufactured goods) to N$ 1.3 billion in 2010. During a visit to China, Agriculture Minister John Mutorwa signed a bilateral trade agreement on 16 December 2010, which paved the way for the future export of meat and fish, grapes and dates to the Chinese market. Bilateral trade soon recovered again and reached new peaks. In August 2015, the Namibian Minister of Agriculture signed another Protocol, sealing the planned export of beef to China as the first country from the continent.

When celebrating the 65th anniversary of the founding of the People's Republic of China on 2 October 2014, the Chinese Ambassador to Namibia, Xin Shunkang, stated that 40 Chinese companies had operations in the country, managing about N$ 38 billion worth of investments (US$ 3.4 billion), and employing a total of 4000 local people (New Era 2014). But some of these investments were at the centre of public controversy and debate. A major dispute erupted during 2015, when it was announced that the Regional Governor of the Zambezi region had offered the Chinese company Namibia Oriental Tobacco 10,000 hectares of land for a tobacco plantation. Protest was voiced by some land activists of the

SWAPO Youth League who were facing disciplinary punishment from the party for their initiatives to occupy urban land. While the Minister of Health opposed the intended use of land for tobacco production, local people complained that they need access to land for their subsistence instead. Controversy surrounded also, in 2015, the awarding of an N$ 7 billion tender to the Chinese Anhui Foreign Economic Construction Cooperation (AFECC) for the upgrading and expansion of Windhoek's international airport. Amidst accusations of irregularities in the awarding process, President Geingob revoked the decision and cancelled the contract at the end of the year. Instead, the tender was readvertised. In February 2016, the Chinese company announced that it planned to seek an interdict from the Namibian High Court to set aside the government's decision as unlawful and invalid, since it had already taken significant steps towards the implementation of the contract.

Other incidents with the involvement of Chinese individuals adding to a negative image were repeated reports in the media about humiliating treatment of local employees in the retail shops as well as employment conditions in violation of the labour regulations. In the vicinity of the Northern industrial area of Windhoek, some 50 Chinese shops are accommodated in a garage compound dubbed "Chinatown". In February 2012, the local weekly newspaper "The Economist" claimed in an article that the monthly salary for the on average two local employees (mainly young women from the Oshivambo-speaking majority who among others are tasked to serve as translators, since the shop-owners hardly speak any of the local languages, including English) ranged between 300 and 400 N$ as the minimum and 1600 N$ as the maximum (the latter is around US$ 100 at the 2015/16 exchange rate). A survey by Niikondo and Coetzee (2009: 30) established that 76 % of their respondents in Chinese retail shops had wages in the range of N$ 100 to N$ 500 per month compared to 44 % employed in local small–scale retail shops, while only 16 % of those employed in Chinese shops earned between N$ 500 and N$ 1000 per month. Their employment generally includes neither social security payments nor medical aid, lacks any holiday benefits or other work-related entitlements and does not protect from immediate dismissal without compensation. They concluded,

> that a large number of people working for the Chinese are just hanging in there, either while they are looking for other jobs or because they failed to get jobs elsewhere in the labour market. The problem would be that these people are extremely at risk of being abused because they have very limited hope of finding other jobs if they quit from their Chinese employment. (Niikondo and Coetzee 2009: 33)

Several cases of robbery, in which reportedly large amounts of money in different currencies were stolen from Chinese victims, suggested in the popular opinion that these are hoarding money. Criminal offences by Chinese when caught red handed for illegally trying to smuggle large sums in cash abroad were adding to the image that Chinese are exploiting the locals unashamedly. In June 2013, it was reported that the Namibian custom services confiscated cheap knock off goods amounting to the value of N$ 10 million from one trader who was also accused of tax-evasion. Other activities damaging the reputation of Chinese individuals were the suspected involvement in the violation of laws protecting the nature and especially wildlife. A spectacular court case since early 2015 implicates four Chinese citizens in smuggling rhino horns and other illegal hunting trophies. In February 2016, another Chinese citizen was arrested for the possession of 90 kg of protected abalone and 1.15 kg of different pieces of rhino horn. It is estimated that since the beginning of 2015, more than 100 rhinos have been poached. There are also allegations that high-ranking Namibian officials are involved in such organised crimes with Chinese partners. While the Chinese–Namibian friendship seemed to be effective in multiple aspects, growing sentiment among ordinary people in response to such reported crimes seemed to suggest that it was not welcomed by all.

9.5 Assessing the Namibian–Chinese "All-Weather Friendship"

Chinese economic engagement receives controversial assessments. In 2007, the President of the Namibian Chamber of Commerce and Industry (NCCI) expressed strong concern over Chinese investors who venture into so-called *kapana* business (i.e. local street vendors who try to make a living by selling prepared food). In an interview six years later, he recognized the existence of "Chinese businesspersons who uphold good virtues of investment", who should be differentiated from others "who do not respect Namibia's labour laws and further avoid paying taxes" (Mushelenga 2015: 206 and 207). The NCCI's Chief Executive Officer, in an interview in 2010, negative behaviour by Chinese investors as "isolated events". But he also identified problems where Chinese "venture into small businesses that should have been left to local investors" (Mushelenga 2015: 210).

The retail enterprises and construction companies are indeed the most visible presence of Chinese in Namibia (since mining operations happen mostly at locations away from human settlements), and both are having a bad image among the ordinary Namibians. Chinese traders are flexible in exploiting, on ad hoc basis, business opportunities but move on when these decline. Oshikango is the classical case. But they are also vulnerable, since they often depend for trade and residence licenses and their business operations on Namibian officials in home affairs and customs, who are needed for political and administrative protection. They secure such protection through an alliance, which "merely creates an additional rent income for some Namibians without changing their economic behaviour, and it prevents economic development … rather than fostering it" (Dobler 2009b: 710).

Trade union related labour perspectives have been critically assessing the nature and impact of Chinese investments also in the construction sector. They list numerous violations of the Labour Act. Strained labour relations are characterised by mutual suspicion and mistrust. A low degree of organised labour is partly a result of intimidation by the employer. Health and safety issues at the workplace are often neglected and there is generally a lack of training beyond on-the-job. Tenders are awarded to companies who do not comply with national laws and regulations:

> Such practices undermine not only Namibia's legal foundation but also erode the country's social fabric. (…) This is why many Namibian workers indicated that they regarded the working conditions at Chinese companies as a new form of colonialism. They simply reminded them of conditions they had to endure before 1990 (Jauch and Sakaria 2009: 39)

In contrast to the critical undertones articulated at times by higher officials and representatives of the private sector, the political establishment in the SWAPO government has always been strongly in favour and defence of its "Go East" policy. The iconic SWAPO leader and first Head of State (1990–2005), Sam Nujoma, a frequent visitor to China, maintained in an interview in 2011 "that people who complain about the Chinese are narrow-minded, as they do not appreciate the role played by Chinese, in the course of Namibia's liberation struggle" (Mushelenga 2015: 207). While the author, being Namibia's Deputy Foreign Minister, in his PhD thesis, is in tendency justifying the Chinese engagement as part of a largely beneficial economic diplomacy, he also acknowledges the side effects of what he terms a "deep-pocket/cheque-book diplomacy", which makes high-ranking political office bearers beneficiaries of preferential treatment bordering to bribery (Mushelenga 2015).

Certain investments by the Chinese government beyond the red carpet have indeed exceeded the ordinary friendly diplomatic relations. China has in the past made financial donations to SWAPO as a political party in independent Namibia; China has also translated the biography of Sam Nujoma into Chinese and launched it with pomp on 20 July 2004 in Beijing, in the presence of the Namibian President, who was on his 12th visit to the country. Most spectacular, however, was the case of stipends to family members of the party elite. Some investigative local journalists had disclosed that one of the daughters of President Pohamba was among the beneficiaries of study grants secretly offered by the Chinese government to nine Namibian students from privileged (politically highly influential) families for studies in the People's Republic, while thousands of young Namibians have no financial means to translate the educational qualifications obtained under much harsher conditions into an opportunity for academic study. This provoked a public outcry over the preferential treatment and even became a newsworthy item in the established US media (LaFraniere 2009).

In his first State of the Nation Address in April 2015, President Geingob was careful to mention in his appreciation of "significant contributions made by our development partners", (in this order) China, the USA, Germany, the World Bank and Japan (Republic of Namibia/Office of the President 2015a: 17). While this embraced a plurality of bi- and multi-lateral partners, the President was less diplomatically pluralistic when he rebuked at the FOCAC Summit, in early December 2015, any criticism of the Chinese engagement in no uncertain terms:

> It is ironic that those who warn us are the same nations who sat around the table at the Berlin Conference in 1884 and carved out colonies in Africa with the sole intent to develop their countries with our mineral resources and the blood and sweat of our forced labour.
>
> The same countries who complain about Chinese investment in Africa are themselves recipients of large scale Chinese investment. As these nations have faith in their capacity to negotiate the best deals for themselves, Africans too have this same capacity.
>
> Africa is free now and so is our ability to deal with those we choose to deal with, in our terms. (Republic of Namibia/Office of the President 2015b: 3).

Mentioning the Husab Mine as a prominent example, Geingob at the FOCAC Summit praised the project as having "brought meaning and purpose to the life of previously unemployed Namibians" (Republic of Namibia/Office of the President 2015b: 4). Just weeks before, wild strikes by locally employed workers, who also damaged property, had been triggered by what was perceived as unfair labour practices and had interrupted the final construction phase of the mine for several days. As not only this example shows, the view on the ground differs at times, substantially, from that at the top echelons of society. As succinctly summarised in a comprehensive MA thesis, the grassroots perception is suspicious of the official praises:

> China's seemingly aggressive economic presence in the construction and retail industry is mostly responsible for shaping negative perceptions of Sino-Namibian relations. Citizens are very much aware of the economic and social threat of the use of Chinese companies and workers in the construction of public and private projects and the increase in the number of Chinese traders in the country. China is perceived to be an emerging economic power that has no concern for the rights and wellbeing of the Namibian

> people. The apparent disinterest of the government in taking action against China's dominant economic and social presence in the country is causing widespread criticism of Sino-Namibian relations. Despite the positive perceptions that lower-income citizens have of small Chinese retailers and their affordable goods, they pale in comparison to the overall negative perceptions of Chinese presence in Namibia. (Amadhila 2013: 94f.)

9.6 Concluding Remarks

The increased competition for entering favourable relations with African countries is in itself of course not negative to the interests of the African people. But it requires that the tiny elites benefiting from the currently existing unequal structures put their own interest in trans-nationally linked self-enrichment schemes behind the public interest. The priority should be to create investment and exchange patterns, which provide in the first place benefits for the majority of the people. As the African Economic Outlook 2011 suggested, most African countries still need to enhance their bargaining position vis-à-vis traditional and emerging partners to ensure that these partnerships are actually mutually beneficial (African Development Bank et al. 2011). This was somewhat reinforced and echoed again by the United Nations Economic Commission for Africa (2013).

But the times of the Berlin Conference, 1884/1885, when external powers sliced up the continent into colonial territorial entities without any meaningful participation of local agencies are past. Decolonisation has created new realities by establishing sovereign states governed by local policy makers. The principle of self-determination and territorial sovereignty does apply, even though it seems all too often a hollow declamatory reference in the absence of meaningful power over a country's own affairs and the use of its resources. But at the end, the local power constellation does play a role and it could well be decisive. There is manoeuvring space and room for negotiations with any external interests seeking own gains which could be used if the political will exist. The interaction between Africa and China brings us back to the roles of the policies of the governments, of the state, of political office bearers, civil servants and the all too weak local bourgeoisie, anything from acting "patriotic". If and to which extent the majority of the African people benefit from the old and new actors on their continent depends, at the end as so often, once again to a large extent upon their rulers—and not least but most importantly on their own social struggles. But it also requires the state as an actor, who provides the arena for such struggles without being the machinery for oppression and the vehicle for the interests of tiny elite. Establishing additional state control is in principle a step in the right direction—provided that this is not limited once again to a self-enrichment scheme through appropriation of revenue and rent seeking by the elites in control over the state. As Dobler (2007: 108) concludes:

> African governments will not change China's role in the world economy nor the leverage that comes with it, but policy measures they implement now may contribute to transforming its consequences and may determine whether China's emergence will reshuffle the cards in Africa's international economic relations or simply change the players.

Many remain sceptical over the dominant exchange mechanisms. The motive of such scepticism is not to protect Western or Northern interests at stake. On the contrary: the fear is that China at the end merely offers more of the same and continues business as usual. The ultimate challenge therefore remains with the government of Namibia. It needs to show to which extent it has the political will to turn the "all-weather friendship" into the win–win situation, so often declared as the ultimate rationale by the Chinese policy makers when justifying its political and economic partnerships. As the second Vice President of the NCCI declared in an interview 2013, "the problem is not the Chinese investors" but "rather how Namibians relate to the Chinese" (Mushelenga 2015: 210). But the local responses to the Chinese presence are a result of the laissez-faire policy of their government towards the Chinese investors, which led to "increasing xenophobia and resentment against Chinese in general and Chinese shop owners in particular" (Dobler 2009b: 718). According to Odada and Kakujaha-Matundu (2008: 22f.), local economists "bemoan the absence of a coherent strategy … to engage local industry in the Sino-Namibian trade". They believe "that this relationship would not go beyond the exports of minerals and agricultural products, unless deliberate efforts are made". After all: "Apart from some job creation and popular access to cheaper goods", the presence of Chinese traders and companies "is not likely to contribute much to the Namibian economy" (Dobler 2009b: 725). As regards the obvious discrepancy between the official bilateral "all-weather friendship" and the far more critical views from the grassroots, Namibia seems to be a typical case similar to those observed by Mohan et al. (2014), where a lack of policy intervention and protective measures opens space for abuse by foreign, in this case Chinese, economic actors. This in return triggers sentiments bordering to racism from those ordinary citizens feeling negatively affected on the ground.

References

African Development Bank/OECD Development Centre/United Nations Development Programme/Economic Commission for Africa. (2011). *African Economic Outlook 2011 Africa and its emerging partners. Summary*. OECD. http://www.africaneconomicoutlook.org. Accessed 03 Mar 2015.

Amadhila, N. (2012). Grassroots perceptions of China in Namibia: Effects on domestic politics and foreign policy. *The China Monitor* (2), 17–45.

Amadhila, N. (2013). *China in Africa. The effects on Namibia's foreign policy and domestic politics*. Saarbrücken: LAP Lambert Academic Publishing.

Bräutigam, D. (2010). *The dragon's gift. The real story of China in Africa*. Oxford: Oxford University Press.

Cheru, F., & Obi, C. (Eds.). (2010). *The rise of China & India in Africa*. London: Zed.

Cissé, D. (2016). Chinese traders in Windhoek. *Pambazuka News* 760, 3 February. http://www.pambazuka.net/en/category.php/features/96524. Accessed 03 Feb 2016.

Dobler, G. (2007). Old ties or new shackles? China in Namibia. In H. Melber (Ed.), *Transitions in Namibia. Which changes for whom?* (pp. 94–109). Uppsala: Nordic Africa Institute.

Dobler, G. (2008a). Solidarity, xenophobia, and the regulation of Chinese business in Namibia. In C. Alden, D. Large, & R. S. de Oliveira (Eds.), *China Returns to Africa: A rising power and a continent embrace* (pp. 237–255). London: Hurst.

Dobler, G. (2008b). From Scotch Whisky to Chinese Sneakers: International commodity flows and new trade networks in Oshikango, Namibia. *Africa, 78*(3), 410–432.

Dobler, G. (2009a). Oshikango: The dynamics of growth and regulation in a Namibian Boom Town. *Journal of Southern African Studies, 35*(1), 115–131.

Dobler, G. (2009b). Chinese shops and the formation of a Chinese Expatriate Community in Namibia. *The China Quarterly, 199*, 707–727.

Du Pisani, A. (2014). Namibia and China: Profile and appraisal of a relationship. In A. Bösl, A. du Pisani, & D. U. Zaire (Eds.), *Namibia's foreign relations. Historic contexts, current dimensions, and perspectives for the 21st century* (pp. 111–134). Windhoek: Macmillan Education Namibia.

Gibson, R. (1972). *African liberation movements. Contemporary struggles against white minority rule*. London: Oxford University Press.

Hamutenya, H. (2014). Namibia and Angola: Analysis of a symbiotic relationship. In A. Bösl, A. du Pisani, & D. U. Zaire (Eds.), *Namibia's foreign relations. Historic contexts, current dimensions, and perspectives for the 21st century* (pp. 81–109). Windhoek: Macmillan Education Namibia.

Harneit-Sievers, A., Marks, S., & Naidu, S. (Eds.). (2010). *Chinese and African Perspectives on China in Africa*. Oxford and Nairobi: Fahamu Books/Pambazuka Press.

Iileka, M. (2016). Crisis of epic proportions. *Namibian Sun*, 3 March. http://www.namibiansun.com/economics/crisis-epic-proportions.91925. Accessed 03 Mar 2016.

Jauch, H (comp.). (2009). Chinese investments in Africa. Opportunity or threat for workers? Accra: African Labour Research Network

Jauch, H., & Sakaria, I. (2009). *Chinese investments in Namibia: A labour perspective*. Windhoek: Labour Resource and Research Institute (LaRRI).

LaFraniere, S. (2009, November 19). China helps the powerful in Namibia. *The New York Times*. http://www.nytimes.com/2009/11/20/world/asia/20namibia.html?_r=0. Accessed 17 Jan 2016.

Lee, M. C., Melber, H., Naidu, S., & Taylor, I. (2007). *China in Africa* (Current African issues; no. 35). Uppsala: The Nordic Africa Institute.

Melber, H. (2010). China in Africa: Any impact on development and aid? In J. S. Sörensen (Ed.), *Challenging the aid paradigm Western currents and Asian alternatives* (pp. 214–240). Houndsmills: Palgrave Macmillan.

Melber, H. (2013a). Africa and China. Old stories or new opportunities? In T. Murithi (Ed.), *Handbook of Africa's international relations* (pp. 333–342). London: Routledge.

Melber, H. (2013b). Reviewing China in Africa: Old interests, new trends – Or new interests, old trends? *Development Southern Africa, 30*(4/5), 437–450.

Melber, H. (2016). *A decade of Namibia. Politics economy and society – The era Pohamba, 2004–2015*. Brill: Leiden.

Mohan, G., Lampert, B., Tan-Mullins, M., & Chang, D. (2014). *Chinese migrants and Africa's development. New imperialists of agents of change?* London: Zed.

Mushelenga, S. A. P. (2015). *The economic diplomacy of a small state: The case of Namibia.* PhD thesis (unpublished), University of South Africa, Pretoria

New Era. (2014). *Remarkable progress in China-Namibia trade*, 3 October. https://www.newera.com.na/2014/10/03/remarkable-progress-china-namibia-trade/. Accessed 29 Feb 2016.

New Era. (2016). *Hundreds retrenched as businesses fold at Oshikango*, 1 March. https://www.newera.com.na/2016/03/01/hundreds-retrenched-businesses-fold-oshikango/. Accessed 03 Mar 2016.

Nikondo, A., & Coetzee, J. (2009). *Perceptions on the impact of Chinese businesses in Namibia: A case study of the retail and construction sector in Windhoek.* Windhoek: Polytechnic. http://hdl.handle.net/10628/166. Accessed 09 Feb 2016.

Odada, J. E., & Kakujaha-Matundu, O. (2008). *China-Africa economic relations: The case of Namibia.* Windhoek: Department of Economics/University of Namibia. http://dspace.africaportal.org/jspui/bitstream/123456789/32046/1/Namibia-China.pdf?1. Accessed 24 Feb 2016.

Oshili. (2016). *Cement: Ohorongo wary of Southern Africa oversupply*, 2 March. http://www.oshili24.com.na/article.php?sid=1068. Accessed 03 Mar 2016.

Republic of Namibia/Office of the President. (2015a, April 21), *State of the Nation Address 2015 by His Excellency Dr. Hage G. Geingob, President of the Republic of Namibia.* Windhoek.

Republic of Namibia/Office of the President. (2015b, December 5). *Statement by His Excellency Hage G. Geingob, President of the Republic of Namibia at the Opening of the Forum on China-Africa Cooperation (FOCAC) Summit.* Johannesburg.

Sherbourne, R. (2007). China's growing presence in Namibia. In: Garth Le Pere (Ed.), *China in Africa. Mercantilist predator, or partner in development?* Midrand: Institute for Global Dialogue and Johannesburg: South African Institute of International Affairs.

Shinn, D. H., & Eisenman, J. (2012). *China and Africa. A century of engagement.* Philadelphia: University of Pennsylvania Press.

Taylor, I. (1997). China and SWAPO: The role of the People's Republic in Namibia's liberation and post-independence relations. *The South African Journal of International Affairs, 5*(1), 110–122.

United Nations Economic Commission for Africa. (2013). *Africa-BRICS cooperation: Implications for growth, employment and structural transformation in Africa.* Addis Ababa: United Nations Economic Commission for Africa.

Xinhua. (2013, March 19). *Quality, corporate image stressed in China-Africa cooperation.*

10

"Unequal Sino-African Relations": A Perspective from Africans in Guangzhou

Dong Niu

10.1 Introduction

In past decades, with the fast growth of infrastructural investment and international aid from the People's Republic of China (PRC) to Africa, the international trade between China and Africa has developed rapidly, while the Sino–African relations have also been entering into a new period of development, which bred diversified official interaction and non-governmental contacts between Chinese and Africans. Within the people of Chinese origin (ethnic Chinese) in continental Africa, contractual migrants constitute a highlighted sizable group (Mung 2008). Differing from Chinese moving to Africa, the occupations of Africans coming to China, however, are mostly small traders and international students. Most of Africans travel back and forth frequently between China and Africa while still producing a remarked African landscape in Guangzhou.

D. Niu (✉)
Tsinghua University, Beijing, China
e-mail: niudong.winter@gmail.com

Y. C. Kim (ed.), *China and Africa*, The Palgrave Macmillan Asian Business Series, DOI 10.1007/978-3-319-47030-6_10

About ten years ago, the emergence of Africans in Guangzhou/China as a research topic started to receive scholarly attention from around the world. In the eyes of scholars, it seemed that China, as a new emerging migration destination, had been attracting the arrival of immigrants from sub-Saharan Africa. Scholars regarded the topic as virgin soil and so produced a small body of academic literature. Those publications mostly contributed to a whole understanding of the appearance of Africans in Guangzhou in terms of space, business, education, language, health care and ethnicity. For the present, however, the Sino–African relations from the perspectives of Africans in Guangzhou is still less systematically described and analysed.

In the context of "The Road and Belt" initiated by the Chinese Government, more appearance of Africans in Guangzhou epitomises the general trend in the development of Sino–African Relations. However, the legislative fact that China is still a migration country determines that the local authorities' measures for regulating foreigners are limited. The current conflicts between Africans and relevant Guangzhou authorities, especially Guangzhou police, which have been depicted by Africans as the significant enforcement of "unequal Sino–African Relations" can reflect an uncertain barrier in Sino–African relations.

This chapter describes the barrier in the development of Sino–Africa relations, which will be posed or may have been posed, through the comparison of Africans' imagination before coming to China and their experience in Guangzhou. The structure of the analysis follows Africans' migration from Africa to China: imagining China before coming to China, experiencing China when living in Guangzhou and then responding to China through emerging public opinions.

10.2 International Migration and International Relations

As individuals are the primary actors within all human societies, nation-states are the primary actors within the current international society. Besides nation-states, non-state actors like intergovernmental organisations, non-governmental organisations, multinational corporations and super-empowered politicians are also playing the game of international politics. Compared with *aforesaid* big actors, international migrants, who normally move across country borders in the unit of individual or family, obviously, are not the typical research objects in the study of international relations. However, due to improvements in modern transportation coupled with advances in communication technology, population mobility has become a common phenomenon, immigration and emigration has become a common social problem, and international migrants are getting more and more visible within the actors acting and influencing the global or international system.

International migrants have been the focus of attention since they can connect different countries and societies officially or unofficially as 1985, Myro Weiner (Weiner 1985) suggested three propositions in connection between international migration and international relations: The first is that relations between states are often influenced by the actions or inactions of states vis-à-vis international migration. The second is that states affect international migration by the rules they create regarding exit and entry. The third is that international migrants have often become a political force in the country in which they reside. Christopher Mitchell (Mitchell 1989) summarised similar relationships: international relations help to shape international migration. Migration may influence and serve the goals of national foreign policies. "Domestic" immigration laws and policies may have an unavoidable international political projection. Since the structures and patterns of migration systems are determined not only by economic factors but also by political incentives, "migration diplomacy" and administrative practices shaped by political representations ought to be analysed so as to obtain a better understanding of the politics of regional integration (Thiollet 2011). Furthermore, some normative qualities of domestic regimes increasingly affect international relations and some international structures reinforce particular norms and institutions within states. In other words, norms and institutions help to explain matters of migration and the circumstances of immigrants in host societies (Heisler 1992).

In contrast with impacts brought about by intergovernmental organisations, non-governmental organisations, multinational corporations, and super-empowered politicians, international migrants' effects on international relations operate essentially with cross-border flow of population. As "agents", migrants not only respond to opportunities and constraints created by international social structures but also create pressures on states and subvert state authority (Klotz 1997). Free movement of population enables people of different countries to get acquainted with one another and with its cultures, which also shape perceptions people have of the respective other country and subsequently the relations between the countries. In other words, international migration can drive international relations "from below" (Düvell 2014).

In terms of the research on Sino–African migration and relations, African traders in China distribute Chinese consumer goods in Africa through their business networks with other traders around the world. They manage to connect African traders, Chinese manufacturers and wholesalers, thus playing an important role in China's exports to Africa and shape the business ness environment in Africa–China relations (Cissé 2015). When examining the role of Africans in China, Adams Bodomo sees the socio-economic and socio-cultural contributions by Africans in China as the basic of nascent African soft power in China. Under the background of initiating a people-to-people approach to Africa–China cooperation, he mentioned that some prominent members of the African communities in China are helping African diplomatic personnel perform official consular duties away from Beijing in places like Guangzhou, Yiwu, and Hong Kong (Bodomo 2015). Africans in Guangzhou function as a linguistic, cultural and economic bridge between China and Africa (Bodomo 2010). The fact that Africans' social organisations in Guangzhou have been involved in the administration of foreigners of Chinese government has been demonstrated. Dong Niu found such social organisations usually based on a common nationality, centred around leaders, required the provision of internal aid and guidance, and represent their people to interact with other organisations or groups (Niu 2015). In fact, China does not have an effective legal framework and enforcement capacity in place to manage high immigration pressure, so that the policing of migrants and other forms of control measures have been intensified as an ad hoc response in places where the immigrant population is perceived to have grown too large (Haugen 2012). Under the background of continued intensified relations between Guangzhou authorities and Africans, the strict regulation of undocumented Africans was interpreted as an "anti-immigrant campaign", which leads to a discrepancy between the local level and the national and international levels, with the pro- African political ideology at the latter ones (Lan 2015).

There is already ample documentation to explain the importance of international migration in international relations and international politics. Compared with fierce national confrontation like armed conflicts, migration's impacts on international relations might be mild and subtle. However, the enormous complexity of international relations where international migrants are involved will be more and more apparent as time goes by. This chapter contributes to revealing the relation between grassroots foreigners and international relations by describing the "unequal Sino–African relations" from the perspective of Africans in Guangzhou, discussing the potential setbacks in the development of Sino–African relations, and emphasising the importance of Africans in Guangzhou, who have the ability to affect their countries' relations with China.

10.3 Methodology

This chapter is based on 22 months of fieldwork that was conducted in Guangzhou from July 2013 to May 2015, which was carried out in conjunction with a larger study on Africans' daily experiences in Guangzhou—which is commonly regarded as being a popular area of residence for Africans residing in China. Over the course of the study, I acknowledged that although the term "Africans" encompasses a wide range of diverse groups, all of them encountered similar difficulties when trying to enter the country due to the strenuous visa provision scheme. In other words, the fragile nature of the visa status greatly undermines their ability to settle down with ease. Africans, however, may complain that the law enforcement of the Guangzhou authorities, especially the Guangzhou police, has been stringent and difficult. The matter had not been a subject of much consideration until several African nations started to adopt measures to check the validity of the visas of Chinese migrants, from the end of 2014. They utilised similar techniques to that of the Guangzhou police in combatting the problems of illegal residence, and it was this phenomenon which prompted me to solely focus on Africans in Guangzhou and the future of Sino–African relations in this chapter.

Data were collected via participant observation, semi-structured interviews, and unstructured interviews. The consequent findings showed that

Africans in Guangzhou were somewhat untrusting towards strangers and unwilling to answer questionnaires. During the start-up stage of the fieldwork, I drafted anthropological research methods that endeavoured to comprehend the intricacies of Sino–African relations in relatively isolated societies to urban studies. As a registered social worker, professional social work methods were further utilised to integrate the perspectives of those who I dealt with on a day-to-day basis to obtain an impartial idea of the nature of the relation. Ultimately, it was beneficial to become accustomed to the experiences of the African migrant society in Guangzhou. It also made me acknowledge the fact that the logic and the mechanisms of the "acquaintance society" is the way forward for the African community in Guangzhou as it would be the ideal way in which they could combat the problem of low trust and high mobility.

English and Chinese were utilised during my fieldwork, with Chinese being the main language I used to communicate with the majority of my informants. Some of my informants had lived in Guangzhou for more than 10 years, while some had been here for 20 plus years, which made Chinese the most appropriate and apt language for communication. The social centre I worked in was based in a neighbourhood where there was a significant concentration of Francophone Africans; thus, when I had to communicate with newcomers who were not proficient English speakers, I received interpretation assistance from several volunteers who were mostly university students majoring in French.

Unique research methods make it impossible to count the number of interviews that I conducted with the informants, which included not only Africans but also people that were in any way or form related to Africans, like their Chinese spouses, social workers, landlords who rented apartments to Africans, taxi drivers, security guards, police working in the local police station and the Exit-Entry Management Division in Guangzhou. I established communication with more than 300 Africans and kept strong ties with approximately 90 of them via mobile applications like Whatsapp and Wechat. I further interviewed 19 people around 30 times, and thus those informants could be regarded as being key informants whose details are as follows: 15 were male, 4 were female, aged between 18 and 41 years; they were mainly traders, students and asylum seekers; nationalities mostly refer to sub-Saharan African countries like

Democratic Republic of Congo, Congo (Brazzaville), Niger, Cameroon, Senegal, Mali, Nigeria, Kenya, Uganda, Somalia, and Tanzania. In addition, it should be noticeable that some of my key informants are the leaders of their social organisations.

Doing fieldwork as a social worker differentiated me from other researchers in the orientation of methodology, which not only gave me an advantage in approaching Africans in understanding their thoughts and experiences but also made me encounter a multidimensional ethical challenge. My customers wished for me to stand on their side to feel their negative experiences in Guangzhou and to help them solve their problems while protecting their respective privacy. The local authorities, especially the police, hoped that I would take the responsibility of "Wei Wen" (meaning, "maintain social stability") by reporting suspicious undocumented activity by Africans. Some scholars hoped to get acquainted with more Africans via my membership in the social work centre. Finally, I chose to maintain the value orientation of African interests and refused the desires of the local police, media personnel and scholars who attempted to direct my social work, which enabled me to gain the trust of more Africans.

10.4 Africans in Guangzhou

Guangzhou, as one of the most important international trade port cities in China, is South China's economic, political and cultural hub. It was called "the capital of the Third World" mainly as it was the ideal place where you could see Africans from almost all the African countries (Huang 2008). While observing such phenomena of "Africans in Guangzhou", many scholars tend to look for clues in their long history to strengthen the base of Sino–African exchanges and cooperation. However, in fact, present Africans in Guangzhou have little to no connection with their ancestors in Guangzhou.

One of the most important backgrounds for Africans coming into Guangzhou is the ever growing economic and trade cooperation between Guangzhou and Africa. As an experimental city, Guangzhou's exports to Africa in 1983 were only 6,216,900 dollars, but by the end of 2012, this figure increased to 2,686,850,000 dollars (Guangzhou-Yearbook-Compilation-Committee 1983–2014). The expanding economic and trade cooperation was promoted by the authorities in Guangzhou, who encouraged Guangzhou enterprises to export goods to Africa and look further for business and investment opportunities in Africa. The spread of cheap and welcomed goods provided Africans with the required force to kick-start their development process. One of my interviewees informed me that it was then that Africans started to come into Guangzhou. "At that time, there were a lot of foreigners here. I could only speak a little English, and couldn't speak Chinese, so couldn't communicate with the Chinese people... The first hotel where I slept in Guangzhou was called Astro Hotel (It was said that the hotel was destroyed in an uncontrollable fire in 2005, where Guangzhou Children's activity centre is located now). It was a well-known hotel, but has now closed. It was located in Xiaobei (the name came from the Small North gate in the ancient city of Guangzhou). The first Chinese food I ate in Guangzhou was noodles, Chinese Muslim noodles. I remember that the male chef was not very tall. At that time, the Chinese Muslim restaurant was the only restaurant here", my Congolese informant recalled. Indeed, as brave pioneers, the Africans coming to Guangzhou near the second millennium provided the incumbent Africans with the absolutely necessary social and ethnic ties.

There were no official statistics on the size of the African population in Guangzhou until 2014, which led to many scholarly deductions to gain an accurate deduction of the relative figures. However, with the escalating and expending Ebola haemorrhagic fever horror among the Chinese public, "uncontrolled illegal Africans in Guangzhou" became a very hot topic on the Internet in China. Due to the increase in public pressure, the Guangzhou authorities began to release official statistics, "There are around 15,000–20,000 Africans in Guangzhou" (Guangzhou-Government 2014, Guangzhou-Public-Security-Bureau 2014, Suo 2014). Nevertheless, it deserves noting that China's local governments didn't have enough efficient resources or measures to obtain a precise statistic regarding the number of foreigners at that moment in time. Guangzhou police managed to obtain relative statistics regarding the size of foreigners at a specific time by adding the population registered in hotels to the ones living in rental estates and updated the statistics by checking visas and residence registrations on the streets and in the neighbourhoods Africans were known to be concentrated in. However, as the majority of Africans travelled back and forth frequently between China and Africa, and as some are known to be newcomers, who are not subject to the registration formalities in their places of residence within 24 hours after their arrival if they aren't residing in hotels, and others can't even finish the normal registration procedure if they do not have a valid visa, the released statistics were challenged by the Chinese general public. Facing the potential "migration pressure" and the fervour of public opinion, the Guangzhou police had to enhance their enforcement actions, and even still, the prospects of there being precise statistics are narrow.

There is a great variety within the African community in Guangzhou. First of all, in terms of age, gender, occupation, and stay time, Africans in Guangzhou mainly refer to ones who are 20–40 years old male traders with a stay time of less than 180 days. Some Africans are unmarried and impoverished but have the dream that one day they'll accumulate wealth via importing cheap Chinese goods to Africa to obtain profits. It should be noted that a considerable number of African visas don't belong in the business criteria. In order to extend their visas, some traders have to apply to Chinese universities to become students so that they are able to stay in Guangzhou for another 6–12 months to continue their businesses, although such actions are regarded as illegal by Chinese laws and regulations. The aims of some Africans, however, are not business. One of my Ugandan informants wanted to be an English teacher at first but she didn't realise that it was a fraud by dangerous Chinese and African agents, until she reached Guangzhou and lost all of her money. Second, in terms of ethnicity, different ethnic groups, in theory, tend to communicate via their native languages. However, Africans in Guangzhou interact by using a mixture of English and French because Chinese traders in Guangzhou are more or less able to speak English. Furthermore, Africans share a language tradition that descended from their colonial days that enables them to liaise with ease with one another. Ultimately, however, the use of a global language doesn't shadow the ethnic diversity of Africans but reveals it instead. Third, it seems that Nigerians are largely responsible for the crimes committed by foreigners in Guangzhou. In the past few years, drug smuggling, marriage frauds, gang crimes, and other breaking Chinese news have more or less been connected to Nigerians in Guangzhou. Generally, other Africans are willing to keep a distance from Nigerians in order to retain their reputation, and other ethnic groups from Nigeria tend to declare that they are different from

Igbo Nigerians. In other words, although Africans in Guangzhou are a differentiated community in the eyes of the Chinese, business secrets, ethnic backgrounds, and national reputation have shaped a culture with a high degree of mistrust within the community. Considering the high mobility of Africans and China's tightened visa policy, it is doubtful whether an integrated immigrant society will ever exist.

10.5 Africans' Imagination Before Coming to Guangzhou

The motivation and determination of Africans to leave their country for China greatly depends on whether their attitude is positive for the development of Sino–African relations. As some studies have shown, the determinants of Africans' perspectives on China–Africa are nuanced and encompass both economic and political factors. Africans perceive imports from China as being damaging to local economies, dampening support for Chinese presence in African countries, but the negative effect of trade on Africans' perspectives is counter-balanced by the effect that Chinese engagement has on poverty alleviation (Hanusch 2012). Although African views on China–Africa links are variegated and complex, most Africans are positive about China–Africa links (Sautman and Yan 2009). Since the 2008 Olympic Games in Beijing, "Africans in Guangzhou" as a new topic has been appearing in the Chinese public and ever since, it has continued to become a hot spot for academic attention as well as it being an issue of governance for local governments and a top focus of public opinion. In any case, the continued appearance of Africans in Guangzhou demonstrates that the majority of Africans' imagination of China is relatively positive before coming to China, which is reflected in the following four features:

First of all, coming to China means that business success is relatively easier. As already indicated above, the most important background for Africans coming to Guangzhou is the growing economic and trade cooperation between Guangzhou and Africa. Many of my informants told me that "Made in China" has occupied all of the markets in their countries, and people can't live without Chinese goods as man cannot live without air. As a Nigerian stressed, "Although the quality of Chinese goods are not good,

Africans do not care about that. They only care about the price, the lowest price is always the most welcomed. Africans also like a lot of styles, colours and patterns, which China can make. In China, as long as you have the money, you can buy everything you need". Some small traders are hoping to come to China to import goods and then to obtain high profits in Africa, which is a particularly evident trend with single African men. For them, it is a good opportunity to go to China to achieve business success, so that they can find love, establish families, get respect and realise the upward social mobility in their societies.

Second, coming to China means that people can gain opportunities to learn the Chinese language and the intricacies regarding advanced technologies. Some Africans have the work experience in Chinese enterprises in Africa (including small supermarkets run by the Chinese). For some of them, it will be an enviable achievement to work in the large Chinese enterprises. In this context, they want to come to China to learn the Chinese language (Mandarin), computer technology, traditional Chinese medicine or international trade, with the dream that they may obtain employment in the near future when they return home. One of my Malian informants had obtained a master's degree in international law before he came to China, but when he observed the influx of migrants coming to do business in China, he proceeded to make a career change. In Guangzhou, he acknowledged that the Chinese people did not speak French and Malian native languages, so he first decided to learn Chinese and then start his business.

Third, when coming to China, the Africans will be welcomed by the Chinese people. Generally, Africans have witnessed the Chinese people's hard work in Africa. When liaising with the Chinese in their own country, they acknowledged that the Chinese people respect the hardworking man so they believe that if they work hard in China, the Chinese people will also welcome and respect them. Some of my informants told me that in Africa, some Chinese people had told them that there are many foreigners in China's cities, and foreigners are welcomed there. If they marry Chinese wives successfully, they can make money easily in China and live in China for the rest of their lives. Africans looked forward to being welcomed by Chinese people in China as the Chinese were welcomed in Africa.

Fourth, coming to China means that people can have peace and freedom. Compared with China, some African countries have no stable political environment. A Congolese (Kinshasa) informant once told a sad story, "Congo is divided into eastern, central and western regions. Eastern Congo is closer to Rwanda, and people there died every day because of the wars. My father, mother and a brother lived in the eastern region. Every holiday, I would go there to visit relatives, but now I can't because of the war... which has killed my brother". In this context, he decided to come to China to live freely and peacefully. The desire for peace and freedom is most evident in most Somalis. Many Somalis have told me that there is no peace and freedom in Somalia so they can't live and do business there. As a result, some of them came to China as asylum seekers to wait for the judgment procedures of the United Nations High Commissioner for Refugees in the hope that one day they qualify as refugees to migrate to Western countries like America or Canada. In this sense, China is a peaceful transit country for some Africans.

In short, the dream of successful business, sufficient study opportunities, friendly people and peaceful social environment have drawn up a grand blueprint for Africans in Africa. The imagination constitutes a built-in incentive for Africans to move to Guangzhou. Although some Africans have heard of the conflicts between the Guangzhou police and Nigerians, some of them believe that they will not encounter such a dilemma if they do not break Chinese laws.

10.6 Africans' Experience in Guangzhou: "Unequal Sino–African Relations"

Although Africans in Guangzhou take it for granted that Exit and Entry Administration Law and Regulations on Administration of the PRC are "the Chinese immigration laws", they refer to Entry-Exit Management Division of Guangzhou public security bureau as "the Chinese immigration", as there are no official immigration laws and immigration bureaus in the Chinese legislative framework and administrative system. In other words, the whole task of regulating domestic foreigners are carried out by the Guangzhou police, which makes the law enforcement of Guangzhou police the trigger-point between Africans and the migration environment of China. In July 2009 and June 2012, two African parades were initiated in protest against police violence, which happened around the international trade markets of Guangzhou (Kong and Liu 2009, Yuexiu-District-Public-Security-Bureau 2012). It attracted the attention of almost all of China, including those at the top, and since then, Africans have been attributed as being a societal problem in Chinese society. In recent years, more negative news about Africans in Guangzhou has spread like wild fire on the Chinese Internet. The panic of civil society for Africans in Guangzhou helped to raise the public opinion that "laws were not strictly enforced by the Guangzhou police, and illegal African immigrants have gone out of control". The anxiety of senior government officials about public opinion was transferred effectively to the Guangzhou police to strengthen their law enforcement units.

In the name of cracking against "Sanfei" ("三非", literally means illegal immigration, residence and employment of foreigners), Guangzhou police detained and deported 768 foreigners from January 2014 to August 2014 (Fu 2014). Although there is no statistics on the proportion of Africans, Africans are probably the majority of all illegal foreigners according to Guangzhou police's frequent actions in the African neighbourhood, "Xiaobei". Xiaobei has a great reputation among Africans. The African traders who have just arrived in China will soon leave for Xiaobei; a few Chinese words that the Africans first learn include "Xiaobei". Xiaobei is so famous that a Xinhua News Agency reporter came here to find materials on Tanzania, Congo (Brazzaville), and South Africa before Chinese President Xi Jinping visited those three countries in March 2013.

However, as I stated above, Chinese local authorities' measures for regulating foreigners are limited. Guangzhou police can't identify whether one African is illegal or not until they initialise contact to check the one's visa and residence registration, so all Africans will be suspects and potential "Sanfei". In this context, a very severe environment for Africans is formed in Guangzhou, which was described by some Africans as "unequal Sino–African relations", because they think the Chinese people in Africa are better served by African police and at least didn't suffer the strict regulation by African governments the severity of this environment is embodied in the following aspects.

First of all, the means of law enforcement are "rude" and "impolite". Guangzhou police control the mobility of Africans by checking visas and residence registrations around the international trade markets and African neighbourhoods. Although all the documents are valid and legal, still some Africans try to avoid encountering police. In the perspective of Africans, Guangzhou police can't speak English and French, don't respect humanity and the means of their law enforcement process are "rude" and "impolite". The expression that "Guangzhou police take Africans as animals" occurred repeatedly from my African informants a Guinean trader said, "I have the paper (means valid residence registrations), and I also have (valid) visa, but they (Guangzhou police) took away my passport. They took me aboard on a bus and took me to the police station. They don't provided seats for me. I just sat on the ground outdoors. A fence enclosed me. I spent nearly two hours there and nobody came to inquire me. I was scared, that is the most terrible time in my life... (At last,) they gave me the passport, said nothing, just let me go".

Second, the social support network for Africans in Guangzhou has been destroyed. Since around 2006, an African neighbourhood has formed in Xiaobei, where some Africans opened dozens of restaurants and hairdressing salons without licenses, or operated restaurants and hairdressing salons in the names of Chinese partners. Africans could taste their home dishes and make African haircuts in those stores to relieve their homesickness. Actually, the stores that Africans operated are the key notes in the social support network of Africans in Guangzhou. According to China's laws, however, such actions like running stores without necessary licenses and documents and employing African students who usually have no authorised work permits are illegal. In this context, some African students have been detained and fined, and some stores have been closed by Guangzhou police, especially in 2014. For the majority of Africans, the law enforcement of Guangzhou police is unreasonable, because the Chinese people are not the customers of those stores. As a Uganda student said, "Unless Chinese can make us African haircuts and Matoke (A traditional Uganda food)... I didn't hurt anyone there and we didn't make any money from the Chinese. We make money from African people, not Chinese".

Third, Africans from other provinces and cities of China "got entrapped" in Guangzhou. Because Guangzhou, especially Xiaobei, is the hub of Africans in China, some Africans from Shanghai, Beijing, Wuhan, Yiwu and other cities of China described the negative experience in Guangzhou. They said that Chinese police in other cities wouldn't check visas on the street or in their rental estates. Some Africans feel so shocked by the strict law enforcement of Guangzhou police because they have never even registered in the police stations of their places. In their opinion, Xiaobei is a place where law is the strictest for Africans in China. A Congolese (Brazzaville) student was studying in the city of Wuhan, Hubei province, but he had the experience of "being entrapped" in Guangzhou. As he stated, "When I came here last night, I saw many police standing there. A police asked me, "why do you come here?"... They are not polite. Such matter will not happen in France. Police in France are polite... They could say "Hello. Can I look at your passport?" but they (Guangzhou police) said "Here! Here! Here!' They found my visa was issued at Hubei province, so said, 'you can't live anywhere except in hotel! You must live in hotel!' Then I went to a hotel, pay the money. When I left the hotel, I was so afraid, I was afraid to see police again. You know? A lot of police! You know"?

Fourth, there is no enough screening operation in the law enforcement. As I stated above, Guangzhou police can't identify whether one African is illegal or not until they initialise contact to check the one's visa and residence registration. For the Africans with valid visas and documents, the law enforcement of Guangzhou police is unnecessary harassment. Some Africans are the political elites in their hometowns. For example, one of my Cameron informants is called as "Princess" by Cameroonian in Guangzhou because her father is a powerful chief of a tribe in Cameron, and a Congolese informant's father is working in the Congo Embassy in Angola. Besides political elites, some Africans have great economic power. Those who have bought private cars and real estates in Guangzhou (usually in the name of their Chinese couples) think they are different from other Africans. In the context, they would feel strong passionate snatches in the law enforcement. As one successful representative of a multinational corporation complained, "I have been in China for more than 10 years, and they should have to respect me"! A leader of an African social organisation stated, "If the police want to catch those drug dealers, we would support certainly, but the actions should not affect the others' normal lives. Not all Africans are bad. Many Mama (A title of respect for African women) came to do business here, but they get more and more scared. Some are so scared that didn't come again. Like here around Xiaobei, sometimes there were one hundred police catching people. How do the Chinese people walking on the street look on Africans? How do our Chinese neighbours look on us? If you don't have enough evidence, you'd better not do like this. Now, you check people one by one. That has really bad effects on us".

In conclusion, the experience of most Africans in Guangzhou, no matter illegal or legal according to China's laws, is in strong contrast to their imagination before coming to Guangzhou. Obviously, they think Chinese in Africa are better served by African police, which was described by some Africans as "unequal Sino–African relations". The description on Sino–African relations from African community in Guangzhou contributed to a public opinion. This public opinion was passed to African embassies and consulates in China by their social organisations, which will pose, or even has posed, a barrier to the development of Sino–African relations.

10.7 Conclusion

At the end of 2014, several African police actions towards the Chinese people in African countries require our particular attention. First, 45 Chinese were arrested in a sweep by Uganda Immigration, because they were found to be lacking valid documents. Among them, 15 were deported and the other 30 were advised to apply for work permits so as to formalise their stay (Candia 2014). Second, 77 Chinese in Kenya were charged because they stayed in the country illegally and operated radio equipment without the necessary permits (Unknown 2014b). Third, more than 300 Chinese were arrested by Angolan police in what the government described as an effort to deter illegal immigrants working in Angola (Unknown 2014a). In such police actions, African police didn't claim that they were taking retaliatory measures against the Chinese government, as Guangzhou police never admitted that their law enforcement was against Africans or a specific African country, which makes it hard to find some direct evidence to reveal the complex relation between grassroots foreigners and international relations. However, based on the analysis of this chapter, it can be assumed that those African police actions were not accidental, especially in the era of globalisation, when modern transportation and communication technology have made every corner of the earth connected, and when African social organisations in Guangzhou have made grassroots Africans there and their embassies in China connected tightly. If grassroots foreigners can affect both the national interests of their countries and the countries where they stay, they will also have the ability to affect the relations between these countries.

This chapter has demonstrated the "unequal Sino–African relations" from the perspective of Africans in Guangzhou by comparing the Africans' positive imagination before coming to China and their negative experience in Guangzhou. Although the "unequal Sino–African relations" will not be admitted by China and African countries absolutely in the context of "The Road and Belt Initiative" because it was just produced by the personal passionate snatches of Africans, it represents a setback in Sino–African relations, which deserves greater attention from the Chinese government.

It is undoubted that China's current development model is different from that of Western countries. An important feature of the China model may be its high-performance institution. However, the institution didn't produce enough efficient measures to regulate domestic foreigners, which made Africans' normal appeal present as a social problem and then as a possible barrier to affect the development of Sino–African relations. Some Africans, although very seldom, have lived in China for 10 or even 20 years, so that sometimes give a feeling that they are Chinese with just different skin colour. However, according to the current laws of China, they will not gain stable migrant status or citizenship. If laws are established to meet the needs of practice and to regulate the practice, then obviously, China's laws on domestic foreigners will be lagging behind the reality of its foreign relations with other countries.

Currently, China is still a typical migration country. In this context, sufficient coordination, understanding and political mutual trust between China and African countries are needed on the problem of grassroots Africans in China or grass-root Chinese in Africa. Maybe it should be better, first, to set up an international police cooperation mechanism between China and African countries. Luckily, Nigerian police have appeared on the streets of Xiaobei, Guangzhou, in November 2015, which is a good beginning to break the barrier in the development of Sino–African relations, the "unequal Sino-African relations" from the perspective of Africans in Guangzhou.

References

Bodomo, A. (2010). The African trading community in Guangzhou: An emerging bridge for Africa–China relations. *The China Quarterly, 203*(1), 693–707.

Bodomo, A. (2015). African soft power in China. *African East-Asian Affairs, 1*(2), 76–97.

Candia, S. (2014, December 3). Uganda deports 15 Chinese over Illegal entry, new vision. *Uganda's Leading Daily.* http://www.newvision.co.ug/news/662468-uganda-deports-15-chinese-over-illgal-entry.html

Cissé, D. (2015). African traders in Yiwu: Their trade networks and their role in the distribution of 'Made in China' products in Africa. *The Journal of Pan African Studies, 7*(10), 44.

Düvell, F. (2014). International relations and migration management: The case of Turkey. *Insight Turkey, 16*(1), 35–44.

Fu, Q. (2014, September 4). Guangzhou, 768 foreigners were in detention and deportation in the first 8 months. *Xinhua Net.* http://news.xinhuanet.com/local/2014-09/04/c_1112367857.htm

Guangzhou-Government. (2014, November 1). *XIE Xiaodan attended the Twenty-seventh Government Press Conference and Answered Reporters' Questions.* Guangzhou Government Website.

Guangzhou-Public-Security-Bureau. (2014, December 1). Foreign population in Guangzhou is 118 thousand, Japanese and South Koreans ranks first and second. *New Express.* http://epaper.xkb.com.cn/view/968112

Guangzhou-Yearbook-Compilation-Committee. (1983–2014). *Guangzhou yearbook 1983–2014.* Guangzhou: Guangzhou Yearbook. http://www.gz.gov.cn/publicfiles/business/htmlfiles/gzgov/s2342/201411/2766116.html

Hanusch, M. (2012). African perspectives on China–Africa: Modelling popular perceptions and their economic and political determinants. *Oxford Development Studies, 40*(4), 492–516.

Haugen, H. Ø. (2012). Nigerians in China: A second state of immobility. *International Migration, 50*(2), 65–80.

Heisler, M. O. (1992). Migration, international relations and the New Europe: Theoretical perspectives from institutional political sociology. *International Migration Review, 26*(2), 596–622.

Huang, J. J. (2008). Guangzhou is the capital of "the third world"? *New Weekly*, (11), 68.

Klotz, A. (1997). International relations and migration in Southern Africa. *African Security Review, 6*(3), 38–45.

Kong, B., & Liu, W. L. (2009, July 15). A gathering event of Africans happened around a police station in Guangzhou. *Xinhua Net.* http://news.xinhuanet.com/society/2009-07/15/content_11713880.htm.

Lan, S. (2015). State regulation of undocumented African migrants in China: A multi-scalar analysis. *Journal of Asian and African Studies, 50*(3), 289–304.

Mitchell, C. (1989). International migration, international relations and foreign policy. *International Migration Review, 23*(3), 681–708.

Mung, E. M. (2008). Chinese migration and China's foreign policy in Africa. *Journal of Chinese Overseas, 4*(1), 91–109.

Niu, D. (2015). "Transient Association": Africans' Social Organizations in Guangzhou. *Sociological Studies*, (2), 124–148, 244.

Sautman, B., & Yan, H. R. (2009, September). African perspectives on China–Africa Links. *The China Quarterly*, 728–759.

Suo, Y. W. (2014, June 13). Mayor of Guangzhou: About twenty thousand Africans are doing business in Guangzhou. *China News Service.* http://finance.chinanews.com/cj/2014/06-13/6279575.shtml

Thiollet, H. (2011). Migration as diplomacy: Labor migrants, refugees, and Arab regional politics in the oil-rich countries, *International Labor and Working-Class. History, 79*(1), 103–121.

Unknown mimeo. (2014a, December 23). Angolan police arrest, detain foreigners. *Angola News Network*. http://www.angolanewsnetwork.com/news/2014/12/23/angolan-police-arrest-detain-foreigners.html

Unknown mimeo. (2014b, December 4). Kenya breaks 'Chinese-run Cyber Crime Network'. *BBC News.* http://www.bbc.com/news/world-africa-30327412?mc_cid=070fe8be63&mc_eid=c4816424bb

Weiner, M. (1985). On international migration and international relations. *Population and Development Review, 11*(3), 441–455.

Yuexiu-District-Public-Security-Bureau. (2012, June 19). *A number of foreigners gathered and blocked traffic in Guangyuan West Road, Yuexiu police legally and properly handled it*. Guangzhou Public Security Bureau Website. http://www.gzjd.gov.cn/pub/index_jsp_catid_14_154_id_106713.html

11

Conclusion: An Argument for a Development Paradigm in Africa That Reconciles the Washington Consensus with the Beijing Model

Simplice A. Asongu and Jacinta C.Nwachukwu

11.1 Introduction

This chapter is presented as an argument to address two types of readership: policy makers who can easily grasp the arguments without the cumbersome exercise of references and scholars in the academic community without prior knowledge of the underlying concepts, who may need substantive references to comprehend the nature of the matter in question.

Three main schools of thought dominate Sino–African relations: the Pessimistic, Optimistic and Accommodation schools. Pessimists view the

S.A. Asongu (✉)
Africa Governance and Development Institute, Yaounde, Cameroon
e-mail: asongusimplice@yahoo.com

J.C. Nwachukwu
School of Economics, Finance and Accounting, Faculty of Business and Law, Coventry University Priory Street, Coventry, CV1 5FB, UK
e-mail: jacinta.nwachukwu@coventry.ac.uk

Y. C. Kim (ed.), *China and Africa*, The Palgrave Macmillan Asian Business Series, DOI 10.1007/978-3-319-47030-6_11

nexus as an asymmetric relation that favours China. Optimists contend that China is offering Africa an opportunity to charter its own development course without Western policy prescriptions in order to stimulate further economic growth. The third school is founded on the premise that the relationship is an ineluctable process that can be mutually beneficial if African countries adopt a common 'China strategy' based on rational economic arguments in order to balance the asymmetric relationship (Asongu and Aminkeng 2013). Pessimists are advocates of the Washington Consensus (WC) for the most part, optimists are sympathetic to the Beijing Model (BM) whereas proponents of the Accommodation school view Sino–African relations in the light of a paradigm shift or/and contemporary African Consensus as an instrument that incorporates both the BM and the WC (Asongu and Aminkeng 2013).

The WC can be defined as being a '*liberal democracy, private capitalism and priority in political rights*', while the BM is commonly perceived as being a '*de-emphasised democracy, state capitalism and priority in economic rights*' (Asongu 2016a). The current African consensus or New Partnership for Africa's Development (NEPAD) consists of: (i) the promotion of strong institutions, good governance, democracy and human rights and (ii) 'African sovereignty'. The first is consistent with the BM whereas the second is in accordance with the WC, for the most part. Whereas the WC promotes human rights and democracy that are advocated by the NEPAD, the non-interference policy of the BM is also in accordance with the NEPAD's core value of African ownership. The NEPAD therefore incorporates both the WC and the BM. Furthermore, the NEPAD reconciles both the first and second schools siding, respectively, with the WC and BM.

In this chapter, we articulate the highlighted reconciliation into more perspectives, notably: optimists versus pessimists; preferences in rights (national vs. human, sovereign vs. idiosyncratic) and economic versus political rights. The Accommodation school posits that the optimistic or balance-development school can build on the criticisms levelled by the pessimistic or neo-colonial school to improve on the development issues surrounding the Sino–African nexus. According to the narrative, China is simply playing by the globalisation standards that are embraced by the pessimistic school. Globalisation is now an ineluctable process whose challenges cannot be neglected without jeopardising the prosperity of nation states. Hence, given the growing relevance of China in an increasingly globalised world, Sino–African relations can be viewed as a historic process that is steadily evolving to mutually beneficial development, if the right policies are put in place at the right time.

Concerns about the preferences in rights motivating the pessimistic and optimistic schools merit further emphasis. The WC versus BM or the first school's versus the second school's ideology is respectively consistent with the following analogies: human versus national rights, idiosyncratic versus sovereign rights and political versus economic rights. First, on the debate over human versus national rights, China's non-interference policy is based on the preference of national over human rights. There is a longstanding suspicion by African countries of Western bias when it comes to the conception and definition of human rights. Recently, gay rights have become fundamental human rights and considered to stand before national rights (legislative, judiciary and executive). An example is the humiliating suspension of loans and grants issued to Uganda as a result of a bill, which was voted by the legislative power that was made into a law by the executive authority. Furthermore, the West has been overtly hypocritical in the criticisms she has been levelling on Sino–African relations, especially with regard to China's policy of non-interference. Two facts merit emphasis here: Historically, France's policy towards Africa has not been greased by her cherished values of 'liberty, fraternity and equality'. China's 'resource diplomacy' in Africa is further consistent with the USA's oil diplomacy in Saudi Arabia, which exemplifies the fact that there is some correlation in the ways in which the West and China dictate their foreign policies when working with African nations.

Furthermore, idiosyncratic or specific-individual rights are perceived as being equipollent to sovereign rights. Hence, one should not take precedence over the other, according to Chinese foreign policy. African countries are waking up to the realisation that foreign policy should be an amicable affair that is void of hegemony. Moreover, international law should not be skewed to favour the more affluent sovereign nations by giving them the right to critique and punish subsequent sovereign states on issues that are legitimate and sanctioned by domestic principles of democracy and law. The underlying suspicion further extends to the selective application of law by the International Criminal Court.

Thirdly, with regard to the priorities between 'the right to vote' and 'the right to food' advocated by the WC and BM respectively, it is no longer a moderate consensus that political rights are more endogenous than economic rights. It is very likely that a person with an empty stomach would sell his/her 'right to vote' in exchange for daily supplies of bread. The BM has cultivated a burgeoning middle class within a breathtaking period of time. Once a burgeoning middle class has been established, liberal democracy would be credible and sustainable because the middle class is very likely to prefer the 'right to vote' independently of the 'right to food'. In addition, it is apparent that the WC is essentially a long-term development strategy. This is not suspiring because it took the Western icons of liberal democracy more than 150 years to provide equal rights to their citizens. In the sections that follow, we substantiate the points highlighted above in greater depth.

The rest of the chapter is organised as follows; Sect. 11.2 engages historical and contemporary perspectives, while the dominant schools of thought are presented and reconciled in Sect. 11.3. Section 11.4 discusses the practical and contemporary relevance of such issues, whereas Sect. 11.5 concludes with a summary of the core arguments.

11.2 Historical and Contemporary Perspectives

This section is discussed in five main strands: a brief summary of the literature on the possible causes of Africa's underdevelopment, foremost development models, contemporary development proposals, recent trends regarding African poverty in the light of the Millennium Development Goals (MDGs) poverty targets and the most recent perspectives on solutions to the continent's underdevelopment.

Consistent with Asongu and Kodila-Tedika (2015), Africa's development tragedy can be discussed in 15 main strands, namely (i) the loss of traditional institutions (Lewis 1955; Amavilah 2006, 2014) and/or African de-institutionalisation (Nunn 2008, 2009; Nunn and Puga 2012); (ii) neglecting art as an expression of technological know-how (Amavilah 2014); (iii) the juxtaposition between 'private property rights' and 'private use rights' (Amavilah 2015); (iv) the overly idle handling of natural resources (Doftman 1939; Lewis 1955; Amavilah 2014); (v) the overvaluation of foreign knowledge and the devaluation of local knowledge (Asongu et al. 2014a, b; Amavilah et al. 2014; Tchamyou 2015; Lwoga et al. 2010; Raseroka 2008; Brush and Stabinsky 1996); (vi) the inability to acknowledge scarcity (Dorfman 1939; Lucas 1993; Drine 2013; Fosu 2013; America 2013; Asongu 2014a, b; Looney 2013); (vii) excessive consumption of luxurious goods by the rich elite (Efobi et al. 2013; Adewole and Osabuohien 2007); (viii) the false economics of preconditions (Monga 2014) and the decades that were lost due to the WC (Lin 2015); (ix) issues surrounding colonialism, neo-colonialism and Western imperialism (Ndlovu-Gatsheni 2013); (x0) over-reliance on Western policies (Fofack 2014) and development assistance (Asongu 2014c; Obeng-Odoom 2013; Moyo 2009); (xi) failure to integrate qualitative development measurements in development paradigms (Obeng-Odoom 2013) and the 'Africa rising' narrative (Obeng-Odoom 2015); (xii2) the need for a paradigm shift from strong economics (or structural adjustment policies) to soft economics (or human capability) development (Kuada 2015); (xiii3) low depth of regional integration (Kayizzi-Mugerwa, et al. 2014); (xiv) fragile institutions, the absence of conducive local conditions and ineffective negotiations in receiving foreign aid (Kayizzi-Mugerwa 2001) and less stringent property rights that are essential for reverse engineering and the imitation of foreign technology (Asongu 2014d) and (xv) corruption in international trade (Musila and Sigué 2010).

The argument for a reconciliation between the WC and the BM deviates from mainstream literature regarding African development models. These consist of, among others: the Lagos Plan of Action for Economic Development (LPA, 1980–2000), the Africa's Priority for Economic Recovery initiative (APPER, 1986–1990), the African Alternative Framework to Structural Adjustment Programme for Socioeconomic Recovery and Transformation (AAF-SAP, 1989), the African Charter for Popular Participation for Development (1990), the 2001 NEPAD (OAU 1980, 2001; Bujra 2004; Adedeji 1999), self-reliance as a sustainable path to African development (Fofack 2014, p. 13) and development strategies from developing countries based on the lessons that were learnt from both the WC and the BM (Fosu 2013).

Further development models that were introduced post-WC further sustain the argument we laid out afore and also entails the New Structural Economics (NSE) and Liberal Institutional Pluralism (LIP) initiative. The NSE posits, without necessarily tailoring, a unified economic theory that some convergence between ideologies of structuralism and liberalism are needed. The approach which recognises both state and market failures (see Fofack 2014, p. 14) is advanced by, *inter alia,* Chang (2002), Lin and Monga (2011), Norman and Stiglitz (2012), Stiglitz and others (2013a, b) and Stiglitz and Lin (2013). The second or LIP school is oriented towards, among others, institutions for effective delivery of public services, institutional conditions for successful growth and institutional diversity (see North 1990; Acemoglu et al. 2005; Brett 2009).

An April 2015 World Bank report on MDGs has shown that extreme poverty has been decreasing in all regions of the world with the exception of Africa (World Bank 2015; Asongu and Nwachukwu 2016a), despite more than two decades of resurgence in growth that began in the mid-1990s (Fosu 2015a, p. 44). This is despite narratives of Africa rising (Leautier 2012), Africa persistently achieving their MDG poverty target (Pinkivskiy and Sala-i-Martin 2014) and an Africa growth miracle (Young 2012). Obeng-Odoom (2013, 2015) has documented that such narratives may be more concerned with extolling the neoliberal ideology and capital accumulation, therefore neglecting fundamental ethical concerns like inequality, ecological crisis and sustainable jobs.

A more recent stream of the literature has been devoted to proposing measures towards understanding and solving Africa's poverty tragedy. The concern about exclusive growth in the continent served as the motivation for a recent book by Kuada (2015) which proposes a new paradigm of 'soft economics' as a mechanism by which one can understand Africa's development trends. Fosu (2015b, c) also responded with a book devoted to elucidating myths behind Africa's recent growth resurgence and the role of institutions in the underlying growth resurgence. According to Kuada (2015), it is important to deviate from strong economics (neoliberal economics and structural adjustment debates) and focus on soft economics (or human capability development) in order to understand, *inter alia*, immiserising growth, increasing poverty and low employment levels. The paradigm shift of Kuada (2015) is broadly in accordance with a recent stream of African development literature which is tailored towards reinventing foreign aid for inclusive and sustainable development (Simpasa et al. 2015; Page and Shimeles 2015; Jones et al. 2015; Asongu 2015a; Jones and Tarp 2015; Page and Söderbom 2015; Asongu and Jellal 2016; Asongu and Nwachukwu 2016b).

In the light of the above, reconciling the dominant schools on Sino–African relations for an African development model is important for a twofold reason. On the one hand, in the post-independent era, Africa and China were both economically fragile. Whereas China opted to chart its own development course, most African countries endeavoured to emulate the WC. On the other hand, contemporary differences in development are self-evident because China has progressed at a spectacular pace and is now providing development aid to Africa.

11.3 Reconciling Dominant Schools of Thought

There are three main schools of thought in Sino–African literature, namely, optimists, pessimists and accommodators (Asongu and Aminkeng 2013; Asongu 2016a). The first group (or the Optimists school) are Chinese optimists who argue that cooperation with China provides Africa with the opportunity of charting its own development course without a great deal of Western interference and policy prescriptions. This group is sympathetic to the 'Beijing model' of governance, which focuses on state control and national sovereignty. The second group (or Pessimists school) consists of Chinese pessimists who are wary of the fact that the Sino–African relationship is skewed in China's favour. This category instead prefers the democracy-oriented approach of the West which articulates in the WC that political rights should be underpinned by free market competition. The third group (or Accommodation school) consists of 'China accommodators' who combine both the pessimists' wariness and optimists' goals. They argue that a common development strategy is required that minimises the asymmetries in the China–African relations as much as possible. The values that are promoted by this group are consistent with the NEPAD initiative which emphasises both African sovereignty/ownership and the process of liberal democracy as a solid foundation for economic development.

We reconcile the three groups into four principal categories: pessimists versus optimists; right preferences (human vs. national, idiosyncratic vs. sovereign and political vs. economic); the Beijing Model versus the WC and an African development model that integrates both the WC and the BM (Asongu 2016a).

First, from a recent survey of the literature (see Asongu 2016a; Asongu and Ssozi 2016), authors are most sympathetic to the Accommodation school because there are strong reasons to be both optimistic and pessimistic about Sino–African relations. On the one hand, in the light of Tull (2006) and Asongu and others (2014a, b), the West has been overly hypocritical when criticising the foreign policy of China in Sino–African relations. This is essentially based on the fact that the foreign policy of the United States of America (USA) towards Saudi Arabia is not sanctioned by the USA's ideals of liberal democracy and human rights. Accordingly, like China, USA's foreign policy is guided by the same terms of resource/oil diplomacy. Moreover, notable developed countries or former colonial powers are no exceptions to the yardstick policy of 'resource diplomacy'. The moral compass of French foreign policy towards her colonies were not historically orientated by her much cherished ideals of 'liberty, fraternity and equality'. On the other hand, the Sino–African nexus like most historical processes is bound to evolve steadily and sustainably as China is growingly asserting her footprint in an increasingly globalised world. Accordingly, globalisation has come to stay: it has become an ineluctable phenomenon whose challenges cannot be overlooked without jeopardising the prosperity of nation states (Tchamyou 2016). In the light of these facts, the Accommodation school argues that the Optimists school can leverage on criticisms from the Pessimists school in order to balance the asymmetry in contemporary Sino–African relations. The reconciliatory arguments are consolidated by the fact that China is playing by the same globalisation standards that are embraced by the Pessimists school.

Next, fundamental concerns about the rights' preference which animated the first and second schools require some clarification, namely, human versus national (see Taylor 2006); idiosyncratic versus sovereign rights (Asongu et al. 2014a, b) and political versus economic rights (Lalountas et al. 2011; Moyo 2013; Asongu 2014c, 2015a, b). It is important to note that the second set of rights (national, sovereign and economic) is consistent with the Optimists school, whereas the first set (human, idiosyncratic and political) is in accordance with the Pessimists school.

Three points merit critical emphasis here.

1. The foreign policy of China that articulates non-interference is partially based on the imperative desire to give priority to national rights over human rights. Africa has been very suspicious of bias from Western nations when it comes to the manner in which human rights are conceived and defined. For instance, gay rights, which are being increasingly acknowledged as a fundamental human right, is deemed to preside over national rights (executive, legislative and judiciary).[1] It follows that African countries who are passing and enforcing anti-gay laws are doing so at the price of hurting the WC and limiting their eligibility for development assistance from the West. For instance, very recently the World Bank and some Western donors have suspended foreign aid to Uganda because of an anti-gay legislation bill that was passed as a law by the president of the republic (Asongu 2015b).
2. Consistent with Taylor (2006), China's foreign policy is guided by the principle that sovereign rights should not be preceded by specific-individual or idiosyncratic rights. Hence, given that African countries are constantly decrying neo-colonial and hegemonic influences in their domestic policies, it is reasonable for China to leverage on their frustrations by articulating her position that under international law, sovereign nations should not be critical of other sovereign nations regarding their dealings with domestic affairs that are sanctioned by their principles of democracy and law. If the Pessimists school were to

[1] It is also relevant to note that the selective application of laws by the International Criminal Court is also an eloquent example of African suspicions towards her Western counterparts' bias re the concept of human rights.

acknowledge this point, they would be in tandem with the Accommodation school —who are more in line with the status quo.

3. Differentiating between 'the right to food' and 'the right to vote' has been the subject of intense debate in recent Sino–African development literature (see Moyo 2013; Asongu and Ssozi 2016; Asongu 2016a, b, c). There is also an evolving stream of literature documenting the fact that economic rights (economic prosperity and productive structures) are more exogenous to political rights (see Anyanwu and Erhijakpor 2014). In this light, the Pessimists school could acknowledge that developing nations are more in need of economic rights when compared to political rights, which would enable them to join the ranks of the Accommodation school, as the majority of her criticisms on Sino–African relations would be appropriately and more constructively addressed.

Third, on the debate over whether economic rights should precede political rights, there is some consensus in the literature that the BM should be prioritised as a short-term development model, whereas the WC should be regarded as the long-term development goal (Moyo 2013; Asongu 2016a; Asongu and Ssozi 2016). This is essentially based on the: (i) reality that the BM has cultivated a burgeoning middle class in China within a spectacularly short spell of time and (ii) the hypothesis that the WC is a more sustainable and inclusive model. Hence, the Accommodation School also posits that both the Pessimists and Optimists schools can make viable cases for priorities in the long term and short run, respectively.

In the light of the above, the two schools of thought are reconciled in the perspective that a sustainable middle class is necessary before political rights can be demanded genuinely because in average terms, a sustainable middle class would be less likely to trade its vote for basic necessities such as food and shelter. The relevance of income levels in the demand for political rights has been established in both developing (Lalountas et al. 2011) and African (Asongu 2014e) countries.

Fourth, a reconciliation of the two schools of thought is consistent with the rules guiding the (NEPAD). Hence, both the WC and the BM are accounted for in the NEPAD essentially because the NEPAD recognises both African ownership/sovereignty and the need for democratic processes in sustainable development. Hence, the priorities of the WC (or democratic and human rights) and the BM (or sovereign and economic rights) are both incorporated into the NEPAD and the Accommodation School. The NEPAD which is deemed to be the current African consensus has been espoused by African nations that adamantly wish to drive the continent forward, economically and politically. It is worthwhile noting that the NEPAD is a consensus for the development of Africa that articulates a number of principles on its charter that are sympathetic to both the BM and the WC, namely good governance, human rights, democracy, sustainable development, non-interference and sovereignty.

11.4 Practical and Contemporary Implications

The 2011 Arab Spring experiment is an eloquent testimony of the need for multi-polar development strategies on the African continent that incorporates both the BM and the WC. In Egypt, the overthrowing of President Morsi was deemed by the United States Secretary of State, John Kerry, as being a legitimate endeavour to restore democracy and not a coup d'état. A few days later, Senator John McCain stated that it was indeed a coup d'état that overthrew a legitimate government. A few months after, we were informed by Abdel Fattah that it may take around 25 years for Egypt to experience the liberal democracy that is embraced in the West. In Tunisia, the current president is a product of the regime that was overthrown in 2011. There is a growing consensus that post-Gaddafi, Libya has become a failed state, with many rebel factions and conflicting governments attempting, without success, to dictate the law of the land.

The fact we cite the Arab Spring as a case study demonstrates the fact that sovereign rights are needed as much as individual rights. Hence, consensus-building for political breakthroughs is better than resorting to military strengths to resolve conflicts. For instance, the Western slogan of 'Assad must go' that was greatly publicised before any negotiations has consolidated the Islamic State of Iraq and Levant (ISIL). Today, at least three facts are difficult to refute: (i) Libya is substantially worse-off than it was before 2011 because her citizens still do not have the politico-economic rights that they demanded; (ii) the citizens of Iraq are also worse-off than they were, prior to the US invasion in 2003 and (iii) the 'Assad must go first' policy has strengthened ISIL. This narrative should not be construed as condoning the policies of Bashar al-Assad, Saddam Hussein and Muammar Gaddafi. What we seek to articulate is that, had the West reconciled her priority for political rights with ideals of the Beijing model, Libya, Syria and Iraq may not be the failed states that they are today.

Growing South–South relations and challenges to the Bretton Wood institutions with new establishments (e.g. New Development Bank, Contingency Reserve Arrangement and Asian Infrastructure Investment Bank) are due to increase in the levels of dissatisfaction that are experienced by developing countries to the WC (Desai and Vreeland 2014; Asongu 2016b). Accordingly, the architecture of power on which the Bretton Woods institutions were founded is no longer deemed to be legitimate based on geo-demographic and politico-economic perspectives (see Cooper and Farooq 2015; Dixon 2015). With more than 45 % of African countries off-track from achieving the MDG extreme poverty target, there is a growing realisation that it would require a paradigm shift in the post-2015 development agenda. A new paradigm that reconciles, *inter alia*, (i) human rights with national rights; (ii) idiosyncratic rights with sovereign rights and (iii) political rights with economic rights is required.

11.5 Concluding Remarks

There are two opposing camps when it comes to Sino–African relations. In this study, we have argued that an approach that will bring the most progress is a 'middle passage', one that greases contradictions and offers an accommodative, balanced and pragmatic vision on which Africans can unite.

There are three main schools of thought in Sino-African literature, namely optimists, pessimists and accommodators (Asongu and Aminkeng 2013; Asongu 2016a, c). The first group (or Optimists school) are Chinese optimists who argue that cooperation with China provides Africa with the ideal opportunity of charting its own development course without a great deal of Western interference via their policy prescriptions. This group is sympathetic to the BM of governance, which focuses on state control and national sovereignty. The second group (or Pessimists school) consists of Chinese pessimists who are wary that the Sino–African relationship is skewed in favour of China. This category instead prefers the democracy-oriented approach of the West which articulates, as stated in the WC, that political rights underpinned by free market competition is the ideal way forward. The third group (or Accommodation school) consists of 'Chinese accommodators' who combine both the pessimists' wariness and optimists' goals. They argue that a common development strategy towards China that minimises asymmetries in the relationship is needed to mutually benefit both parties as much as possible. The values promoted by this group are consistent with the NEPAD which emphasises both African sovereignty/ownership and the processes of liberal democracy as solid foundations for development.

A reason for the non-interference principle is that China, like many African countries, has long suspected a Western bias when it comes to the definition and conception of 'fundamental human rights'. For instance, with increasing moves by Western countries to protect the rights of gays, it is expected that the recipients of foreign aid should follow suit, which places the demand for such rights above 'national/sovereign rights'. To substantiate this position, we have discussed a scenario in 2014 in which development assistance was cut to Uganda because she passed a law which permitted the use of violence when dealing with homosexual activities.

Another bias that is apparent is the so-called 'resource diplomacy' of China by Africa's pro-Western China pessimists. But China's approach is similar to America's long-standing oil-based foreign policy with countries like Saudi Arabia. Moreover, the historical involvement of France in Africa has not been guided by her cherished values of 'liberty, fraternity, and equality'.

Within this framework, although it is apparent that countries in Africa protect the citizens' individual rights, foreign perspectives of what constitutes a right should not take precedence over sovereign authority. In the same vein, space should not be created by international law so that some countries punish and criticise other countries on matters that should be settled by domestic democracy and law. This dimension entails the selectivity of the International Criminal Court in her application of international law that supposedly favours certain nations. An important issue being tackled by the NEPAD is the precedence between 'the right to bread', or economic rights, which the 'BM' camp emphasises and 'the right to vote', or political rights, which the pro-Western supporters prioritise. Here, the key aspect to address is sequencing.

Based on the fact that a starving person is most likely to give up his/her vote in exchange for basic economic rights like the rights to bread and shelter, it can be surmised that a certain level of economic prosperity is required before genuine political rights can be demanded or prioritised. However, entrenched pessimists on Sino-–African relations ultimately favour the free market policies approach as it is difficult to deny the fact that the BM has rapidly created a burgeoning middle class by lifting millions of people out of absolute and relative poverty. In the light of this evidence, African countries too can now focus on a similar orientation of prioritising economic rights instead of placing greater emphasis on political rights as a precondition for productive structures and economic prosperity.

While pessimists of Sino–African relations may not be at ease with the fact that the nexus between China and Africa is growing stronger, China is only leveraging on the principles of globalisation which these pessimists so greatly embrace. Hence, China is also playing by the same rules espoused by the advocates of the WC. However, a burgeoning middle class is needed before a sustainable shift to credible liberal democracy is initiated.

The need for a development approach that is two-pronged by incorporating elements of both the WC and the BM has been underscored by the outcome of the 2011 Arab Spring revolts. Although the lack of economic opportunities substantially fuelled pro-democracy uprisings in Tunisia, Libya, Egypt and subsequent countries, the dream that 'the right to vote' would take precedence over 'the right to bread' has steadily become a nightmare.

In essence, despite the overthrowing of authoritarian regimes, Egypt, for instance, has been unable to build a democratic government that is credible and one that can effectively enforce the rule of law; Libya is considerably worse off, and change in Tunisia remains very unpredictable.

If the rights of sovereignty had perhaps been considered, with foreign powers acknowledging the need to form a general consensus, instead of funding vehement politically and economically driven rebellions, political breakthroughs could have been reached, paving the path towards sustainable economy-boosting policies.

From a more contemporary view, it appears that the West has not learnt her lesson because of her long-standing demand for the Syrian President Bashar al-Assad to stand down before any credible peace-building process can be initiated. Although Western leaders have softened their stances in recent months, the consequences have been greatly damaging because President Assad has also leveraged on the position of the West to create an environment whereby his enemies have become those of the West as well. This however has not been feasible as many members of the Western funded rebellion are proceeding to join the ranks of the Islamic State and are consequently turning against both Assad and the West.

The above narratives are not designed to condone policies of repression from authoritarian leaders whose regimes were ousted. The position of this study, however, is to emphasise the potential rewards of greater stability-related approaches that build on a consensus between Western interests in promoting political rights and national/sovereign rights that are espoused by the BM.

The growing involvement of China in Africa is crucial not only exclusively for direct economic rewards but also for alternative-development strategies. It has been argued throughout the course of this study that African countries can substantially enhance the prospect of development if an African consensus builds on a merger between Western and Chinese models: a balance that articulates national interest with human rights, sovereign authority with individual rights and economic goals with political rights.

References

Acemoglu, D., Johnson, S., & Robinson, J. (2005). Institutions as a fundamental cause of long-run growth. In *Handbook of economic growth* (Vol. 1, Part A). North Holland: Elsevier.

Adedeji, A., (1999). "Structural adjustment policies in Africa". *International Social Science Journal, 51*(162), 521–528.

Adewole, M. A., & Osabuohien, E. S. (2007). Analysis of cost of governance and its reduction options in Nigeria, Nigerian. *Journal of Economic and Social Studies, 49*(1), 137–159.

Amavilah, V. H. (2006). "Institutional change and economic performance: An off-the-cuff comment on Professors Daron Acemoglu, Simon Johnson, and James Robinson's three papers", Glendale College, United States.

Amavilah, V. H. (2014). *Sir W. Arthur Lewis and the Africans: Overlooked economic growth lessons* (MPRA Paper No. 57126). Munich.

Amavilah, V. H. (2015). *Social obstacles to technology, technological change, and the economic growth of African countries: Some anecdotal evidence from economic history* (MPRA Paper No. 63273). Munich.

Amavilah, V. H., Asongu, S. A., & Andrés, A. R. (2014). *Globalization, peace & stability, governance, and knowledge economy* (African Governance and Development Institute Working Paper No. 14/012). Yaoundé.

America, R. (2013). Economic development with limited supplies of management. What to do about it – the case of Africa. *Challenge, 56*(1), 61–71.

Anyanwu, J., & Erhijakpor, A. E. O. (2014). Does oil wealth affect democracy in Africa? *African Development Review, 26*(1), 15–37.

Asongu, S. A. (2014a). *Knowledge economy gaps, policy syndromes and catch-up strategies: Fresh South Korean lessons to Africa* (African Governance and Development Institute Working Paper No. 14/014). Yaoundé.

Asongu, S. A. (2014b). Knowledge economy and financial sector competition in African countries. *African Development Review, 26*(2), 333–346.

Asongu, S. A. (2014c). The questionable economics of development assistance in Africa: Hot-fresh evidence, 1996–2010. *The Review of Black Political Economy, 41*(4), 455–480.

Asongu, S. A. (2014d). Software piracy and scientific publications: Knowledge economy evidence from Africa. *African Development Review, 26*(4), 572–583.

Asongu, S. A. (2014e). Globalization (fighting) corruption and development: How are these phenomena linearly and nonlinearly related in wealth effects. *Journal of Economic Studies, 41*(3), 346–369.

Asongu, S. A. (2015a). Reinventing foreign aid for inclusive and sustainable development: Kuznets, Piketty and the great policy reversal. *Journal of Economic Surveys*, Forthcoming. doi:10.1111/joes.12109.

Asongu, S. A. (2015b). On taxation, political accountability and foreign aid: Empirics to a celebrated literature. *South African Journal of Economics, 83*(2), 180–198.

Asongu, S. A. (2016a). Sino-African relations: a review and reconciliation of dominant schools of thought. *Politics and Policy*, 44(2), 351–383.

Asongu, S. A. (2016b). Drivers of growth in fast developing countries: Evidence from bundling and unbundling Institutions. *Politics and Policy*, *44*(1), 97–134.

Asongu, S. A. (2016c). "Africa's middle passage to development", Project Syndicate. https://www.project-syndicate.org/commentary/africa-development-china-accommodation-by-simplice-asongu-2016-03. Accessed 16/03/2016.

Asongu, S. A., & Aminkeng, G. (2013). The economic consequences of China–Africa relations: Debunking myths in the debate. *Journal of Chinese Economic and Business Studies, 11*(4), 261–277.

Asongu, S. A., & Jellal, M. (2016). Foreign aid fiscal policy: Theory and evidence. *Comparative Economics Studies.* http://www.palgrave-journals.com/ces/journal/vaop/ncurrent/abs/ces20167a.html.

Asongu, S. A., & Kodila-Tedika, O. (2015). Is poverty in the African DNA(gene)? African Governance and Development Institute No. 15/11, Yaoundé.

Asongu, S. A., & Nwachukwu, J. (2016a). Finance and inclusive human development: Evidence from Africa. *Brussels Economic Review*, Forthcoming.

Asongu, S. A., & Nwachukwu, J. (2016b). Foreign aid and inclusive development: Updated evidence from Africa, 2005–2012. *Social Science Quarterly*, DOI:10.1111/ssqu.12275.

Asongu, S. A., & Ssozi, J. (2016). Sino-African relations: Some solutions and strategies to the policy syndromes. *Journal of African Business, 17*(1), 35–51.

Asongu, S. A., Amavilah, V. H., & Andrés, A. R. (2014a). *Economic implications of business dynamics for KE-associated economic growth and inclusive development in African Countries* (African Governance and Development Institute Working Paper No. 14/023). Yaoundé.

Asongu, S. A., Nwachukwu, J., & Aminkeng, G. (2014b). *China's strategies in economic diplomacy: updated lessons for Africa, the West and China* (African Governance and Development Institute Working Paper, No. 14/036). Yaoundé.

Brett, E., (2009). *Reconstructing development theory: International inequality, Institutional Reform and Social Emancipation.* Palgrave Macmillan.

Brush, S. B., & Stabinsky, D. (1996). *Valuing local knowledge: Indigenous people and intellectual property rights.* Washington, DC: Island Press.

Bujra, A. (2004). *Pan-African political and economic vision of development: From OAU to the AU, from the Lagos Plan of Action (LPA) to the New Partnership for African Development (NEPAD). DPMF* (Occasional Paper 13). Addis Ababa: Development Policy Management Forum.

Chang, H.-J. (2002). *Kicking away the ladder: development strategy in historical perspective*. London: Anthem Press.

Cooper, A., & Farooq, A. (2015). Testing the club dynamics of the BRICS: The new development bank from conception to establishment. Department of Political Science and Balsillie School of International Affairs at the University of Waterloo. http://www.brics.utoronto.ca/biblio/iorj-2015-02-cooper-farooq.pdf. Accessed 19/10/2015.

Desai, R, & Vreeland, J. (2014). What the new bank of BRICS is all about. *The Washington Post.* http://www.washingtonpost.com/blogs/monkey-cage/wp/2014/07/17/what-the-new-bank-of-brics-is-all-about/. Accessed 14/02/2015.

Dixon, C. (2015). The new BRICS bank: Challenging the International financial order? *Global Policy Institute Policy Paper, 28*, 1–13.

Dorfman, J. (1939). Predecessors of Adam Smith: The growth of British economic thought. by E. A. J. Johnson. *Political Science Quarterly, 54*(1), 103–105.

Drine, I. (2013). 'Successful' development models: Lessons from the MENA region. In A. Fosu (Ed.), *Achieving development success: Strategies and lessons from the developing world.* Oxford: Oxford University Press.

Efobi, U., Osabuohien, E., & Beecroft, I. (2013). The macroeconomic consequences of the Black Sunday in Nigeria. In J. Adibe (Ed.), *The politics and economics of removing subsidies on petroleum products in Nigeria*. London/Abuja: Adonis & Abbey Publishers.

Fofack, H. (2014). *The idea of economic development: views from Africa* (WIDER Working Paper 2014/093). Helsinki.

Fosu, A. (2013). Achieving development success: Strategies and lessons from the developing world. *UNU-WIDER Policy Brief* (November).

Fosu, A. (2015a). Growth, inequality and poverty in Sub-Saharan Africa: Recent progress in a global context. *Oxford Development Studies, 43*(1), 44–59.

Fosu, A. K. (2015b). *Growth and institutions in African development*. Abingdon/New York: Routledge.

Fosu, A. K. (2015c). Growth and institutions in African development, in growth and Institutions in African Development. In Augustin K. Fosu (Ed.), Chapter 1, (pp 1–17). Routledge.

Jones, S., & Tarp, F. (2015). Priorities for boosting employment in Sub-Saharan Africa: Evidence for Mozambique. *African Development Review*, Supplement: Special issue on "aid and employment, *27*(S1), 56–70.

Jones, S., Page, J., Shimeles, A., & Tarp, F. (2015). Aid, growth and employment in Africa. *African Development Review*, Supplement: Special issue on "aid and employment", *27*(S1), 1–4.

Kayizzi-Mugerwa, S. (2001). *Globalisation, growth and income inequality: The African experience* (Working Paper No. 186). Paris: OECD Development Centre.

Kayizzi-Mugerwa, S., Anyanwu, J. C., & Conceição, P. (2014). Regional Integration in Africa: An Introduction. *African Development Review, 26*(S1), 1–6.

Kuada, J. (2015). *Private enterprise-led economic development in Sub-Saharan Africa the human side of growth*. Basingstoke: Palgrave Macmillan.

Lalountas, D. A., Manolas, G. A., & Vavouras, I. S. (2011). Corruption, globalization and development: How are these three phenomena related? *Journal of Policy Modeling, 33*, 636–648.

Leautier, F. A. (2012). What role for Africa after 50 years of independence: Provider of natural resources or a new global leader? *Journal of African Development, 14*(1), 127–151.

Lewis, A. (1955). *Theory of economic growth*. London: Routledge.

Lin, J. Y. (2015). The Washington consensus revisited a new structural economics perspective. *Journal of Economic Policy Reform, 18*(2), 96–113.

Lin, J., & Monga, C. (2011). Growth identification and facilitation: The role of the state in the dynamics of structural change. *Development Policy Review, 29*(3), 264–290.

Looney, R. E. (2013). The Omani and the Bahraini paths to development: Rare and contrasting oil-based economic success stories. In Fosu, A. (Ed.), *Achieving development success: strategies and lessons from the developing world.* Oxford Oxford University Press

Lucas, R. E. (1993). Making a miracle. *Econometrica, 61*(2), 251–272.

Lwoga, E. T., Ngulube, P., & Stilwell, C. (2010). Managing indigenous knowledge for sustainable agricultural development in developing countries: Knowledge management approaches in the social context. *The International Information & Library Review, 42*(3), 172–185.

Monga, C., (2014). "The False Economics of Pre-Conditions: Policymaking in the African Context", *Journal of African Development, 16*(2), pp. 121-140.

Moyo, D. (2013). "Is China a new idol for developing countries", TED Talks, New Ideas Every day. https://www.youtube.com/watch?v=4Q2aznfmcYU. Accessed 07/05/2014.

Moyo, D., (2009), Dead Aid: Why Aid Is Not Working and How There is Another Way for Africa. New York: Farrar, Straus and Giroux.

Musila, J. W., & Sigué, S. P. (2010). Corruption and international trade: An empirical investigation of African countries. *World Economy, 33*(1), 129–146.

Ndlovu-Gatsheni, S. J. (2013). The entrapment of African within the global colonial matrices of power: Eurocentrism, coloniality and deimperialization in the twenty-first century. *Journal of Developing Societies, 29*(4), 331–353.
Norman, A., & Stiglitz, J. (2012). African development prospects and possibilities. In E. Aryeetey et al. (Eds.), *The Oxford companion to the economics of Africa*. Oxford: Oxford University Press.
North, D. (1990). *Institutions, institutional change and economic performance*. Cambridge/New York: Cambridge University Press.
Nunn, N. (2008). The long-term effects of Africa's slave trades. *Quarterly Journal of Economics, 123*, 139–176.
Nunn, N. (2009). The importance of history for economic development. *Annual Review of Economics, 1*(1), 65–92.
Nunn, N., & Puga, G. (2012). Ruggedness: The blessing of bad geography in Africa. *Review of Economics and Statistics, 94*(4), 20–36.
OAU. (2001). The New Partnership for African Development (NEPAD). Addis Ababa: OAU.
Obeng-Odoom, F. (2013). Africa's failed economic development trajectory a critique. *African Review of Economics and Finance, 4*(2), 151–175.
Obeng-Odoom, F. (2015). Africa: On the rise, but to where? *Forum for Social Economics, 44*(3), 234–250.
Organisation of African Unity (OAU). (1980). *Lagos Plan of Action for the Economic Development of Africa*. Addis Ababa: OAU.
Page, J., & Shimeles, A. (2015). Aid, employment and poverty reduction in Africa. *African Development Review*, Supplement: Special issue on "aid and employment" *27*(S1), 17–30.
Page, J., & Söderbom, M. (2015). Is small beautiful? small enterprise, aid and employment in Africa. *African Development Review*, Supplement: Special issue on "aid and employment" *27*(S1), 44–55.
Pinkivskiy, M., & Sala-i-Martin, X. (2014). Africa is on time. *Journal of Economic Growth, 19*(3), 311–333.
Raseroka, K. (2008). Information transformation Africa: Indigenous knowledge – Securing space in the knowledge society. *The International Information and Library Review, 40*, 243–250.
Simpasa, A, Shimeles, A. & Salami, A. O. (2015). Employment effects of multilateral development bank support: The case of the African development bank, *African Development Review*, Supplement: Special issue on "aid and employment". 27(S1), 31–43.

Stiglitz, J., & Lin, J. (Eds.). (2013). *The industrial policy revolution I: The role of government beyond ideology*. Basingstoke: Palgrave Macmillan.

Stiglitz, J., Lin, J., & Monga, C. (2013a). *The rejuvenation of industrial policy* (*Policy Research Working Paper 6628*). Washington, DC: World Bank.

Stiglitz, J., Lin, J., Monga, C., & Patel, E. (2013b). *Industrial policy in the African context* (Policy Research Working Paper 6633).. Washington, DC: World Bank.

Taylor, I. (2006). China's oil diplomacy in Africa. *International Affairs, 82*(5), 937–959.

Tchamyou, V. (2016). The role of knowledge economy in African business, *Journal of the Knowledge Economy*: DOI: 10.13140/RG.2.2.13707.69922.

Tull, D. M. (2006). China's engagement in Africa: scope, significance and consequences. *The Journal of Modern African Studies, 44*(3), 459–479.

World Bank. (2015). World development indicators. World Bank publications. http://www.gopa.de/fr/news/world-bank-release-world-development--indicators-2015. Accessed 25/04/2015.

Young, A. (2012). The African growth miracle. *Journal of Political Economy, 120*(4), 696–739.

Index[1]

[1] Notes: Page number followed by 'n' denotes notes

Y. C. Kim (ed.), *China and Africa*, The Palgrave Macmillan Asian Business Series, DOI 10.1007/978-3-319-47030-6